Versions of Pygmalion

Versions of Pygmalion

J. HILLIS MILLER

HARVARD UNIVERSITY PRESS
CAMBRIDGE, MASSACHUSETTS
LONDON, ENGLAND
1990

Library of Congress Cataloging-in-Publication Data

Miller, J. Hillis (Joseph Hillis), 1928–
   Versions of Pygmalion / J. Hillis Miller.
     p. cm.
   Includes bibliographical references.
   ISBN 0-674-93485-7 (alk. paper)
   1. Metamorphosis in literature. 2. Personification in literature.
3. Narration (Rhetoric) I. Title.
PN56.M53M55 1990   89-24729
809'.93353—dc20   CIP

To my students and colleagues at Irvine

Preface

At first there may seem little relation among the stories discussed here. The intricacies and scrupulosities of Maisie's coming to know, in James's *What Maisie Knew,* may seem to have little similarity to the violence and rapidity of the strange events in Kleist's "Der Findling." Neither of those is much like Bartleby's celebrated immobility, the passive resistance of his "I would prefer not to," in Melville's "Bartleby the Scrivener," nor like the two strange dreamlike narratives of death suspended that make up Blanchot's *L'arrêt de mort.* Nor does there even seem much connection between *What Maisie Knew* and an earlier story by James, "The Last of the Valerii," the subject of the final chapter. Each chapter takes its own way and is primarily concerned to read a work on its own terms. But all these stories are in one way or another versions of the story of Pygmalion. Each contains a character who does something like falling in love with a statue.

The coming alive of a statue that one has made and then fallen in love with expresses in a fable the act of personification essential to all storytelling and storyreading. Unless the storyteller can create out of words characters in whom we can believe, characters who seem to have a vivid independent life, we will not have much interest in the story. In the narratives discussed here characters in the story do something like what its author, reader, or critic must do in order to write, read, teach, or write about the story. This book investigates that doubling of the author or reader by the character.

The book continues my investigation of the ethical side of writing, reading, and teaching literature. I ask, by way of the particular examples, not only how a work of literature can be known in its historical context, though that is also one of my topics. Rather I ask whether writing literature, reading it, teaching it, and writing about it make anything happen in the real historical world. If so, how? And what? Who must take responsibility for this? Stories show people acting, choosing, and evaluating, "doing things that do other things in their turn." (That is Henry James's phrase for the way writing stories is part of what he calls, echoing Emerson, "the conduct of life.") The characters in the stories I discuss are shown as obligated to take responsibility for what they do. In diverse ways, the stories read here show how ethical doing and evaluating are related to personification.

But storytelling itself is also an ethical act involving personification for which the storyteller must be held responsible, as must reader, teacher, or critic for bringing the story to life by reading it, talking about it, writing about it. These ethical acts have had political, historical, and social consequences. But the line from reading to action is by no means so simple as to allow us to say that we read a story, identify its "moral," evaluate the characters as ethically good or bad, and then act on that knowledge. In the case of those relatively few world historical events where reading is known to have led to action, for example Ghandi's reading of Thoreau, the work cannot be shown to have directly counseled the acts its reading has instigated. Even more difficult to assess is the effect on conduct of reading by multitudes of small players on the stage of history, say American students in a thousand classrooms reading the canonical works of American literature, such as "Bartleby the Scrivener." All the stories read here contain thematic and textual elements that make them especially appropriate for investigating the difficult question of how reading makes something happen. What happens in the story suggests what may happen when we read the story.

I have been motivated here, as in all my previous books, by a fascination with what seems strange and unaccountable in particular works. I want to account for that "unaccountable" as clearly as possible and to make what I have found available to whoever is interested in literature. But my obligation is not only to transmit something I know. I also want to make the work effective here and now, to reactivate its performative power, not simply let it be known as a piece of literary history. The two obligations may not be symmetrical, as my stories show. The stories also show how such double doing is related to personification, and in what sense it may properly be called ethical.

Deer Isle, Maine
September 1989

Contents

Thou shalt not make unto thee any graven image.
—Exodus 20:4

ishment fits the crime. The sins of the fathers and mothers are visited on the children from generation to generation. The guilt is always passed on in new desires demanding the compensation of yet another literalizing metamorphosis.

But to say "materialization of desire" or "literalizing metamorphosis" does not quite do justice to what these transformations are. In an adjacent story, the Cerastae, so called because they have horns on their foreheads, have made sacrifice to Jupiter, god of hospitality, by slaying their guests. It is a grotesque perversion of the obligation of a host. "Sacris offensa nefandis . . ." (Sickened by their unspeakable offerings), Venus says, "exsilio poenam potius gens inpia pendat, / vel nece; vel siquid medium est mortisque fugaeque. / idque quid esse potest, nisi versae poena figurae?" (Rather let these wicked people be punished either by exile or by death, or by something intermediary between the two: and what could that be, except to be transformed into something other than they are?).[1] Venus changes the Cerastae into bullocks, in fulfillment of the destiny inscribed on their foreheads. A metamorphosis is not exile from the human community, such as Ovid himself was to suffer, and it is not the ultimate separation of death. It is halfway between the two, neither death nor life. The one who has been transformed remains as a memorial example still present within the human community—in the form of a tree, a fountain, a bullock, a flower. The halfway state of the victim of a metamorphosis is a sign that his or her fault has not been completely punished or expiated. The changed state may be read this way or that way, as life-giving or death-dealing, depending on how you look at it.

The story of Pygmalion in book 10 of the *Metamorphoses,* with its adjacent stories, is a splendid example of all this. The narratives in this book represent only a few of the innumerable stories that could be called "versions of Pygmalion." My discussions do not add up to a total repertory of possibilities, nor do they make in their sequence a coherent narrative, with each chapter leading logically to the next. Each of my chapters begins again each time more or less from scratch, that is, from the incitement to thinking anew about the personifications of a particular text. The reading takes the line that incitement indicates. But in their range my examples indicate what is at stake when someone becomes infatuated with a statue or a painting or, for that matter, when someone reads or hears a story and thinks of its characters as "real people." This proem is a reading of the prototypical version of Pygmalion.

Ovid's "Pygmalion" differs from most of the stories in the *Metamorphoses*. It is a tale in which something inanimate comes alive, rather than the other way around. The story is flanked by two stories in which the transformation goes the usual way, from human to inanimate. The three stories, as well as others before and after in book 10, are held together by the fact that all involve the pleasure or displeasure of the goddess of love.

In the story just before Pygmalion (10.238–242), Venus punishes the "loathsome Propoetides," who have dared to deny her divinity. The goddess in her wrath makes them the first women to become public prostitutes. The blood hardens in their cheeks as they become shameless, spiritually hard. Venus then punishes them again, in punishment for a punishment she has herself inflicted. She makes them literally stone: "in rigidum parvo silicem discrimine versae" (turned by a slight alteration into stony flints).

Pygmalion's horror at these wicked, stony-hearted women leads him to remain celibate, "sine coniuge caelebs" (10.245). In an attempt to compensate for the Propoetides, Pygmalion fashions "a snowy ivory statue . . . lovelier than any woman born" (231). This compensatory gesture does not quite make sense. To make up for women who have become painted ladies with hearts of stone, Pygmalion fashions another painted lady out of another hard, inanimate substance. The crisscross substitution begins when he falls in love with his own creation, "operisque sui concepit amorem": "The statue had all the appearance of a real girl, so that it seemed to be alive, to want to move, did not modesty forbid. So cleverly did his art conceal its art [ars adeo latet arte sua]. Pygmalion gazed in wonder, and in his heart there rose a passionate love for this image of a human form" [simulati corporis] (10.249–253; 231).

If most of the metamorphoses in the *Metamorphoses* go from human to inhuman, life to death, animate to inanimate, the coming alive of Galatea goes the other way. The name for the figure of speech of which this metamorphosis is the literalizing allegory is *prosopopoeia.* This trope ascribes a face, a name, or a voice to the absent, the inanimate, or the dead. But prosopopoeia is already the basic operative trope in the more usual transformations in the *Metamorphoses.* The two kinds of metamorphosis meet, the criss-cross lines intersect, because both are forms of prosopopoeia.

In most of the metamorphoses, the dead do not completely die. They remain to be memorialized in a work of mourning that may never be completed. The irreducible otherness of my neighbor or of my beloved may be expressed by saying that he or she may die. My relation to the person is always shadowed from the beginning by death. That we are certain, if we live even a minute longer than whatever is taken as "now," to be the survivors of the deaths of others is a determining feature of the human condition. If proso-popoeia is a cover-up of death or of absence, a compensation, its power is needed even in my relation to my living companions. My neighbor is always somehow absent even in moments of the most intimate presence. Personification both covers over these blank places in the midst of life and, sooner or later, brings them into the open.

That prosopopoeia is the trope of mourning is indicated by the way that the more usual changes in the *Metamorphoses,* though they go from life halfway toward death, are personfications too. They are etiological myths expressing our sense that an obscure human life is diffused throughout nature—in the sighing of branches, in the whispering of water in a fountain, in the dancing of a daffodil. In the story just after Pygmalion, for example, the dripping of the sap of the myrrh tree is the tears of Myrrha: "Though she lost her former feelings when she lost her body, yet she still weeps, and warm drops flow from the tree" (238).

Pygmalion's happy love for a Galatea brought to life by the ur-gency of prosopopoeia is the reversal of these more usual features of metamorphosis. The story of Pygmalion shows prosopopoeia functioning not to hide the absolute absence of death but to give life to the inanimate in a dream come true. For Pygmalion, the other is not really other. Pygmalion has himself made Galatea. She is the mirror image of his desire. His relation to her is not love for another, in an attachment always shadowed by the certain death of the other. It is a reciprocity in which the same loves the same. Here

Narcissus' vain desire seems fulfilled: "timidumque ad lumina lumen / attollens pariter cum caelo vidi amantem" (And timidly raising her eyes, [the just-awakened Galatea sees] her lover and the light of day together; 10.293–294; 232). For Galatea, to see at all is to see Pygmalion and to be subject to him. It is as if Narcissus' reflection in the pool had come alive and could return his love.

If anthropomorphisms exceed the ordinary opposition between literal and figurative language, since they posit as given an identification at the level of substance,[2] even the most traditional rhetorical definition of prosopopoeia begins with language. Prosopopoeia is the ascription to entities that are not really alive first of a *name*, then of a face, and finally, in a return to language, of a voice. The entity I have personified is given the power to respond to the name I invoke, to speak in answer to my speech. Another way to put this would be to say that though prosopopoeia is a fact of language, a member of the family of tropes, this tends to be hidden because the trope is posited a priori. Many prosopopoeias are part of ordinary language and so exist prior to the distinction between figurative and literal speech—many prosopopoeias are also catachreses, neither literal nor figurative, like "headland," "eye of a storm," or "face of a mountain."

But a proper name may also be a strange species of catachresis. There is an equivocation in the definition of a prosopopoeia as the ascription of a *name*. The name may be proper or generic, though in either case the process goes from the name to the substance named. Hardy used two lines from *Two Gentleman of Verona* (I.ii. 114–115) as the epigraph for *Tess of the d'Urbervilles*: "Poor wounded name! My bosom, as a bed, / Shall lodge thee." The epigraph defines the act of narration as an extended prosopopoeia, invoking Tess and keeping her alive within the covers of a book. In Shakespeare's play Julia says she will hide in her bosom Proteus' name on the fragment of the love letter she has torn to pieces. The paper serves as a personification of the beloved because it bears his name. But that name is both proper and conceptual. The name "Proteus" foreshadows its bearer's faithlessness.

Ovid's *Metamorphoses* already dramatizes this doubleness of prosopopoetic naming in its stories of why a certain flower is called a narcissus, a certain tree a myrrh. On the one hand, these are the generic names for this kind of flower or tree. On the other hand, behind each of these generic names is a proper name, behind each proper name a story that presupposes the anthropomorphizing of the flower or the tree. Hidden within each narcissus is Narcissus and his story, within each myrrh tree, Myrrha and her sad tale.

The story of Pygmalion dramatizes the process by which an anthropomorphism takes place, whereas in most of the stories of the *Metamorphoses* the anthropomorphism is already complete at the beginning. This makes the story of Pygmalion a prosopopoeia of prosopopoeia. Myrrha is already a girl; she becomes a tree. Galatea is an ivory statue that becomes a girl.

Ovid's description of the anthropomorphizing of Galatea strongly emphasizes the autoerotic side of this process. Autoeroticism is a region of human experience in which prosopopoeia appears to be least verbal, most bodily, tactile, and affective. Even here, however, a murmured proper name may invoke the absent, personify the inanimate, or repersonify the dead:

> saepe manus operi temptantes admovet, an sit
> corpus an illud ebur: nec adhuc ebur esse fatetur.
> oscula dat reddique putat loquiturque tenetque
> et credit tactis digitos insidere membris
> et metuit, pressos veniat ne livor in artus. (10.254–258).

> Often he ran his hands over the work, feeling it to see whether it was flesh or ivory, and would not yet admit that ivory was all it was. He kissed the statue, and imagined that it kissed him back, spoke to it and embraced it, and thought he felt his fingers sink into the limbs he touched, so that he was afraid lest a bruise appear where he had pressed the flesh. (231)

Only in this imaginative caressing of the statue does the reversal of the previous story, redressing the imbalance, begin to occur. Ultimately Pygmalion places the statue on a couch and, as Ovid tactfully puts it, "appellat tori sociam" (called it his bedfellow; 10.268; 232). So passionate is Pygmalion's love for the girl he has made with his own hands that, with some help from Venus, Galatea comes alive. His patience is rewarded when he prays submissively to Venus, who hears his prayer. It may be better for her to let him marry a statue brought to life than for him to remain a bachelor, in defiance of her power. So she grants his not quite spoken wish.

The ivory does become flesh, in the magical substantiation of what began as a trope. The passage describing this merits analysis:

> When Pygmalion returned home [from praying to Venus], he made straight for the statue of the girl he loved, leaned over the couch, and kissed her. She seemed warm: he laid his lips on hers again, and touched her breast with his hands—at his touch the ivory lost its hardness, and grew soft: his fingers made an imprint on the yielding surface, just as wax of Hymettus melts in the sun and, worked by men's fingers, is fashioned into many different shapes, and made fit for use by being used [ut Hymettia sole / cera remollescit tractataque pollice multas / flectitur in facies ipsoque fit utilis usu]. The lover stood, amazed, afraid of being mistaken, his joy tempered with doubt, and again and again stroked the object of his prayers. It was indeed a human body! (10.280–289; 232)

Though the birth of Galatea takes the help of a goddess, Ovid emphasizes the way it is the result of human work, even of specifically male work. The work is both sexual and at the same time simply one of manufacture, in the literal sense of a making by hand: "at his touch the ivory lost its hardness." This story embodies a male fantasy whereby a woman cannot be the object of sexual desire and cannot desire in return unless she has been made so by male effort. The process is likened to the procedure whereby a passive and formless raw material is given shape by man's productive power.

Is this fantasy exclusively male? Not necessarily, if there is any truth in the many versions of the Pygmalion story in which the woman rather than the man idolizes a statue or a painting. Examples are Kleist's "Der Findling," Hardy's "Barbara of the House of Grebe," or James's "The Last of the Valerii," two of which are discussed in this book. Though these stories are by male writers, they would at least authorize saying that men have ascribed to women as well as to men the error of taking prosopopoeia literally. The word "versions" in my title is meant to suggest not only different tellings of the same story, but also deflections, or one might even say "metamorphoses," of that story. Are the versions of Pygmalion in which the gender of the protagonist is changed so radical a transformation as no longer to be "versions" in the sense of "redactions"? That question must remain open for now and abide the readings that follow.

"Fit utilis usu" (made fit for use by being used)—the phrase, in

Latin or English, vibrates with various meanings of the noun or verb, "usus," "utor," "use," including its negative forms, since "use" is a double antithetical word: "use value" as against "exchange value," "use" of a word or phrase as against its "mention," the mistreatment of one person by another—as in Miss Havisham's question to Pip about Estella in *Great Expectations*, "How does she use you?"—or the notion of exhaustion in the phrase "all used up," with its overtones of usury as wearing away or "usura." But Ovid's usage also vibrates with the meaning of the word when it is given negative prefixes, as in "abutor" (to make full use of, to waste, or to use a word wrongly) or, in English, "misuse," "abuse," and even, as I have suggested, "self-abuse." What the word "usu" literally names here is all that caressing and stroking by Pygmalion of the ivory statue.

Perhaps most obscurely and profoundly, Ovid's phrase "fit utilis usu" expresses the paradox in all inaugural acts of creation—artistic, sexual, ethical, or political. The shapeless wax is not yet fit for use, but it must be used in order to become useful. It must be at the beginning both usable and not usable. The initial using, the shaping manipulation by man, both makes something not yet useful fit for use and at the same time does this by using it, by using the unusable. To put this in terms of speech-act theory, such acts of shaping are, against reason, both constative and performative at once. They identify a usefulness that is already there, as in the old notion that the sculptor does no more than remove the excess stone from around a statue that is hidden in the shapeless material. On the other hand, such shapings bring something absolutely new into existence by a performative gesture that makes the useless useful, gives the shapeless shape.

"Made fit for use by being used" echoes the similar self-reflexive phrase in a passage already cited: "ars adeo latet arte sua" (so cleverly did his art conceal its art). That phrase succinctly expresses what is self-deceitful and idolatrous about prosopopoeia. A prosopopoeia is a human creation, a product of the capacity within language for tropological substitution. We can, for example, shift the name of a part of the human body to a feature of the landscape and speak of the face of a mountain. This operation is concealed when the anthropomorphism then becomes part of ordinary language. We forget that we ourselves have artfully personified the mountain and are fooled into taking our own creation literally. It comes to seem that there is a real personality in the mountain, so that, like Wordsworth, we talk of the "speaking face" of nature within which is diffused "a soul divine which we participate" (1805 *Prelude*, 5.12, 15, 16). Pygmalion is so skillful an artist, skilled even in concealing his art from himself, that he is taken in by his own fabrication: it seems to him that Galatea must be a real girl.

The image of the wax of Hymettus melting in the sun so that it may be fashioned by men's fingers into many different shapes, made fit for use by being used, indicates what is equivocal and even ominous in Pygmalion's artful metamorphosis of a chunk of ivory into a living maiden. The transformation requires the cooperation of the gods. But what Pygmalion does is a usurpation of divine power as manifested in the sun god's sovereignty over shapeless matter. In another story told in the *Metamorphoses* Icarus flies too close to the sun, and the wax binding his wings melts. This is a punishment for Daedalus' temerity. In the phrase Joyce cites in part as the epigraph for *A Portrait of the Artist as a Young Man*, "ignotas animum dimittit in artes / naturamque novat" (He set his mind to sciences never explored before, and altered the laws of nature; 8.188–189; 184). Yeats's "Nineteen Hundred and Nineteen" picks up on what is ominous about this traditional figure of the melting wax as a trope for man's shaping power. The fragility of "Phidias' famous ivories" is analogous to the fragility of "habits that made old wrong / Melt down, as it were wax in the sun's rays." But if old wrong can melt in this way, new right is equally destructible, as "the Platonic Year / Whirls out new right and wrong, / Whirls in the old instead" (lines 7, 11–12, 54–56). Ultimately the sovereign sun, seeming natural symbol of a transcendent power, conquers all man's attempts to achieve stability in art or politics, and with open mouths and blinded eyes, like Yeats's wise old men, we "but gape at the sun" (102).

Pygmalion seems to have escaped scot-free from all this. Rather than concluding with the terse announcement of a metamorphosis as punishment, his story ends with the birth of Paphos. Paphos is the child conceived, apparently, just after Galatea is born and sees her lover and the light of day together: "when the moon's horns

had nine times been rounded into a full circle, Pygmalion's bride
bore a child, Paphos, from whom the island takes its name." Who
could blame Pygmalion for his wistful affection for the beautiful
statue he has made? And who could blame Venus for granting a
wish that so benignly acknowledges her sovereignty?

Ovid's judgment of Pygmalion, however, is not so simple or so
positive as this happy ending suggests. For Ovid the appropriate
punishment always comes, though in this case it is deferred. The
payment for Pygmalion's happiness is made not by his daughter
Paphos, but by his grandson Cinyras and, especially, by his great-
granddaughter Myrrha.

The narrative of Myrrha's incestuous love for her father is a retrospective reading of the story of Pygmalion. Myrrha's story has
great power. It is longer than most of the stories in the *Metamorphoses,* and it is prefaced with a stern warning: "The story I am
going to tell is a horrible one [Dira canam—this is a good example
of how Ovid's laconic Latin inevitably becomes somewhat verbose
in translation]: I beg that daughters and fathers should hold themselves aloof, while I sing, or if they find my songs enchanting, let
them refuse to believe this part of my tale, and suppose that it
never happened: or else, if they believe that it did happen, they
must believe also in the punishment that followed" (10.300–303;
233). Father-daughter incest, like the Oedipal incest of mother and
son, is so shocking that it cannot be looked at directly by civilized
men and women. Parental guidance will not avail in this case. The
taboo against confronting such incest was still strong in the late
nineteenth century, when Freud changed the relation in one of the
case histories in *Studies in Hysteria* from father-daughter incest to
uncle-niece incest, and then added a footnote years later castigating
himself for having hidden the truth.

In Ovid, Myrrha's irresistible passion leads her, with her nurse's
help, to trick her father into sleeping with her, night after night,
not knowing it is his daughter. The story is a good example of that
cunning method of enchainment whereby one story in the *Metamorphoses* functions as a commentary on previous ones. Pygmalion
too, Myrrha's story implies, is guilty not only of Narcissism and
of a strange kind of onanism but also of incest. Pygmalion is Galatea's fathering maker as well as her husband. To sleep with her is

to sleep with his own daughter. Pygmalion avoided the painful encounter with the otherness of other persons in ordinary human relations. But a relation in which there is no otherness, in which the same mates with the same, is, precisely, incest. Poor Myrrha pays for the sins of her great-grandfather by repeating his crime in her violent infatuation with her father. Her punishment is to be turned into a perpetually weeping myrrh tree.

The sequence of stories comes full circle back to its initiator, Venus, in a final story, the last in book 10. This story shows that even a goddess is not exempt from punishment meted out by the strict justice of the *Metamorphoses*. The child born out of the trunk of the myrrh tree is Adonis, "offspring of his sister and his grandfather," fruit of the horrible union of Cinyras and Myrrha. This leads Ovid to tell the tale of Venus' doomed love for the mortal Adonis. If Venus punished the Propoetides for denying her divinity and allowed Pygmalion to get away with falling in love with a statue he made, she pays for this by experiencing human loss. At least to that degree she loses her divinity. She falls in love with a mortal and then, when Adonis dies, suffers the human pain of being the survivor of the death of the beloved. As Ovid puts it, Adonis "now became the darling of Venus, and avenged the passion which had assailed his mother."

I have spoken of guilt and its punishment as governing the narratives in the *Metamorphoses*. The most general definition of this guilt would label it the error of taking a figure of speech literally. Such a mistake, like all such illusions, aberrations, or misreadings, can cause great social, historical, and personal grief. To treat something dead as if it were alive is an error in reading. It is also an ethical error that can be exposed by another act of reading. Whether this knowledge can be gained without repeating the error that the knowledge warns against remains to be seen.

My book will explore the ethics of narrative in its connection with the trope of prosopopoeia. But we have already learned something a little unsettling. Though none of us, of course, would take a statue as a real person, in order to "read" the *Metamorphoses* it is necessary to yield to its basic narrative personifications, by a certain willing suspension of disbelief. We must think of Pygmalion, Galatea, Cinyras, Myrrha, and even Venus to some degree as if they were real persons, not just black marks on the page. This does not bode well for the hope that the reader of these stories can be exempt from the error the tales describe. In order to understand the "crime," it may be necessary to commit it again. Whether this is really the case must remain an open question, to be tested by the readings that follow.

CHAPTER I

The Ethics of Narration

In *The Ethics of Reading* (1987) I investigated in a preliminary way the question posed by that title. I propose here to exemplify further the claim that the rhetorical study of literature is indispensable to exploration of the so-called extrinsic relations of literature: the relations of literature to history, politics, and society, to personal and institutional relations. *The Ethics of Reading* ends with a promise, the promise to read some actual narratives rather than passages where authors write about what they have written.

This book is the attempt to fulfill my promise. It presents readings of a series of stories that exemplify the relation between ethics and narrative. I do this with special attention to prosopopoeia as the fundamental generative linguistic act making a given story possible. If there is no ethics without story and no story without prosopopoeia, then understanding that figure of speech is essential to an understanding of ethics and especially of the ethics of reading.

My inaugural or constitutive questions remain what they were at the beginning of *The Ethics of Reading*. This new book has been undertaken in the hope that a careful reading of some actual stories may take me closer to answers. Is there an ethical dimension to the act of reading as such (as opposed to the expression of ethical themes in the text read)? Does some moral good come to me out of the solitary act of reading? How would one measure that good accurately, and what kind of good, exactly, would it be? Reinforcement and creation of my values, my further incorporation into the values of my society?

A. Bartlett Giamatti seemed to be affirming something like the latter in a vigorous attack on literary theory written while he was still president of Yale University. He was of course implicitly criticizing some influential colleagues at Yale. The address was delivered, of all places, before the Signet Society at Harvard. It was reported in some detail in the *Boston Globe* for Wednesday, April 17, 1985. The function of the mass media in sustaining the attack on literary theory or the resistance to it deserves analysis. It has received some discussion since then. Literary study, Giamatti reportedly said, "is meant to be a means to clarify the values and strengthen the lessons that make life bearable or even joyful . . . language shapes and transmits values, creates the environment for a rational, decent and civilized life." This seems so reasonable and plausible a claim that one would hesitate to quarrel with it, beyond asking for some demonstration of just how this happens in a given case and perhaps asking what the difference is between "shaping" and "transmitting" values. Just how much autonomous power was Giamatti willing to allow in that word "shapes"? In any event, if the study of literature does so much good and demonstrates that language has this humane value as creator and sustainer of civilization, does my reading diffuse that good to others, to my students if I am a teacher, to my readers if I am a critic? What good is reading?

Reading would seem to be initially and perhaps primarily a matter of getting the meaning of what is read right, that is, a cognitive or epistemological matter, not an ethical matter having to do with conduct and responsibility. Nevertheless, just as Henry James in the eloquent paragraph ending the preface to *The Golden Bowl* claims that the act of writing is a privileged part of what he calls "the conduct of life,"[1] so I claim that the act of reading is also part of the conduct of life. I propose to demonstrate this by readings of narratives by James, Kleist, Melville, and Blanchot, returning at the end to another story by James. These stories are all versions of Pygmalion and Galatea, that is, stories in which the act of prosopopoeia essential to any storytelling is overtly thematized, as when someone falls in love with a statue.

My questions are the following: In the pragmatic, "real-life" situation of reading a work of literature, or teaching it to a class, or writing an essay about it, what exactly are the ethical responsibilities of the reader, teacher, or critic? To what or to whom are we obligated, and what, exactly, does that obligation require us to do? Are we primarily responsible to society in general or to our particular local community or, if one is a teacher, to the institution that hires and pays us, or are teachers primarily responsible to their students? Must not the work of reading, on the other hand, all grow out of what is traditionally called "respect for the text"? How can the reader fulfill all those perhaps conflicting obligations at once? What power adjudicates in case of a conflict among these responsibilities? The "conscience" of the reader? Some external authority? If respect for the text takes priority, exactly to what or to whom are we responsible when we have "respect for the text"? At exactly what point, in relation to the total transaction with a text, including cognitive responsibility to "get the text right," does a properly ethical moment intervene for the reader, teacher, or critic of literature?

But, first, what do I mean by "ethics" in the phrase "the ethics of reading"? I mean more or less what Henry James means in that preface to *The Golden Bowl,* when he says that "the whole conduct of life consists of things done, which do other things in their turn."[2] If James is correct to say that writing, say writing *The Golden Bowl,* is a thing done that does other things in its turn, my question is concrete and specific. In what sense is reading novels, poems, or philosophical texts, teaching them, or writing about them a thing done that does other things in its turn? Does reading have a proper and unavoidable ethical dimension, along with its cognitive or epistemological one, and, if so, what is it? How does reading differ from other ethical acts, such as making promises and keeping them, proferring a true report, giving and receiving gifts, or greeting my neighbor?

But I mean by an ethical act not only a doing that does other things in its turn. An ethical act must also be free, free in the sense that I must be free to do it or not to do it, therefore taking responsibility for it. How can I be held responsible for something I cannot *not* do? At the same time, in any act properly to be called ethical, I must be directed by some imperative "I must; I cannot do otherwise." Some such demand or exigence is an essential feature of ethical acts, including acts of reading insofar as they are ethical. Examples of ethical acts represented *in* works of literature (which is by no means the same thing as the ethical moment involved in reading those works) are Nora Rowley's decision to refuse Mr. Glascock's offer of marriage because she does not love him, in Anthony Trollope's *He Knew He Was Right:* "She must refuse the offer that was so brilliant, and give up the idea of reigning as queen at Monkhams"[3]; or Maisie's offer, at the end of James's *What Maisie Knew,* to give up Mrs. Wix if Sir Claude will give up Mrs. Beale. Maisie's "I must," James's narrator says, is based on "something still deeper than a moral sense."[4] What is the source of this "I must," and is it analogous to the demand James responded to when he wrote the novel, the demand we respond to when we read it, teach it, write about it?

It will be seen from my use of examples that I think my topic is one that cannot be adequately discussed in the abstract. It *must* be analyzed and demonstrated in terms of specific cases. The relation between examples and conceptual generalizations is one of the problematic areas in any theory of the ethics of reading. It is easy to see that no selection of an example is innocent. Each is a somewhat arbitrary choice for which the chooser must take responsibility. On the other hand, there is no doing, in this region of the conduct of life, without examples. This is as true of philosophical treatises on ethics as it is in literary study. Narratives, examples, stories, such as Kant's little story in the *Grundlegung zur Metaphysik der Sitten* of the man who makes a promise intending not to keep it, are indispensable to thinking about ethics. An understanding of ethics as a region of philosophical or conceptual investigation depends, perhaps surprisingly, on a mastery of the ability to interpret written stories, that is, on a kind of mastery usually thought to be the province of the literary critic. If this is true, it has important implications for my claim that the rhetorical study of literature has crucial practical implications for our moral, social, and political life. Narrative examples are especially appropriate for an investigation of the ethics of reading. But it is not because stories contain the thematic dramatization of ethical situations, choices, and judgments that makes them especially appropriate for my topic; it is, on the contrary, because ethics itself has a peculiar relation to that form of language we call narrative. The thematic dramatizations of ethical topics in narratives are the oblique allegorization of this linguistic necessity. On this difficult point I shall have more to say later.

Some theories of ethics would contest my claim that an ethical act must be both free and at the same time a response to a categorical imperative. The history of speculation about ethics since Kant is the story of attempts to deal with this apparent contradiction. It is possible to argue, for example, that one is as ethically responsible for acts done inadvertently or automatically as for those that are done by free choice. Not only is ignorance of the law no excuse—ignorance of what I have done unintentionally, as when I was sleepwalking, is no excuse either. Being able to say "I did not mean to do it" does not free me of ethical responsibility. This issue is precisely one of those ethical themes often dramatized within works of literature, as in the opening sentence and all the ensuing action of Kafka's *The Trial:* "Someone must have been telling lies about Joseph K., for without having done anything wrong he was arrested one fine morning."[5] The novel turns on the question of whether Joseph K. has done anything wrong, whether it is just that he should be condemned to death for the infraction of a law of which he is not only initially ignorant but which he has no possibility of ever confronting face to face or reading as an ascertainable written law. The parable within the text of *The Trial*, "Before the Law," dramatizes this situation as subjection to a law that is invisible but sovereign.

A different result is obtained when one shifts, as I am trying to do, from the thematic representation within a work of ethical issues to the ethical issues involved in the act of reading itself. It is easy to see that the act of reading is in a curious way both free and not free. Surely I am relatively free to read or not to read a given book, to teach it, or to write about it. Or am I? If my department or institution has charged me with teaching a certain course, or if I am a student forced to take a required course within a certain curriculum, then I can hardly be said to be free not to read the books on the curriculum of that course. This freedom would be even more radically curtailed if the current movement back to the establishment of a basic canon of works of literature that all American schoolchildren *must* read were successful.

Let me try to clarify this curious constraint on my freedom to read or not to read. Imagine a situation in which by accident I take a certain book down from the shelf or spot an open book on someone's desk. If I know the language, I may be said to read it whether or not I want to do so. And I must take responsibility for the consequences of that act. Reading is in a certain sense automatic, involuntary. I just happen to have read a certain book, say one I find in a hotel room or in a rented summer house. This accidental encounter may have the most extensive ethical consequences in my own life, and in those of others, as my act of reading causes other things to be done in their turn. My own reading of the criticism of Georges Poulet, for example, occurred in just this fortuitous way. It was nevertheless decisive for my professional career as teacher and critic, even for my personal life.

It is an intrinsic feature of written pieces of language that they demand to be read, even though they may never find their readers. All those books lining the shelves of all the libraries do not just passively sit there. They cry out to be read. They do not cease day and night to clamor for readers, just as, according to Walter Benjamin in "The Task of the Translator," each text demands to be translated, even though it may never find its translator. This demand will be met only when the text is turned into another language, perhaps into all other languages. The ethics of reading begins with the reader's response to a parallel demand that each text be read, and even read again and again.

This response begins and remains in a painful double bind. Each book, text, essay, scrap of written language, even those in languages I do not know, asks to be read. The call is directed to me personally and with equal force by each text. I *must* read them all. There is no initial way or principle, other than arbitrary or contingent ones, by which I can decide an order of priority among all the books. I must get on with it and begin where I can. But in choosing to respond to the demand made by the book that has fallen by accident into my hands, I am betraying my responsibility to all the other books. This is a responsibility I can never fulfill. So I live in a perpetual condition of guilty arrears, which is my fate as soon as I have learned to read. I shall go to my grave still in debt and unable by the most heroic efforts to pay off my obligation. Thomas Wolfe reports how as a student at Harvard he was tormented not only by the impossibility of ever reading through all the books in Widener Library, but also by learning that there were a hundred thousand new books in German published each year, that is, in a language he did not even know. His ignorance did not lessen one whit the obligation he felt to read all the books in German as well.

The situation is made even worse by the fact that my decision to read means a suspension of other responsibilities and contractual obligations, to my family, to my institution, to my students and colleagues, whose "secondary" texts I have a perpetually mounting obligation to assess, to all those committees and advisory boards on which I serve. Proust, in his description of the youthful reading of Marcel, has dramatized what is furtive, guilty, private about reading, the way someone, the reader's grandmother for example, is always trying to get him to do something else, to get out in the sunlight and take part in the world of action. There are many other representations *in* novels of what the reader of the novel is at that moment doing. Examples are George Eliot's description of Maggie Tulliver's childhood readings, the decisive effect on Conrad's Jim of his reading of adventure stories, or the effects of reading novels on Don Quixote and Emma Bovary. These novels warn against what the reader must do in order to understand the warning. It might be better not to read. Nor does this manifold pressure not to read disappear as you get older. By a familiar paradox of the teaching profession, the older and more established you get, the less and less time you are allowed for what was your vocation in the first place, that is, a calling to read works of literature, as many as possible in all the languages, and a commitment to talking and writing about what you have read.

Nor is this initial demand, command, or exigency that I read all the books a fantasy or mere theoretical concept. It is a concrete and real experience, the experience of an implacable and at the same time entirely unfulfillable obligation. Any reader who takes reading at all seriously will have felt the force of this responsibility, however successfully one may have suppressed it as an absurdity. Who or what says I must read all the books? My situation as reader is a little as if I had signed an impossible contract without having in fact signed it, as if I were born into the world encumbered with a debt I have no chance of ever paying off. It is as if someone or something else had signed in my stead. As soon as I learn to read I am already bound by an obligation I had no idea I was taking on. I am in this like Joseph K. arrested one fine day without having done anything wrong.

In this ethical emergency, as in other unbreakable double binds, the only way to live with it in the most responsible way is to do something. A parallel may be made with that irreconcilability between spiritual love and bodily love demonstrated so irrefutably in Shakespeare's *As You Like It*. Both the verbal texture and the dramatic action of this play demonstrate that you cannot, logically, love in both ways at once. Nevertheless, the denouement of *As You Like It* is the celebration of four marriages. These marriages do not break the knot of the double bind by tying new bonds within which lust is lawful and compatible with spiritual love. Instead they put all the protagonists, high and low, in the situation of dwelling with the greatest tension within that double bind, as anyone who has been married will know.

In the case of the double bind of reading, the analogous leap in the dark is clear. In all desperation I must take up the first book that falls into my hands and begin reading. *Tolle, lege* is the first law of reading. In order to fulfill the obligations involved in the ethics of reading, I must first read something, some one book, poem, novel, or essay, in spite of the fact that to single out one over all the others is not only an arbitrary and unjustified choice, but also a betrayal of my obligation to all the other books. They call out with equal peremptoriness to be read. To read one book is therefore to get even further behind in fulfilling my duty to read all those other books. Still I must read. The essays that follow in this book are a response to that demand.

What happens when I read, when I *really* read, which does not happen all that often? What happens is something always fortuitous and unpredictable, something surprising, however many times the book in question has been read before, even by me. One way to define this unexpected quality of true acts of reading is to say that they never correspond exactly to what other readers tell me I am going to find when I read that book, however learned, expert, and authoritative those previous readers have been. Another way to describe what is unpredictable about a genuine act of reading is to say that reading is always the disconfirmation or modification of presupposed literary theory rather than its confirmation. What happens when I read a particular book never quite fits my theory (or anyone else's) of what is going to happen. You can never be sure what is going to happen when someone in a particular situation reads a particular book. Rather than thinking of all those books on the shelf as the sure and safe repository of the values of Western culture, the army of unalterable law ranged in rows, it might be better to think of them as so many unexploded bombs that may have who knows what result when they get read by the right (or the wrong) person at the right (or the wrong) place or time. A book is a dangerous object, and perhaps all books should have warning labels. Strange things happen when someone reads a book.

A theory of the ethics of reading that takes seriously the possibility that reading might lead to other morally good or valuable actions would also have to allow for the possibility that the reading even of a morally exemplary book might cause something morally deplorable to occur. This has in fact happened more than once. Paul de Man is right in his shrewd adaptation of Hölderlin's "Es ereignet aber das Wahre" into a formula for what happens in reading. Hölderlin's phrase, says de Man, "can be freely translated, 'What is true is what is bound to take place.' And, in the case of the reading of a text, what takes place is a necessary understanding. What marks the truth of such an understanding is not some abstract universal but the fact that it has to occur regardless of other considerations."[6]

De Man's formulation must not be understood as meaning that exactly the same thing occurs each time a given text is read. "Ereignen" means "happen, come to pass, occur." An act of reading takes place as an event. It is something that happens, with the same inaugural violence, breaking any predictable concatenation, as other events in the real world like birth, copulation, death, or declarations of independence. That such events, including reading, may be in one way or another a repetition by no means disables their disruptive force, as Kierkegaard recognized in his concept of repetition, described as follows by Sylviane Agacinski: repetition "is like a tear or rip that blows or blows up, pops, pierces, opens and shows up. There it was, and now here it is. It happens."[7] The event of reading, like the writing of that text in the first place, "takes place," with all the enigmatic force in this notion of an event as something that comes out of nowhere, so to speak, occupies space, and makes that space into a place, with orienting coordinates. Reading occurs in a certain spot to a certain person in a certain historical, personal, institutional, and political situation, but it always exceeds what was predictable from those circumstances. It makes something happen that is a deviation from its context, and what happens demands a new definition each time. The record of those deviations includes the further language written or spoken in response to the act of reading, such as critical essays or acts of teaching, but of course reading may lead to many other kinds of acts. Another way to put this is to say that reading always has a performative as well as a cognitive dimension. It follows that the historical and practical, as well as the theoretical, study of literature should include attention to the performative force in reading. The following chapters are an attempt to pay such attention. My book is a record of situated acts of reading.

CHAPTER 2

Reading, Doing:
James's *What Maisie Knew*

Suppose the book I pick up and decide to read, to the momentary exclusion and neglect of all others, happens to be Henry James's *What Maisie Knew,* complete with the preface James wrote for the New York Edition. What happens when I do that? In what sense is the reading of *What Maisie Knew* an ethical act, the doing of something that does other things in its turn? How should I go about rendering justice to *Maisie?*

This apparently limited act of reading is accomplished by a deliberate asceticism that gives up, for the moment, reading all other books. Nevertheless, in spite of its apparent limits, it may be an interminable task. A relatively short novel by James like *What Maisie Knew* (simple in comparison to *The Golden Bowl*) turns out to be complex and difficult to read. The reading of *Maisie,* moreover, leads to the reading of its preface of 1908 and then to a reading of the entries about the gestation and writing of *Maisie* in James's notebooks. The preface leads also to a reading of "In the Cage" and "The Pupil," joined with *Maisie* in volume 11 of the New York Edition. *The Princess Casamassima* is mentioned in the preface as analogous in a specific way to *Maisie.* That too would need to be read. *What Maisie Knew* has also been the subject of a number of excellent essays, including some fairly recent ones.[1] Before we know it, we have incurred an obligation to read all of James and all of the criticism about James before daring to write one sentence about *Maisie.* A number of distinguished critics have become permanently lost on that road. The courage to write about James at all may come from a blessed stupidity that blunders ahead in spite of such difficulties.

In the case of *What Maisie Knew,* we have the record of what happened to one exemplary reader of that novel, namely to Henry James himself when he reread it in order to write the preface for the New York Edition of his works. The record is the preface. In the case of reading as a thing done that causes other things to be done, the first new thing is always another act of language. This is so even if that second act remains merely implicit in the "silent" act of reading. Whatever may be the momentous effects of reading in the real world of politics, economics, and family life, those effects must go by way of new words. Criticism or the teaching of a given text is always the displaced expression of what happened when the work was read.

What James says about *What Maisie Knew* in his preface may be taken as exemplary of what any reader might come to say about the novel. The difference is that James can also write about what he remembers or is willing to tell about how he came to write the novel. If the notebook entries are written in anticipation of an act of writing James has not yet accomplished, the preface, on the other hand, is memorial. It may be full of elisions and suppressions. There is no reason to suppose that what James says in the preface to *Maisie* is the last word about the novel. As Sharon Cameron has argued,[2] James's celebrated prefaces do not by any means always say the same thing the novels say. Later readers may find their best chance within the space of that deviation.

The most salient thing that readers of *What Maisie Knew,* as of James's work generally, find themselves obligated to account for is the following: Why is the highest good, the truly moral act, for James always some act of giving up, of abnegation? What does this mean for what I should do on the basis of reading *What Maisie Knew?* Isabel Archer in *The Portrait of a Lady* stays with Gilbert Osmond, though that staying seems to contradict all she has learned about what is most valuable in life. Catherine Sloper in *Washington Square* sticks to Morris Townsend, or rather to her false image of him, even after she discovers he is worthless. Lambert Strether in *The Ambassadors* refuses Maria Gostrey's offer of herself and returns to Woollett, Massachusetts, in order to remain true to his principle: "That, you see, is my only logic. Not, out of the whole affair, to have got anything for myself."[3] Maggie in *The Golden Bowl* tells her lie, denies knowledge of her husband's adultery with Charlotte, and triumphs over both in perhaps the most complex case of giving up in all of James. Milly Theale in *The Wings of the Dove* leaves her money to Merton Densher, knowing he has betrayed her, thereby effectively separating Densher from Kate Croy forever.

All these acts of abnegation, far from bringing "bliss" either to the one who gives up or to those around, only bring more and more lasting "bale," to use James's terms from the preface to *Maisie*.[4] It may be, however, that renunciation gives the one who renounces something even more precious than worldly success and happiness. Just what this treasure is will take more than a little digging to uncover. In all these works by James, knowledge ultimately leads to a climactic choice, decision, and action. This act ends the book. But the act is enigmatic. It does not seem, at least superficially, to follow logically from knowledge, whatever Strether, for example, may say about his "logic."

Maisie takes her place in this long line of Jamesian protagonists who ultimately "give up." The novel might more properly be called "What Maisie Did on the Basis of What She Knew." But once more the phrase "on the basis of" hardly seems right for the non sequitur between knowledge and act. No careful reader of *What Maisie Knew* can doubt that an understanding of the novel depends on a right reading of the concluding two chapters. Maisie's renunciation takes place in these chapters, first in the scene of the long talk with Sir Claude as they breakfast together and then wander about Boulogne, and finally in the climactic scene in the hotel when she publicly reaffirms her choice to renounce Sir Claude and go back to England alone with Mrs. Wix. Or rather that is almost but not quite what she does. The chapter reaches its climax in the extraordinary sentences in which the narrator records Maisie's rejection of Mrs. Wix's insistence that she should decide in terms of the "faint flower" of her moral sense. Maisie replaces "moral sense" with another basis for ethical judgment and action. Any right reading of the novel, no careful reader can doubt, depends on understanding that basis.

BEFORE ATTEMPTING to read the passage, let me try to identify the economic and social realities that set the rules for human behavior in *What Maisie Knew*. The factors of greatest importance are like those unspoken social laws, rules, assumptions, and prescriptions that an anthropologist must identify in order to make sense of the behavior of the peoples she studies or in order to understand the stories they tell. To some degree these rules and assumptions are more difficult to identify for a culture like our own than for a more alien one. We tend to take our own cultural laws as part of nature. James's England, however, is already far enough away from us to seem more than a little strange.

James's presentation of Maisie's gradual initiation into knowledge of the rules of her society is a powerful way of leading the reader to notice this strangeness. We see Victorian culture from the outside, through Maisie's wondering eyes, just as we see through Alice's eyes in *Alice in Wonderland*. This procedure is an effective way of showing the conventions of Maisie's society as cultural and coercive, ideological rather than natural. They could conceivably be otherwise. In this way the writing and then the reading of this novel functions as cultural criticism or as critique of ideology. My basic question here is whether such critique can or should lead to action and, if so, to what action. The answer might well be different for James's English readers in 1898 and for an American reader ninety years later.

One cultural condition presupposed in *What Maisie Knew* has to do with divorce. Though new laws had made divorce somewhat easier in late nineteenth-century England than before, divorce was still expensive and far from common. The main ground was the proved and conspicuous adultery of the wife. Divorce involved lengthy and public litigation. An example is the divorce proceedings of Maisie's parents, Ida and Beale Farange. These are reported by the narrator in the opening sentence of the prologue: "The litigation had seemed interminable and had in fact been complicated" (3). The double standard was still present in the new marital laws.[5] Though both Beale and Ida, so the narrator hints, have been flagrant in their infidelities, custody of Maisie is at first granted exclusively to her father. She is then divided equally between her two parents, six months a year with each, only in remission of the debt of 2600 pounds Beale owes his wife, an amount she gave him three years before, for the child's care, "precisely on a proved understanding that he would take no proceedings: a sum of which he had had the administration and of which he could render not the least account" (3).

Though making adultery public, a matter for gossip and the newspapers, was still scandalous, even so Maisie is born into a set of high-bourgeois people whose way of life seems to involve a perpetual and conspicuous round of adultery. Both Maisie's parents remarry new sexual partners after their divorce. That does not prevent each from proceeding to an apparently endless series of lovers. Maisie hears of Lord Eric and meets Mr. Perriam and the Captain, with whom Ida takes up, one after the other. She also meets the ugly, brown American lady, a "Countess," with whom Beale Farange "bolts." The narrator discreetly indicates his disapproval of this set of people. An undercurrent of deep disgust with sex flows through *Maisie*. On the other hand, James, the narrator, Maisie, and the reader all capitalize on this social situation. Each makes something, or claims to make something, of priceless value out of it.

The new English marital laws that allow the divorce of Maisie's parents registered a further dissolution of traditional patriarchal society. In that society the woman was a possession of her father, if unmarried, or of her husband, if married. She had few legal rights of her own. She was flesh of her husband's flesh. As Lawrence Stone and many other scholars have demonstrated, this patriarchy had been weakening since the seventeenth century, through the passing of new laws as well as through changes in customary behavior.[6] By the time of *What Maisie Knew* the old model of a proper marriage is no longer dominant. This model presupposed a family in which the husband faced out into the world, fulfilling his civic and financial responsibilities, while his wife remained within the home, as one of his major pieces of property, bearing and bringing up his children, thereby maintaining his line and prudently managing his household.

In English upper middle-class society of the late nineteenth century, if we can trust James's testimony as well as that of other witnesses, some men do not work or fulfill any other social responsibilities. They are more subject to women than sovereign over them. And some women have become free-floating objects of sexual exchange, passed from man to man. Or rather, it would be better to say, even this gender-specific description of sexual transgression has broken down. It would be just as correct to say that the men in *Maisie*, men such as Sir Claude, are free-floating objects of sexual exchange, passed from woman to woman. Marriage has become no more than a way of legitimizing sex, which no longer has procreation as its goal. Sex is no longer a means of preserving property, along with social power, and passing it on to the next generation. Though Maisie is the product of a lawful marriage, after her parents' divorce she no longer has the legitimate girl-child's traditional social function. This would be the daughter's function of being married off as well as possible, so establishing a new economically valuable social bond by assisting another family in maintaining its patrilineal continuity. Maisie, on the contrary, is useful to her parents only as the unconscious mediator of their hatred of one another: "the only link binding her to either parent was this lamentable fact of her being a ready vessel for bitterness, a deep little porcelain cup in which biting acids could be mixed. They had wanted her not for any good they could do her, but for the harm they could, with her unconscious aid, do each other" (5). Later she serves the equally lamentable social function of lending respectability to the adultery of her step-parents. The novel ends when she refuses this role.

If these people are driven by lust (as Mrs. Wix says of Sir Claude: "He's just a poor sunk slave . . . To his passions" [313]), they are also driven by economic need. Ida and Beale, Maisie's biological parents, are among those middle-class persons who, like Becky Sharp and others in Thackeray's *Vanity Fair*, have learned to live on nothing, or almost nothing, a year. The narrator carefully specifies the details of this in the prologue. Beale "had been destined in his youth for diplomacy and momentarily attached, without a salary, to a legation which enabled him often to say 'In *my* time in the East': but contemporary history had somehow had no use for him, had hurried past him and left him in perpetual Piccadilly. Every one knew what he had—only twenty-five hundred. Poor Ida, who had run through everything, had now nothing but her carriage and her paralysed uncle. This old brute, as he was called, was supposed to have a lot put away" (8).

Everyone around Maisie is in perpetually straitened circumstances. She is denied many things that someone in her social class ought to have, a proper education, for example, but it does not occur to anyone to go out and get a job with a wage or a salary. Instead, each uses sexual attractiveness as a means of living off others. Miss Overmore, one of Maisie's governesses, the pretty one, escapes poverty by marrying Maisie's father and becoming "Mrs. Beale." Sir Claude, Ida's second husband, is immensely attractive to women and sustains himself through them, though Mrs. Wix says *he* pays Mrs. Beale just as the brown lady pays Beale (276). Economic and sexual matters, in short, are inextricably intertwined in *What Maisie Knew.* The terminology of economic and sexual exchange, and the exchanges between them, are a basic resource of James's nomenclature. An example is his extravagant use in the preface of economic terminology to describe both ethical and aesthetic value.

Another contextual factor is the assumption that the facts of sexuality, particularly illicit sexuality, should be kept secret from children, especially female children. The whole novel turns on the fact that though Maisie is surrounded by shameful goings-on, she is supposed to know nothing of it. She is forced to find the truth out for herself by prodigious efforts of childish detective work, a reading of the covert signs around her. Hence the title. The central question in *What Maisie Knew* is "what Maisie knew," the gradual process of coming to know what in her society there is a strict prohibition against telling her openly.

Maisie is not even supposed to know anything of the physiological facts of human sexuality. This is so absurd a prohibition that one wonders if it was really adhered to. But it is a basic presupposition of nineteenth-century fiction. Adultery is James's great theme, but it cannot ever be spoken of openly or shown in action. Nanda in *The Awkward Age,* published just after *Maisie* in 1899, is rendered unmarriageable by the fact that her mother does not keep her carefully enough segregated from adult conversation. She loses her sexual innocence before she can be married. She knows too much through hearing the talk of her elders ever to be a proper bride. In this society virginity must be of the mind as well as the body. The reader of *What Maisie Knew* and *The Awkward Age* side by side may wonder what chance Maisie may have to marry, since she comes to know, at a much younger age, at least as much as Nanda knows. Maisie at the age of twelve or thirteen is already, from the point of view of the ideology I have been describing, such a piece of damaged goods that it seems hard to imagine any use for her in society. Such a harsh judgment, however, hardly agrees with the high valuation of Maisie made by James, by his narrator, and by their apparent spokesman at one crucial point in the novel, Sir Claude.

One more social and economic context presupposed in *What Maisie Knew* has to do with the novel itself. James made his income by writing novels and stories. Unlike the people about whom he writes in *Maisie* he worked for a living. During the writing of *Maisie* James began to suffer severe writer's cramp, a terrible occupational disability, and he had to begin dictating his novels. There has been much speculation about what changes this brought in James's style. It seems plausible to assume that the technical means by which a work of fiction is produced might have some effect on its form and meaning. *The Golden Bowl* might have been quite different if it had been written on a word processor.

The writing and publication of fiction in James's day were subject to all sorts of further social, technological, and economic restraints. *Maisie* was the first major work James wrote after the failure of *Guy Domville* and after the collapse of his hopes as a dramatist. That failure was financial as well as artistic. As a writer for magazines and for book publishers, James was subject to a complex set of conventions. One of these was a constraint of length, which James found almost impossible to obey. During the time he was writing *Maisie* James was attempting to train himself to write short stories of 5000 words: "The very essence of such a job is—let me with due vividness remember it—that they consist each, substantially, of a *single incident,* an incident definite, limited, sharp. I must *cultivate* the vision, the observation and notation of that—just as I must sternly master the *faire,* the little hard, fine, repeated process."[7] As we can see, writing such brief tales was a matter of stern self-mastery. Such short stories would no doubt have high artistic values of hardness, economy, and concentration, but they would also have the economic value of being salable. Such short stories were a recognizable genre, with a wide market.

These restraints, however, James almost always found it impossible to obey. *Maisie* is a conspicuous example. The first sentence of the preface ruefully describes *Maisie* as "another instance of the growth of the 'great oak' from the little acorn; since 'What Maisie Knew' is at least a tree that spreads beyond any provision its small germ might on a first handling have appeared likely to make for it" (v). The preface to *The Awkward Age* speaks eloquently of "the quite incalculable tendency of a mere grain of subject-matter to expand and develop and cover the ground when conditions happen to favour it."[8] The notebook entries trace the gradual expansion of *Maisie*. First he promised it to Henry Harland in the form of "a 10,000 (a *real* 10,000) for the April *Yellow Book*" (N147), but it continually outgrew his successive shapely plans for it. The original "8 or 10 little chapters" (N148) of "this interminable little *Maisie*" (N167) became finally a substantial novel in thirty-one chapters that ran serially in the *Chap Book* from January 15 to August 1, 1897.

Three contradictory things can be said about the inordinate length of *Maisie*. On the one hand, the traces remain everywhere of the author's attempt to practice economy, to keep the length down so that he could finish what he was writing, sell it, and have readers. The famous "blest scenic method" about which he writes eloquently in the preface and in the notes about *Maisie* (xxii; N162) is at least in part a way to keep it short, as well as an aesthetic law of proper and effective presentation.

On the other hand, James was never fully successful in such parsimony. It is of the nature of the stories he had to tell to be more or less interminable. James formulates this principle of interminability and the artifice to which it leads in a celebrated passage in the preface to *Roderick Hudson*. "Really, universally, relations stop nowhere, and the exquisite problem of the artist is eternally but to draw, by a geometry of his own, the circle within which they shall happily *appear* to do so."[9] The law of this perpetual excess seems to be that less is more. The more James renounced, the more he limited and concentrated his subject and his point of view, the longer and longer, the richer and richer, the more inexhaustible in appreciable value the novel grew. Though James was continually getting himself in trouble with editors and publishers by being unable to keep to length, still it is this getting of more from less that especially marks James's imagination and valued reputation.

But James wrote under yet another complex social restraint. On the one hand he was painfully conscious of the fact that he wrote for readers who would have little appreciation of the purely artistic value of his work. On the other hand he too was limited, as much as Maisie in his novel, by the taboos against open discussion of sexuality, especially illicit sexuality, even though most of his readers were of course fully aware of these facts. Praising the scenic method, at the end of the preface to *Maisie,* James says: "The great advantage for the total effect is that we feel, with the definite alternation [of scene and preparation for scene], how the theme *is* being treated. That is we feel it when, in such tangled connexions, we happen to care. I shouldn't really go on as if this were the case with many readers" (xxii). Earlier in the preface, James complains bitterly that readers of *Maisie* missed the way his treatment transfigured the ugly social facts. They found the novel simply unpleasant—because its subject was the gradual education of an innocent child in those facts:

> Nothing of course, meanwhile, is an older story to the observer of manners and the painter of life than the grotesque finality with which such terms as "painful," "unpleasant," and "disgusting" are often applied to his results . . . I was punctually to have had read to me the lesson that the "mixing-up" of a child with anything unpleasant confessed itself an aggravation of the unpleasantness, and that nothing could well be more disgusting than to attribute to Maisie so intimate an "acquaintance" with the gross immoralities surrounding her. (xiii)

The preface to *Maisie* can in fact be seen as an elaborate defense against this charge of unpleasantness, even of immorality. James must defend himself against the accusation of a kind of imaginary child abuse or of contributing to the delinquency of a minor.

All of these constraining social and economic factors are presupposed in any adequate reading of the passage I have promised to read. I am aware that to say they are "presupposed" or "constraining," or are the essential "context" of the novel or its own immanent unspoken rules, begs all sorts of questions about the relation of text to context. These questions are essential in present-day concerns for interpreting literature in terms of its social and historical contexts. My reading of *Maisie,* as of the other narratives in this book, has been guided by four assumptions:

(1) The relation of literature to history is a problem, not a solution. Just to establish in all its factual circumstantiality one or another historical context for a work, for example the facts about marital law in England in the late nineteenth century as a context for *Maisie,* is only the beginning of an interpretation of that work. The question still remains of just how the context inheres in the text, is presupposed by it, or is operative within it. Does the text merely represent or reflect its historical conditions, in a correct or distorting mirror? If it does more, what is that more?

(2) It follows that the establishment of the complex content "embedded"[10] in the text does not exempt the scholar-critic from the fulfillment of the patient task of actually *reading* the text. Reading should be guided by the expectation of surprise, that is, the presupposition that what you actually find when you read a given work is likely to be fundamentally different from what you expected or what previous readers have led you to expect. Good reading is also guided by the presupposition of a possible heterogeneity in the text. The ever-present danger in reading is that it will not be reading at all, but just a finding in the text of what the reader already knew he or she was going to find there and therefore has posed as a screen between himself or herself and the actual text.

(3) The relation between text and context does not exist as a physical relation (say a relation of material causality), but as a textual or sign to sign relation. Moreover, this relation is tropological, never straightforwardly referential. This means that the relation of text to context cannot be thought about or formulated except in terms that are figurative, whether that figure is metaphor (representation as mimetic likeness), or metonymical (text side by side with its determining context), or allegorical (text as the concentrated saying otherwise of economic or social conditions, a covert expression of hidden ideological constraints), or some version of an inside-outside figure (text as one side of an exchange by chiasmus in which inside turns into outside, outside into inside). The investigation of the relation of literature to history depends on an awareness of these latent figures and on a skill in manipulating

their implications, not being manipulated by them. Achieving that awareness and skill is a major task of literary studies. To put this another way, study of the relations of literature to history and society is part of rhetoric, not part of physics, however "material" history may be. This fact is not news to good Marxists or to good "new historicists," any more than it is news to good "deconstructionists," but it is all too easy for critics of all three persuasions to forget this essential truth.

(4) A literary text does not merely reflect its historical conditions, in however complex or obscure a way. It also transforms those conditions, does something to them. A work of literature intervenes in history whenever it is read. Literature is productive, performative. It makes something happen. Study of the way the writing and reading of a work of literature are speech acts is another part of rhetoric.

I hold these truths to be self-evident, but even self-evident truths need occasionally to be enunciated, whatever the risks involved in stating them categorically, partly because they may not seem all that self-evident to everyone or, to put this another way, because it is not self-evident whether they are constative or performative.

LET ME TURN now to the passage I have promised to read:

> "Your moral sense. *Haven't* I, after all, brought it out?" She [Mrs. Wix, Maisie's governess] spoke as she had never spoken even in the schoolroom and with the book in her hand.
>
> It brought back to the child's recollection how she sometimes couldn't repeat on Friday the sentence that had been glib on Wednesday, and she dealt all feebly and ruefully with the present tough passage. Sir Claude and Mrs. Beale stood there like visitors at an "exam." She had indeed an instant a whiff of the faint flower that Mrs. Wix pretended to have plucked and now with such a peremptory hand had thrust at her nose. Then it left her, and, as if she were sinking with a slip from a foothold, her arms made a short jerk. What this jerk represented was the spasm within her of something still deeper than a moral sense. She looked at her examiner; she looked at the visitors; she felt the rising of the tears she had kept down at the station. They had nothing—no, distinctly nothing—to do with her moral sense. The only thing was the old flat shameful schoolroom plea. "I don't know—I don't know." (353–354)

What can the reader say of this "present tough passage" in its context, the context ultimately of the whole novel, of the rest of James's work, of social and economic reality in late nineteenth-century England, and of the long tradition of thinking about the grounds of ethical decision, along with traditional thinking about the function of art? What can the reader say initially by renouncing, at first, somewhat artificially, the help of the preface, or at any rate by remembering that the preface may be a treacherous clue that suppresses or distorts as much as it reveals?

The passage opposes two ways of making an ethical decision. One is by way of appeal to an innate moral sense. To be specific, Mrs. Wix expects Maisie to reject Sir Claude and Mrs. Beale because her moral sense will lead her instinctively to condemn the adulterous relation between them. This liaison is in fact a double adultery, the reverse mirror image of the double adultery in Goethe's *Die Wahlverwandtschaften*. In Goethe's novel the lawfully wedded couple commit adultery when they make love. In the midst of the act each is thinking of the person he or she really loves and wishes were there instead. In *What Maisie Knew* Maisie's divorced parents have each remarried, and her step-parents have through her mediation begun a liaison. Each betrays the marriage bond in an adultery that is at a second remove from the adulteries of Maisie's actual parents.

A complex tradition of Enlightenment thinking about ethics, going back to Kant and of course behind Kant to the tradition of Greek, Roman, Judaic, and Christian ethical thought, is ridiculed in Maisie's repudiation of Mrs. Wix's appeal to "moral sense." The other basis for ethical decision and action is here defined negatively as "something still deeper than a moral sense." Just what that is, positively, the reader is left to find out. It is clear, in any case, that when Maisie turns from knowledge to decision and action she does not do so on the basis of innate moral sense.

Some help may be given in understanding what that other basis might be by thinking through the three tropes intertwined in the passage. One is the figure of the schoolroom oral examination, with Maisie the examinee, Mrs. Wix the schoolmistress examiner, and Sir Claude and Mrs. Beale school "visitors" who have come to witness the exam. This figure defines the moral sense as an act of memory in which the one taking an exam refers to what has been memorized in order to answer a question. Plato thought that right moral decision is an act of anamnesia, the remembering of something we brought with us from another world but forgot at birth.[11] Rousseau is often said to have believed that children are naturally good and would remain good if allowed to grow up naturally, like flowers in a garden, a kindergarten.

If the appeal to an innate moral sense invites the "examinee" to an act of memory, the something still deeper might be, on the contrary, an encounter with an unforeseen factor compelling choice. This factor would emerge suddenly, perhaps as a quick access of new knowledge and new desire that are like a "spasm." The something still deeper than a moral sense is not an act of memory, and it is not innate in the way held by all those diverse theories of educational psychology alluded to in the phrase "moral sense."

The second trope in the passage is that of scent. Maisie gets a momentary whiff of the "faint flower" of the moral sense, but it leaves her. The figure ridicules Mrs. Wix's attempt: this process of education is as superficial and evanescent as sticking a flower under someone's nose and telling her to smell it. Though Mrs. Wix claims that her condemnation of Sir Claude and Mrs. Beale is based on an innate moral sense and so should be spontaneously shared by Maisie, in fact it is mere conventional social judgment. It is as exterior as a flower's scent. Maisie, on the other hand, decides and acts on the basis of something genuinely deep down, something not presented in peremptory fashion from the outside.

The figure of the flower's fragrance seems to be wholly negative here, but it should be remembered, and at least kept suspended as an unresolved problem of reading, that James uses the same figure twice in a positive sense in the preface to *Maisie*. James's identification of the "*full* ironic truth" of the germ story is said to be like the digging out of a hidden fragrance: "It lurked in the crude postulate like a buried scent; the more the attention hovered the more aware it became of the fragrance. To which I may add that the more I scratched the surface and penetrated, the more potent, to the intellectual nostril, became this virtue" (vi). If James's search, in the primary act of imagination that generates the novel, is for a buried scent, Maisie's freshness is, later in the preface, figured in a related image. Maisie is shown "drawing some stray fragrance of an ideal across the scent of selfishness" (viii). For the moment, the apparent contradiction in the values of the three versions of the image must remain suspended.

The third image is the most obscure. Its implications are surprising, perhaps even shocking: "as if she were sinking with a slip from a foothold, her arms made a short jerk. What this jerk represented was the spasm within her of something still deeper than a moral sense." The image is an intimate bodily one. For James, here at least, emotions and thoughts are deeply incarnated. We think with our bodies or, to put it another way, our thoughts and emotions are "represented," instantly and spontaneously, by bodily movements, a short jerk of the arms, a spasm deep within. The word "represented" seems to be used here not in the sense of a secondary and mediated delegation, as a sign stands for what it signifies, but in a more immediate sense. The jerk of the arms is the external correlate of the deep spasm, continuous and adjacent, more metonymic than metaphoric. And the deep spasm *is* the "something still deeper than a moral sense." If the jerk of the arms is in any way a representative sign, it functions in that way not for Maisie, for whom it is an immediate part of her emotive thought, but for a spectator. For an exterior witness, the jerk of Maisie's arms is the outer and visible sign of an inner spasm that is bodily and mental at the same time.

What is this spasm? The figure of the slip from a foothold and the adjacent figure of rising tears give the reader a clue. The image is of someone falling from a precarious perch, from the side of a cliff or perhaps even from the scaffold when the trap is sprung. In any case it is a free fall from a situation of danger, a fall with no bottom in sight. The fall is brought up short by the jerk of the arms, the spasm within. The spasm is at one with an instinctive fear and an instinctive gesture, like the jerk of the arms a baby makes when falling. Whether in this case the jerk of the arms means Maisie has stopped falling, has caught herself, or has been caught, or whether it is the first futile gesture before a free fall, is not immediately clear. But the context leaves no doubt that the spasm is also a paroxysm of sexual desire and loss.

This reading of Maisie's spasm is confirmed by the reference to

"the rising tears she had kept down at the station." Those suppressed tears came at the moment she made her decision and knew
she would lose Sir Claude for good. Though her tears have "nothing—no, distinctly nothing—to do with her moral sense," they *do*
have to do with the doubleness of what Maisie means when she
says, repeating the statement twice, as almost everything is said
twice in the final scene, "I love Sir Claude—I love *him*" (359).

The meaning of Maisie's ultimate choice turns on the double
meaning of this assertion. On the one hand, Maisie is still a child.
She is this side of sexual maturity, sexual knowledge, and sexual
desire. She loves Sir Claude as a child might love the step-parent
who has taken better care of her than all her real parents and foster
parents together. On the other hand, Maisie has gradually, before
the reader's eyes, crossed the line into sexual maturity. She adds
herself to all the other women who have become infatuated with
Sir Claude, including Mrs. Wix. Maisie refuses to share Sir Claude
with Mrs. Beale. "Him alone or nobody," she has earlier asserted
(309). When at the train station she is suddenly gifted with an ability to understand and to speak French, her cry of "*Prenny, prenny.
Oh prenny!*" means: "Take tickets for the train for Paris before it is
too late, you and I alone together, leaving my governess, Mrs.
Wix, and your mistress, Mrs. Beale, behind." The ability to speak
French, the language of love, especially illicit love, is the sign of
Maisie's sexual maturity. For a few minutes she is tempted to enter
the world of taking rather than giving up, the endless round of
sexual partners that is social reality in *What Maisie Knew*.

When Maisie sees that Sir Claude will not go to Paris alone with
her, she turns from him to keep down her tears. These tears are
born of her sense of irrevocable loss, the loss of any chance that her
desire for Sir Claude might be satisfied. "I feel as if I had lost everything," she says a little later (353). On the basis of that sense of loss
she tells Sir Claude that she will give up Mrs. Wix if he will give
up Mrs. Beale. Maisie's tears before Mrs. Wix and Mrs. Beale in
the later scene are the repetition of her tears at the station—another
external sign, like the jerk of Maisie's arms, of the spasm of desire
and loss. They resemble Tennyson's "tears, idle tears." Maisie's
tears also rise from depths that are both bodily and psychic, very
far down. Maisie's slip from a foothold is into a deep abyss. Her

tears, like Tennyson's, signify infinite loss, the loss of everything. Maisie has, as James says in the preface, "wonder[ed] . . . to the end, to the death—the death of her childhood" (xi). Maisie makes her decision and commits her act not on the basis of a moral sense, but on this baseless basis, the basis of a sense of loss so total that it is like a fall into a bottomless chasm. This act ends the novel with the end of the reader's knowledge, by way of the narrator's knowledge, or James's, of what Maisie knew.

JUST HOW IS the reader to evaluate Maisie's act? Is it ethically admirable? Should we try to emulate it in our own life? What would it mean to do that? Is Maisie's act (as opposed to her knowledge) at all like the act of James in writing the novel, the act of the imaginary narrator in telling her story, the act of the reader in reading it? The beginning of an answer to these questions may be made by asking an apparently easier one: just whose figures of speech are these anyhow? Are they Maisie's figures or the narrator's? The careful reader will have noticed that the linguistic texture of the passage I have been discussing is made, like the novel as a whole, of the superimposition of two consciousnesses and of two languages, the mind and language of the narrator and the mind and knowledge of Maisie. The narrator differs of course from James himself. The narrator appears to have no knowledge at all that Maisie is a fiction, whereas James knows that he has made her up out of the precious germ or donnée of an anecdote. James knows that he is making up his characters out of language as he writes page after page of the novel. But the narrator knows nothing of that. James, unlike Trollope, say, or Thackeray, keeps his narrator rigorously ignorant of the fact that Maisie is a figment of the author's imagination.

The second rigorous law of the novel is a limitation in the narrator's access to the minds of the characters. He can freely enter Maisie's mind. He shares her feelings and thoughts, her silent inner language. He sees all the other characters, on the other hand, only from the outside, through her seeing and hearing and through her knowledge. He is exactly as much outside them as Maisie is, however superior he is to her in worldly knowledge and sophistication. He knows from the beginning, for example, the facts of extramarital sexuality about Maisie's parents and step-parents, whereas Maisie reaches that knowledge only gradually. The novel ends, one might argue, when Maisie's knowledge coincides with the narrator's knowledge. To put this another way, the narration is generated in the space between what he knows and what she knows. But matters are not quite so simple as that.

What is extraordinary, "unreal," abnormal, about the narrator's ability to penetrate Maisie's mind may escape the reader's notice, since it is so common in nineteenth-century novels. To read a novel like *What Maisie Knew* is to enjoy in imagination the uncanny power to possess from within the mind of another without that other's knowledge. The reader enjoys the pleasure of knowing without being known. Whatever Maisie knew, she did not come to know that it would be known again through the retrospective introspection of another.[12] In real life, we do not have such an opportunity to enter freely into the mind of another. Nor do the characters of *What Maisie Knew* have that privilege with one another. This means, for the most part, that one character can know the mind of another only by an empathy based primarily on a process of reading the signs exposing that mind to the outside. Such signs may be subtle gestures, if the reader of them is, like Maisie, sensitive and intelligent. The reader's evaluation of what Maisie ultimately does is determined in part by answering the question of whether Maisie reads the characters around her correctly, or whether her reading is to any degree projective, transformative.

Nevertheless, as Sharon Cameron has definitively shown, James allows for a good bit of thought-sharing among his characters. This occurs by way of silent communion or mute passing of information. An example is the "communion or telegraphy" (303) that becomes habitual between Maisie and Mrs. Wix. Another is the species of instantaneous telepathy that, in one scene, connects Maisie and her father, though Beale is by no means one of the persons Maisie ordinarily knows with much intimacy: "if he had an idea at the back of his head she had also one in a recess as deep, and for a time, while they sat together, there was an extraordinary mute passage between her vision of this vision of his, his vision of her vision, and her vision of his vision of her vision" (182). Here the characters share an "introspection of another" almost as total as the narrator's inward knowledge of Maisie. The difference is that in this case the "vision" is reciprocal. This creates a curious and hardly comfortable situation of endless feedback in which vision is superimposed on vision. Each character keeps his or her own visionary idea, but at the same time that idea is known a second and a third time, ad infinitum. A little later Maisie is able to read into her father's gesture of embracing her and rubbing his beard against her cheek a long speech, never spoken, in which he implores her to repudiate him so he will not have to repudiate her: "Then she understood as well as if he had spoken . . . It was exactly as if he had broken out to her" (187). There is variety, complexity, and intermittence in the mode of access James's characters have to one another. This might be expressed for Maisie by saying that sometimes she knows without knowing she knows; sometimes she knows and knows she knows; sometimes she thinks she knows but does not know; sometimes she knows she does not know.

The law determining the access one mind has to another is formulated by Maisie in terms of fear, a key emotion in this novel. It is much discussed by Maisie and Sir Claude. Fear is the name, among its other uses, for the emotion one feels about the person to whom one is linked sexually. Sir Claude fears Ida in this way and, later, Mrs. Beale. But fear is also the name for Maisie's feeling toward her mother. And fear can be the name for the characters' relation to themselves. Sir Claude fears that he will not be able to free himself from Mrs. Beale, and he appears to fear that he may succumb to the temptation of child abuse if he accepts Maisie's more or less innocent offer of herself to him. Maisie fears that she may not be strong enough to give up Sir Claude, even if that means sharing him with Mrs. Beale.

The phenomenology of fear in *What Maisie Knew* is as rigorous as the phenomenology of pain in Wittgenstein's analysis. Each person can know only his or her own pain and cannot communicate it to another. On the other hand, pain must be communicable or else all language may turn out to be private language and so mere nonsense, like a private game without fixed rules. According to James, or rather according to Maisie and Sir Claude, I can understand the fear or pain of another only if I am in the same state myself. If you want to know what it feels like to break your leg, break your leg.

If you want to know what it feels like to be afraid of someone or to be in love with someone, you must be afraid or be in love yourself. The novel turns on the question of whether Maisie can "know" the enslavement to sexual desire of the adults around her without herself entering the circle of adultery. That one person can be "in the same state" as another makes it possible for two persons to share the same thought or feeling, as Maisie knows:

> "Fear, unfortunately, [says Sir Claude,] is a very big thing, and there's a great variety of kinds."
> She took this in with complete intelligence. "Then I think I've got them all."
> "You?" her friend cried. "Nonsense! You're thoroughly 'game.'"
> "I'm awfully afraid of Mrs. Beale," Maisie objected.
> He raised his smooth brows. "That charming woman?"
> "Well," she answered, 'you can't understand it because you're not in the same state."
> She had been going on with a luminous "But" when, across the table, he laid his hand on her arm. "I *can* understand it," he confessed. "I *am* in the same state." (114–115)

This limitation of knowledge of another person's mind is not merely a psychological law. It also determines our moral judgment of what Maisie knows and what she does on the basis of this knowing. How can Maisie touch pitch without being defiled? How can she live in the midst of such goings on, gradually and inevitably coming to understand them, without becoming like the others? This question is kept insistently before the reader.

Maisie's knowing is a gradually increasing clairvoyance. She gains an ability to know, or think she knows, what other people are thinking. A good example of a fairly advanced stage of this is the sequence in chapter 20 that shows Maisie's insight into just what is going on in Mrs. Beale's mind, in Mrs. Wix's, but especially in Sir Claude's. The narrator formulates this in one of those relatively few times he speaks in the first person: "It was granted her at this time to arrive at divinations so ample that I shall have no room for the goal if I attempt to trace the stages; as to which therefore I must be content to say that the fullest expression we [he means "I," the narrator] may give to Sir Claude's conduct is a poor and pale copy of the picture it presented to his young friend" (202).

The narrator's limitation here, like Maisie's, is not so much a restriction in knowledge as a restriction in language. Like Maisie, the narrator knows more than he has language for.

A splendid example of Maisie's "divination" is the passage several pages later in which Maisie and Sir Claude carry on an extraordinary conversation without uttering a word:

> Sir Claude appeared absolutely to convey in a wink that a moral influence capable of pulling a string [Mrs. Wix's influence over Sir Claude] was after all a moral influence exposed to the scratching out of its eyes [by Mrs. Beale in her feline jealousy of Mrs. Wix]; and that, this being the case, there was somebody they couldn't afford to leave unprotected [Mrs. Wix] before they should see a little better what Mrs. Beale was likely to do. Maisie, true enough, had not to put it into words to rejoin, in the coffee-room, at luncheon: "What *can* she do but come to you if papa does take a step that will amount to legal desertion?" Neither had he then, in answer, to articulate anything but the jollity of their having found a table at a window from which, as they partook of cold beef and apollinaris . . . they could let their eye hover tenderly on the far-off white cliffs that so often had signalled to the embarrassed English a promise of safety. (206–207)

I have said that the first generative law of *What Maisie Knew* is the narrator's perception of what is going on in Maisie's mind, along with his ability to describe it in language superior to hers, while the second law is that the narrator can for the most part see the other characters only through Maisie's eyes and is most interested in registering the progress of her knowledge. But there is more to say of this. It is not that the narrator is limited to what she knows, but that the core of the novel is his representation of the gradual progress of her coming to know. As James asserts in the preface, "it is her relation, her activity of spirit, that determines all our own concern—we simply take advantage of these things better than she herself" (x). This structuring principle might be formulated by saying that the novel registers not just the narrator's retrospective introspection of Maisie, but his introspection of Maisie's partial, intermittent, progressive, and problematic introspection of others.

The narrator abrogates the strict rule that so narrowly limits the access each mind has to the minds of others. The narrator has continuous direct access to whatever Maisie thinks, feels, and says to herself. He can speak for her. We take this novelistic convention for granted, though it is the preposterous presupposition that makes of the novel a fully developed genre. The linguistic name for this coincidence of two minds and two languages is "free indirect discourse." The passage about moral sense is an example of this strange mode of language. Indirect discourse is the basic technical resource for the part of *What Maisie Knew* that is not direct reporting by the narrator, in the past tense, of dialogue. James's term for the latter is "scenic method." But even the dialogue of others is always in the presence of Maisie. It is therefore implicitly presented by the narrator, until the very end of the novel, as filtered through Maisie even when she does not understand it.

Free indirect speech, however, is more narrowly and properly the name for all those passages in which the narrator speaks in the third person, past tense, for what Maisie thinks, feels, and sees. What is odd here is that the narrator gives words to much that was apparently wordless for Maisie. Here is an example from the passage cited above: "She looked at her examiner; she looked at the visitors; she felt the rising of the tears she had kept down at the station. They had nothing—no, distinctly nothing—to do with her moral sense." Chief among the many peculiarities of indirect discourse, as others have argued, is that it is extremely difficult if not impossible to be sure whether the language used is the character's or the narrator's.[13] The narrator speaks for the character, partly in the character's language, partly in his own. In the case of the passage I have been discussing, Maisie herself makes the analogy between Mrs. Wix's interrogation and a familiar classroom situation, but it is the narrator, maybe, who uses the word "glib" and who goes on to use the figure as if it were the literal truth: "She looked at her examiner; she looked at the visitors." He extends her metaphor and plays with it. There is no evidence that the image of the flower and the image of the slip from a foothold are anything more than language imported by the narrator to describe for Maisie what she does not describe in that way for herself, though Maisie's brief whiff of the moral sense and her sense of falling exist in intimate closeness as appropriate language for what she thinks and feels. The narrator's language always to some degree exceeds Maisie's language, though it is the medium of their closeness. The narrator's words are the means of the narrator's masterful knowledge of Maisie. They are also the indispensable means whereby what Maisie knew becomes what the reader knows. James speaks eloquently in the preface of this strategic law of his narration as a "controlling grace" that "successfully rules it":

> The one presented register of the whole complexity would be the play of the child's confused and obscure notation of it, and yet the whole, as I say, should be unmistakeably, should be honourably there, seen through the faint intelligence, or at the least attested by the imponderable presence, and still advertising its sense.
>
> . . . Small children have many more perceptions than they have terms to translate them; their vision is at any moment much richer, their apprehension even constantly stronger, than their prompt, their at all producible, vocabulary. Amusing therefore as it might at the first blush have seemed to restrict myself in this case to the terms as well as to the experience, it became at once plain that such an attempt would fail. Maisie's terms accordingly play their part—since her simpler conclusions depend on them; but our own commentary constantly attends and amplifies. This it is that on occasion, doubtless, seems to represent us as going so "behind" the facts of her spectacle as to exaggerate the activity of her relation to them. The difference here is but of a shade: it is her relation, her activity of spirit, that determines all our own concern—we simply take advantage of these things better than she herself. Only, even though it is her interest that mainly makes matters interesting for us, we inevitably note this in figures that are not yet at her command and that are nevertheless required whenever those aspects about her and those parts of her experience that she understands darken off into others that she rather tormentedly misses. (ix, x)

"Shade of a difference," the reader may reflect, is something of an understatement for the difference between Maisie's naive childish language and the knowing worldly irony, the wry reserve, of the narrator's presentation. Maisie's own formulations frequently make the adults around her burst into laughter at their ludicrous inappropriateness for the true state of things. The narrator's language, on the other hand, is masterfully adult. His irony can be bitterly judgmental in its presentation of the unseemly set of people around Maisie. An example is the prelude that presents the facts about the divorce of Maisie's parents. The narrator's irony can also be affectionately avuncular in its presentation of the discrepancies between what Maisie knows and what he knows about the events, people, and conversations she experiences.

Irony is the fundamental trope of indirect discourse. It is the appropriate name, in this case, for the "shade of a difference" between Maisie's language and the narrator's language. This difference allows James to write *What Maisie Knew*. It also allows the narrator to create for the reader, in retrospect, a new Maisie, a Maisie who can live again for the reader each time the novel is read.

What is most problematic about *Maisie* is located in the ironic interval between Maisie's language and the narrator's language. The shade of a difference raises all sorts of questions. Just how, for James, is language related to consciousness? Is one the originator of the other, or are they coextensive? Does the relation between the narrator and Maisie figure an ideological presumption about the superiority of male knowledge and language over female powerlessness to speak? Maisie remains until "the death of her childhood" *infans* in the etymological sense of "without language." The decision to make the protagonist of *Maisie* "a slip of a girl" rather than "a rude little boy" was clearly a crucial moment in the genesis of the novel, but just what does this decision presuppose about gender difference and gender relations? Is there, finally, any point or frontier beyond which the narrator's language of male mastery fails to account fully for Maisie?

THIS MAKING of a person, in compensation for a loss, out of what James calls "figures" (in both the economic and rhetorical senses) repeats Pygmalion's gesture in creating Galatea. But this creation occurs in two different ways, in one way for James projecting the character of Maisie and the action of the novel, and in quite a different way for the narrator, who brings Maisie back alive from the past in the figures of his narration. I began this chapter by saying that in the retrospective preface, as in the case of all acts of memory, there is an obscure element of loss, regret, or even of mourning for the dead. This is the case even if the mourning in question is only regret for the death of that moment in the past when the original act of generative insight took place. James in the preface calls this projected moment "the torch of rapture and victory, as the artist's firm hand grasps and plays it—I mean, naturally, of the smothered rapture and the obscure victory" (vi).

If the preface is memorial, so is the narration itself. The sign of this temporal distance, to be crossed only by an ambiguous act of remembering, is the conventional past tense of the narration. Maisie lives her life from moment to moment facing an indeterminate future as she wonders and gradually comes to know, to know more and more, to know ultimately "All." Her final ethical act determines her future and ends the novel. For the narrator, on the other hand, Maisie's childhood is already at the beginning part of the dead past. The narrator writes or speaks from some indeterminate temporal placement after all the narrated events have occurred. The novel must end when the gap closes between what the narrator knows and what Maisie knows.

The name for the imaginative gesture whereby someone who is absent or dead is brought back to life through an act of language is prosopopoeia, the trope this book has been written to interrogate. Prosopopoeia is the figure that insinuates itself a bridge into the temporal gap between then and now. This is the case in *Maisie* both for the author in the preface and for the imaginary narrator, himself the product of another act of prosopopoeia. But this figure also works prospectively, as James, Pygmalion-like, projects the figure of the narrator and the figure of Maisie in the moments in which the as yet unwritten novel is proposed in the notebook entries. The reader of *What Maisie Knew* performs again the act of prosopopoeia as he brings the narrator, Maisie, and the other characters alive from the dead letters lying there, in whatever typeface, on the page.

Let me propose then, as a working hypothesis that it is not enough just to say that prosopopoeia ascribes a name, a face, or a voice to the absent, the inanimate, or the dead. For one thing, this trope is the product of an act of imagination that always goes by way of language or other signs. Like all figures, prosopopoeia turns its medium tropologically, taking one thing for another through words or other signs. A senseless block of ivory is taken for Galatea, words on the page are taken as a person.

The posing of a prosopopoetic transformation in narrative must be presupposed in order for a story to exist. But prosopopoeia, in spite of its apparent orientation toward the past, is also prospective. As retrospective it is memorial, compensation for a loss. In one way or another it is an attempt, necessarily destined to fail, to make up for the ultimate loss of death. We have a foretaste of that loss every time we experience an intermittence or a discontinuity in sequence. James says just this in an extraordinary passage in *Maisie*. Speaking of Maisie's sharp pang when she sees that Sir Claude has not accompanied Mrs. Beale to France, the narrator observes: "She was yet to learn what it would be to recognise in some lapse of a sequence the proof of an extinction, and therefore remained unaware that this momentary pang was a foretaste of the experience of death" (291).

Does the narrator mean by "experience of death" the experience of one's own death or the experience of the death of someone else? One's own death, it might be argued, can never be experienced, if one means "present to consciousness." And, since each person dies his or her own death, how can I experience the death of another? The phrase "experience of death" may be an outrageous oxymoron. We can experience death only indirectly, at a temporal and figurative remove, in "foretaste" or "aftertaste" and covered over by some substitute for it. An example would be some lapse of sequence, such as the failure of a friend to appear when expected, or some tropological death that is not a real extinction, such as the death of Maisie's childhood. If prosopopoeia as oriented toward the past is the repair of a break in sequence that is an extinction, it also produces what it makes by a creative act that moves forward into the future, as Pygmalion carves Galatea or as James first creates Maisie in imagination and then from week to week writes the novel down or dictates it. But in addition, prosopopoeia is a compensation for its creator's own prospective death, or for those future deaths of others that will be the ultimate lapse of a sequence. The figure is, in spite of its positive and productive side, haunted by death. It is an obscure "foretaste of the experience of death."

Taking these hypothetical presuppositions as a starting point, I ask the following questions: If three quite different acts of prosopopoeia characterize the acts of imagination performed by James, by the narrator, and then by the reader, what about Maisie herself? Does she, as the delegate of all three, do anything analogous to what James or the narrator does? It will take some further analysis, and some help from what James says in the preface, to show that this is indeed the case. Let me begin by extending my claim that prosopopoeia, Pygmalion's creative gesture, is the correct name for what author, narrator, and reader do. On that basis I may then return to a reading and evaluation of what Maisie does. Understanding the novel depends on understanding the analogies among these four fictive consciousnesses, themselves products of personification. These are analogies in knowledge and in deed, implicit or explicit, willful or accidental.

IN WHAT SENSE can James's creation of Maisie be said to be a repetition of Pygmalion's carving of Galatea? Beyond the novel itself, we have the notebook entries and the preface, the first prospective, the latter the memorial of an act of imagination long since accomplished. These documents show that James's imagination quickly deviated from the information given in the bit of gossip he heard at a dinner party on November 10, 1892. This transformation involved the decision, apparently not based on the facts as James heard them, to make the child divided between its divorced parents a girl. "Boy or girl would do, but I see a girl" says the first notebook entry (N126). "I see a girl"—this visionary creativity is analogous to what Dickens said of the invention of his first great character: "I thought of Mr. Pickwick." In both cases the act of invention freely exceeds its sources. In the preface to *Maisie* James elaborates on the decision to make his protagonist a girl: "I at once recognised, that my light vessel of consciousness, swaying in such a draught, couldn't be with verisimilitude a rude little boy; since, beyond the fact that little boys are never so 'present,' the sensibility of the female young is indubitably, for early youth, the greater, and my plan would call, on the part of my protagonist, for 'no end' of sensibility. I might impute that amount of it without extravagance to a slip of a girl whose faculties should have been well shaken up" (viii). It will be seen that James quickly went out into a region where he felt free to do anything he liked with his imaginary creation. He was limited by the demands of "verisimilitude." Beyond that, he was constrained only by the intrinsic implications of the "subject," its "*full* ironic truth."

A second major deviation from the historical source is implicit in the first. As James recognizes, the most likely result in the real world of "ugly facts" would be the coarsening and degradation of the child. James decided rather to impute great intelligence and sensitivity to his girl-child. This meant that the full ironic truth of the story could lie in the way the child derives great profit and benefit from her situation, while at the same time, by her very virtues, making the bad people around her even worse. "For satisfaction of the mind, in other words," as he says, "the small expanding consciousness would have to be saved, have to become presentable as a register of impressions; and saved by the experience of certain advantages, by some enjoyed profit and some achieved confidence, rather than coarsened, blurred, sterilised, by ignorance and pain" (vi–vii).

This going beyond not only the historical facts as reported but even normal probabilities in such cases is a curiously double act of imagination. Such doubleness is a version of an intrinsic ambiguity in the notion of invention. "Invent" may mean either "create" or "discover." Though much is at stake in the difference between the two meanings, attempts to choose characteristically end up covertly affirming, in the language used to make the choice, the impossibility of choosing. In James's case, as in most such cases, the undecidability is inherent in the figures chosen to express the inventive act. If James goes beyond the ugly facts he has been told, he does this freely, speculatively. He is governed by no law beyond his own self-generated artistic law. On the other hand, the act of invention is the discovery of a law inherent in the "subject," buried within it like a secret treasure. This law is revealed, not autonomously created, by the act of invention.

This undecidable alternation within the invention of Maisie is expressed in the dual implications of James's description of the imagination as a "light" or a "torch." The imagination is a celebratory torch of victory expressing only its own triumph, but it is also a torch in the sense of a torchlight or flashlight. The imagination is an instrument casting an illuminating ray. Speaking of those ugly facts, James says that "the light of an imagination touched by them couldn't help therefore projecting a further ray" (vi). This sounds as if the imagination were free to make what light it will, free to invent a Maisie who benefits from the "complexity of life" around her rather than being degraded by it. But James then goes on to describe this projection of light as the uncovering of a hidden source of light "that lurked in the crude postulate like a buried scent." The invention of Maisie is discovery by a process of analysis, not free creation. The word "analysis" must be taken here as it is used in chemistry:

> The further analysis is for that matter almost always the torch of rapture and victory, as the artist's firm hand grasps and plays it—I mean, naturally, of the smothered rapture and the obscure victory, enjoyed and celebrated not in the street but before some innermost shrine; the odds being a hundred to one, in almost any connexion, that it doesn't arrive by any easy first process at the *best* residuum of truth . . . At last, accordingly, the residuum, as I have called it, reached, I was in presence of the red dramatic spark that glowed at the core of my vision and that, as I gently blew upon it, burned higher and clearer. This precious particle was the *full* ironic truth— the most interesting item to be read into the child's situation. (vi)

When James here speaks of his "vision" and of the act of "reading into," it is impossible to know for sure whether he means his autonomous creative vision, limited by nothing outside itself, or whether he comes to see something already there but invisible except to his superior power of reading or analysis, taking the latter word in the sense of the reduction of something complex to its primitive elements. The same issue arises in connection with the reader's assessment of what Maisie herself knew. Is her knowing discovery or free invention?

James's making up of Maisie was the creation out of words of an imaginary girl in compensation for the probable real person who resulted from the ugly facts of the case. Having made Galatea, Pygmalion fell in love with her, in a strange love for what was the same and yet other, since invention is always of the other. Pygmalion's inventive personification is repeated in the relation of James and his narrator to Maisie. For James too Maisie is a part of himself, made up out of his own creative power. At the same time, she takes on a life of her own and is to some degree alien.

The notion that the creation of Maisie may be an act of compensation appears in another connection in James's notebook entries, where he talks about the "blest scenic method." This procedure presents a story in scenes dominated by dialogue, not through the narrator's explanation and commentary. James, in a slip of the pen, describes his systematic use of the scenic method in *Maisie* as "vindictive." He then corrects that in a note to "vindicating": "Ah, this *divine* conception of one's little masses and periods in the scenic light—as rounded ACTS; this patient, pious, nobly 'vindictive'[1] [[1](James's note at top of manuscript page): 'vindicating'] application of the scenic philosophy and method" (N162). What is it that James at this point in his career has to be vindictive or vindicating about? *Maisie* was James's first important work of fiction after his failed attempt to have a successful career as a dramatist. I suggest that the systematic use of the scenic method in *Maisie* is a way of compensating for that failure. It is a way of taking revenge on those who did not appreciate James's dramatic powers and a way of vindicating himself for a commitment to artistic principles that were at bottom dramatic. In this way too the creation of Maisie can be seen as compensation for a failure and a lack.

If James describes Maisie herself as deriving paradoxical "profit" from her difficult situation, his terms for what he derived from his creation of Maisie are exactly analogous. He mingles aesthetic terms, primarily "beauty," with an abundance of economic terms to describe the "value," "appreciation," "interest," and "profit" he got out of making Maisie up. He depends on her "wonder," which gives value to the "vulgar" facts around her, to derive his own profit from the work he has made. Here is the essential passage, with the economic terms italicized:

> Our *business* meanwhile therefore is to extract from her current reaction whatever it may be *worth;* and for that matter we recognise in it the highest exhibitional virtue. Truly, I reflect, if the theme had had no other beauty it would still have had this rare and distinguished one of its so expressing the variety of the child's *values.* She is not only the extraordinary "ironic centre" I have already noted; she has the wonderful importance of shedding a light far beyond any reach of her comprehension; of *lending* to *poorer* persons and things, by the mere fact of their being involved with her and by the special

scale she creates for them, a *precious* element of dignity. I lose myself, truly, in *appreciation* of my theme on noting what she does by her "freshness" for appearances in themselves vulgar and *empty* enough. They become, as she deals with them, the stuff of poetry and tragedy and art; she has simply to wonder, as I say, about them, and they begin to have meanings, aspects, solidities, connexions—connexions with the "universal!"—that they could scarce have hoped for. Ida Farange alone, so to speak, or Beale alone, that is either of them otherwise connected—what intensity, what "objectivity" (the most developed degree of *being* [original italics] anyhow thinkable for them) would they have? How would they *repay* at all the favour of our attention? (xi–xii)

Maisie's name, like that of Shakespeare's Miranda, tells her nature. The pun on "amazed" primarily defines her as a wondering spectator, though there may be a secondary suggestion that she is lost in the maze of all the strange signs from the adult world she has to learn to read. Maisie's precious capacity to wonder gives value to otherwise valueless things and people around her. It is as if she has, figuratively speaking, an intrinsic power of coinage. She can turn dross into gold by her special measuring scale. This special power is described as "lending," as "shedding a light," just as James's imagination, when he created Maisie in the first place, was a light source projecting a ray.

But James in his turn finds his creation "wonderful." His wonder is also described in terms that are at once economic, aesthetic, and psychological. They are a matter of "appreciation," "worth," and "repayment." A wonderful reciprocity (the reader here takes a turn at wondering) links what James does and what Maisie does. If James turns the ugly facts of the germ anecdote into "the stuff of poetry and tragedy and art," he can only do this because he imputes to Maisie or discovers in her a corresponding imaginative power, her wonder. By this faculty she measures things by her own scale and transforms Ida, Beale, and the rest into something "*appreciable*" (xii, James's italics), into "striking figured symbol[s]." She transmutes them, that is, into figures that today would be called allegorical. They stand in fact, as James says, for the "universal!"

But these people turned into symbols are figures in an economic as well as tropological sense. They turn little into much, like an investment that brings a spectacular return. Maisie's transmutation of base metal into gold also represents allegorically, in a delegated form, James's act of transmutation in making Maisie up in the first place. If James creates his Galatea, in James's case too, as in Rousseau's version of the Pygmalion story,[14] the fictive woman, created originally as a means of controlling life and as a means of compensating for the way real women escape male control, in the end takes on an autonomous life of her own. The created woman ultimately escapes male domination once more, though she was initially no more than a complex version of a rhetorical figure. This happens against reason, since one would think that what an author has made out of words he should be able to master by knowing.

This drama of Pygmalion's ultimate failure to go on knowing, controlling, and possessing his creation is repeated in a different way for the narrator and for the reader. As I have said, the narrator differs from James himself. The narrator always speaks of Maisie and the others as if they were real people, as much a part of history as Cleopatra, Napoleon, or Lincoln. The narrator speaks of Maisie's knowing and doing as part of the historical past, something that once was but is now over and done, whereas the author knows he is making her up as he goes along. Nevertheless, the narrator too fashions an effigy of Maisie out of language, giving words to Maisie's experience and knowledge that exceed Maisie's own power of articulation.

The narrator speaks for Maisie according to that law of the double language of indirect discourse that James formulates in the preface. The narrator is reticent, ironic, affectionately superior, but appreciatively admiring in his attitude toward Maisie. He is certainly not a person in the ordinary sense of someone with a character and history of his own, but he speaks once or twice as a separate "I" of the difficulties of making a new Maisie out of words: "Oh decidedly I shall never get you to believe the number of things she saw and the number of secrets she discovered!" (205); "Nothing more remarkable had taken place in the first heat of her own departure, no act of perception less to be overtraced by our rough method, than her vision, the rest of that Boulogne day, of the manner in which she figured [figured in Mrs. Wix's vision of her as lacking a moral sense]. I so despair of courting her noiseless mental footsteps here that I must crudely give you my word for its being from this time forward a picture literally present to her" (280–281). The speaker here is not Henry James, who has invented Maisie and can presumably ascribe to her whatever perceptions he likes. The speaker is rather an imaginary narrator, someone who can speak as an "I" of another "I" external to himself of whose mental activities he can give only an imperfect report. The latter is spoken of here in the odd figure of "courting" Maisie's "noiseless mental footsteps." Presumably courting someone's footsteps means here something like "following over again accurately and lovingly" a track already laid down. The narrator cannot convey to the reader his own experience of Maisie's mental experience even though he has an extraordinary and quite "unrealistic" power to penetrate Maisie's mind. His despair is over an inadequacy of language, however, not over an inadequacy of knowledge.

Though the narrator does not speak as openly as James does in the preface of what he gets as a benefit for all the effort of telling her story, it is evident in the tone of his telling that he too gets the value of being able to wonder at Maisie's wonder. He gets Pygmalion's pleasure of knowing through making or of knowing what one has made. If he has not made Maisie, he has given superior words to her experience. He has created an effigy of Maisie out of language. This living monument is a lasting memorial of Maisie, so that what she experienced and knew is not lost wholly with the passage of time. It can be renewed and brought back to life every time what he writes or speaks is read again.

The reader then plays the role of Pygmalion to Maisie's Galatea every time he or she[15] reads the novel and fashions a seemingly living person out of the performative reading of the words on the page. Those words are in themselves inanimate objects, as dead as any corpse. If they have a face, it is only that catachrestic one implicit in the word "typeface." Just how reading is performative I shall try to explain later. The reader's imagination of James and of the narrator as persons, as for example in my reading here, are two more cases of fictional prosopopoeia (but prosopopoeia is always a fiction). In this case it is the ascription of a name, a face, a personality to what after all is only words on the page. Maisie ultimately escapes from the narrator's knowledge at the same moment that she escapes from James's knowledge, since the one is the record or allegorical representation of the other. At that moment the narrator also suffers Pygmalion's fate, the vanishing of what he has made from his full knowledge. And the reader loses the possibility of knowing for sure what Maisie knew.

But to understand how that happens for author, narrator, and reader, it will be necessary to return to Maisie and try to answer a question left dangling. Is Maisie in any sense a maker of compensatory images by a species of personification?

MAISIE IS HERSELF a version of Pygmalion, and she plays as well the role of Galatea for James, the narrator, and the reader as different sorts of Pygmalions. The nature of Maisie's climactic ethical choice is defined by the narrator as a classic example of free and autonomous decision: "I put it to you," says Sir Claude to Maisie. "*Can* you choose freely? . . . *Can* you choose? I mean can you settle it by a word yourself?" (335, 338) "It depended, she had learned, so completely on herself. Her choice, as her friend had called it, was there before her like an impossible sum on a slate" (341). She finally chooses to say she will give up Mrs. Wix if Sir Claude will give up his adulterous liaison with Mrs. Beale. As soon as she makes this proposal, she learns from his reaction that she has lost him for good: "'Oh!' he exclaimed;[16] on which she saw how much, how hopelessly he was afraid" (346). In losing Sir Claude, Maisie feels as if she has lost everything, as she says a little later. Yet what she says, what she does by saying, will remain permanently a barrier between Sir Claude and Mrs. Beale, a judgment on their relation. Maisie's act anticipates that of Maggie in *The Golden Bowl* or of Millie in *The Wings of the Dove*. That all these names begin in "M" suggests the consonance of their bearers. In all three cases the apparently highest ethical act of self-sacrifice, along with the act of measuring others according to the fragrance of a moral ideal, makes things worse rather than better for those around the renouncer. James formulates this irony in detail in the preface:

The child seen as creating by the fact of its forlornness a relation between its step-parents, the more intimate the better, dramatically speaking; the child, by the mere appeal of neglectedness and the mere consciousness of relief, weaving about, with the best faith in the world, the close web of sophistication; the child becoming a centre and pretext for a fresh system of misbehaviour, a system moreover of a nature to spread and ramify: *there* would be the "full" irony, there the promising theme into which the hint I had originally picked up would logically flower. No themes are so human as those that reflect for us, out of the confusion of life, the close connexion of bliss and bale, of the things that help with the things that hurt, so dangling before us for ever that bright hard medal, of so strange an alloy, one face of which is somebody's right and ease and the other somebody's pain and wrong. To live with all intensity and perplexity and felicity in its terribly mixed little world would thus be the part of my interesting small mortal; bringing people together who would be at least more correctly separate; keeping people separate who would be at least more correctly together; flourishing, to a degree, at the cost of many conventions and proprieties, even decencies; really keeping the torch of virtue alive in an air tending infinitely to smother it; really in short making confusion worse confounded by drawing some stray fragrance of an ideal across the scent of selfishness, by sowing on barren strands, through the mere fact of presence, the seed of the moral life. (vii—viii)

This extraordinary passage may be as close as James comes to formulating the strange ethical law that, for him, governs human life, including the function of works of art in human life. The reader is given a precious clue here that may help to read the meaning of all those acts of resignation in James's novels. The moral law involves a strange discrepancy between the ethical act, as a doing, and the results of that act, what that doing does in its turn. The ethical act is good, morally correct. Maisie does the right thing, both at the end and all along, for example in refusing to serve as a mediator for her parents' hatred and in innocently bringing her step-parents together. These acts arise from Maisie's goodness. They lead to bliss for her, whatever bale they bring others. The effects an ethically good act has, what it does in the real world, however good and valuable it is in itself, involve bad for others, "pain and wrong." Understanding James depends fundamentally on understanding why this must be so.

This passage gives the reader no less than four "terribly mixed" metaphors as instruments for thinking about this. The first is economic, implicitly monetary. It uses the symbolism of a coin to name the contradictory rigors of the moral life. The moral life is like an absurd medal whose obverse face contradicts its reverse. It is like a coin that could never be currency, since it has a positive value on one side and a negative value on the other. This strange coin, moreover, is made of two metals, let us say gold on one side and lead on the other.

The second figure describes Maisie as "keeping the torch of virtue alive." James used the same figure earlier to describe his act of imagination as he invented Maisie by analysis of the potentialities of his subject. As applied to the ethical life, to Maisie's keeping the moral life alive, the torch can mean that she has inherited or been endowed with a preexisting standard of virtuous action and has preserved that standard. She has obeyed the moral law in her actions and judgments. On the other hand, as James's use of the figure for his own creative act makes clear, the "torch of virtue" is perhaps a self-kindled flashlight that creates out of nothing, or out of something that is entirely intrinsic to itself, its own self-born ethical standard, the moral light it sheds on those around, illuminating their wickedness and making it more wicked still.

The third image describes Maisie's characteristic ethical act as "really making confusion worse confounded by drawing some stray fragrance of an ideal across the scent of selfishness." The image is the tracking of some animal, as in a foxhunt. Maisie's goodness confounds confusion in the way the dogs in a hunt are put off the scent and the whole hunt reduced to milling confusion if some other scent is accidentally ("stray fragrance") drawn across the fox's scent. This crossing of one scent by another does not set the dogs and hunters off on the new scent of the moral ideal, but brings hopeless confusion to what was at least a somewhat orderly game, as Mrs. Wix calls it (297). In the case of *Maisie,* this game is the perpetual substitution of one lover for another.

The fourth image is a biblical reference. The allusion to the parable of the sower gives the reader yet another formulation of the inscrutable paradox of our ethical life, its deepest irony. Far from making those around her better by her virtue, Maisie makes confusion worse "by sowing on barren strands, through the mere fact of presence, the seed of the moral life." Some of the seeds of the word, in Jesus' parable, "fell upon stony places, where they had not much earth; and forthwith they sprung up, because they had no deepness of earth: And when the sun was up, they were scorched; and because they had no root, they withered away" (Matthew 13:5–6). Jesus explains that the stony places stand for the person who receives the word with joy but "when tribulation or persecution ariseth because of the word, by and by he is offended" (13:21). In short, the bale that Maisie's bliss causes is a version of that terrifying paradox of the moral life as Jesus expresses it: "For whosoever hath, to him shall be given, and he shall have more abundance: but whosoever hath not, from him shall be taken away even that he hath" (13:12). Maisie's virtue is incorruptible, untouched by the vulgarity of those around her. She is like that gold Virgin on the church steeple in Boulogne, high and aloof, implicitly taken as a model by Maisie. The others around her cannot be saved by any means and are in fact made worse by Maisie's fresh capacity for wonder and the fragrance of her moral ideal.

There is deeper irony in James's insight into the ethical import of what Maisie does. Though her act exemplifies what is apparently the highest value for James, the traditional Christian virtue of renunciation, that virtuous act has sorry effects on those around her. Rather than preventing the further spread of adulterous liaisons, innocent Maisie unwittingly brings together those who ought to be separate and keeps separate those who ought to be together. She does this through her very virtue, just as the Word, in the parable, takes away from those who have not even what they have.

In an earlier essay on *Maisie* I concluded that the ethical import of what Maisie ultimately does is undecidable because it cannot be known whether she acts on the basis of the idealism of an innocent child or with an adult's knowledge and sexual desire.[17] When she says, "I love Sir Claude—I love *him*" (359), did she mean filial love or grownup desire? I went on to mention a curious stylistic feature of the last chapter, namely that the characters say almost everything twice or repeat exactly what the other person has said, as a sign of this ethical undecidability: "You're free—you're free";

"Give up Mrs. Beale?" "Give up Mrs. Beale"; "the only right one." "The only right one?"; "She hates you—she hates you"; "she's free—she's free"; "I'll get them back—I'll get them back"; "Let them pass—let them pass!", and so on. Everything said in this scene can be taken in two ways, I claimed, depending on whether the reader sees Maisie as a child or as an adult.

I no longer think that the "undecidability" lies quite in this or that the reader's knowledge is limited in quite that way, though I would still insist that the evaluation of what Maisie does is exceedingly difficult and in that sense undecidable. But the novel makes it clear enough that Maisie has, when she makes her decision, reached just that point where the child's filial affection for her stepfather has definitely turned into sexual desire, child though she still is and "child" as she is called to the end by the narrator. She refuses to go with Sir Claude and Mrs. Beale as the stepchild that will make their liaison respectable because she wants Sir Claude for herself—and she has gradually learned through the adults around her what having Sir Claude to herself would mean. Child she may be, but no longer an innocent child. She is described in one scene, for example, a scene some distance from the end of the novel, as looking into Sir Claude's eyes with a "more than filial gaze" (263). In the last scene, when she insists publicly on sticking to the terms of her decision, her resolution is explicitly said to be based on her knowledge: "What helped the child was that she knew what she wanted. All her learning and learning had made her at last learn that" (357). What she wants is Sir Claude to herself.

But how, the reader may ask, is this compatible with James's description of Maisie in the preface as an example of the fragrance of the moral ideal? To answer this deep question, all the clues the reader is given must be interrogated with great care. The insistent repetitions in the last chapter function, I would now say, to call attention to the fact that even the most common colloquial phrase can be read in many different ways. The meaning does not go without saying, as they say. In short, each phrase, however commonplace and idiomatic, must be *read*. The reader, moreover, must take responsibility for the results of this act of reading. To read the meaning of what Maisie does, the play of possible ways of reading the terms must be looked at with close attention. Here is the most extravagant of the repetitions, just two pages from the end. Mrs. Wix says, "He can't!" and says it "tragically," meaning that Sir Claude cannot bring himself to give up Mrs. Beale. Mrs. Beale repeats the two words as "literal mock[ing]," and then Sir Claude says, "He can't, he can't, he can't!" with a "gay emphasis" that "wonderfully carried it off" (362). "Carried *what* off *where?*" the reader, now alerted to nuances of implication in such phrases, may ask.

I HAVE NOW LOOKED hard at the crucial passage in the preface that describes the way Maisie makes confusion worse confounded by drawing the stray fragrance of virtue across the scent of selfishness. But just what Maisie's "bliss" consists of is still not at all clear. How can she be said to be blissful if, as she correctly says, she loses everything and gets nothing in the end but life with Mrs. Wix? "Him alone or nobody," she says, and then when Mrs. Wix asks, "Not even *me?*" Maisie replies, with the cruel insight and insolence of the young, "Oh, you're nobody" (309). Presumably Maisie gets the bliss of her "wonder," and the bliss of gradually increasing knowledge that her wonder brings. She gets also the bliss of acting, ultimately, on the basis of her knowledge, on the basis of a unique standard of judgment that measures things and people by a scale of its own.

Our judgment must be based on four crucial assertions by Sir Claude. In these Sir Claude, the reader may dare to guess, speaks ironically and indirectly for the narrator's and author's judgment of what Maisie does. In one statement Sir Claude uses the image of the "vicious circle" to define what Maisie cannot enter. In the next he speaks of Maisie or of her choice as "beautiful" and "sacred." In the third he assures the others that she has acted correctly. In the fourth he describes Maisie as something unique and incommensurable, something that cannot be included in their vicious circle. Let me comment on each of these in turn.

Sir Claude, in his appeal to Maisie to sacrifice Mrs. Wix and join him and Mrs. Beale in their doubly adulterous liaison, thereby becoming herself one of the betrayers, defines their unwillingness to give her up: "You're the best thing—you and what we can do for you—that either of us has ever known . . . When I say to her [Mrs.

Beale] 'Give her up, come,' she lets me have it bang in the face:
'Give her up yourself!' It's the same old vicious circle—and when
I say vicious I don't mean a pun, a what-d'-ye-call-'em" (334).
What James wrote here means two incompatible things at once, as
is so often the case when he plays on the figure latent in a cliché. A
vicious circle is a situation in an argument that turns round and
round on itself without the possibility of moving forward. Neither
Mrs. Beale nor Sir Claude can give up Maisie or persuade the other
to give her up. When Sir Claude says he does not "mean a pun, a
what-d'-ye-call-'em" (figure of speech? play on words?), he may
mean that there is nothing "vicious" except the logical impasse in
their situation. Both he and Mrs. Beale have only the most ethically admirable reasons for wanting to take responsibility, in loco
parentis, for Maisie, since each is married to one of her real parents, both of whom have abandoned her. On the other hand, by
having Sir Claude say he does not mean a pun, James invites the
reader to think of what meaning the phrase would have in this
context if it were taken as a pun, that is, if the word "vicious" were
taken in its moral as well as in its strictly logical sense. To put it
another way, the word "vicious" used to describe an impasse in
logical reasoning is a metaphor taken from the terminology of
moral judgment to define something that is neither moral nor immoral. In this reading, Sir Claude restores the word to its literal
meaning in order to define their desire to appropriate Maisie as
morally vicious. The phrase "vicious circle" then describes with
admirable accuracy the nature of the selfish set of people into
which Maisie finds herself born. It describes, that is, what Maisie
comes to know. She gradually learns the facts about sexual desire,
sexual infatuation and servitude, sexual fear. She learns especially
that her parents' community is one continual round of adulterous
betrayal. But she learns all this not merely as physiology but as
primary selfish human acts.[18]

For James, adultery is selfish in being an irresponsible taking
rather than a giving up. It has, moreover, an intrinsic tendency to
ramify, through the perpetual substitution of one sexual partner
for another. This process is economic both in the etymological
sense of having to do with the household, as a travesty of family
relations and obligations, and in the sense that it is an attempt to

get something for nothing, as in financial speculation. One could describe this vicious circle as an infernal parody of the dialectical process that ought to characterize a good society. It is infernal because it is a dialectic without sublation, an endless substitution that goes nowhere. Or one could define this circle as an imperfect substitution by chiasmus. It is a crisscross replacement that does not set things right and always has something left over, like false change for a coin. The new marriages and Maisie's subsequent abandonment by her real parents mean that Sir Claude substitutes for Maisie's mother, Mrs. Beale for Maisie's father. This gives her a new mother and father. But that does not prevent her real mother and father from continuing their series of adulteries, nor does it prevent Maisie's new mother and father from short-circuiting this series by establishing a liaison of their own. This makes them unsuitable parents for Maisie and leaves her with no parents or stepparents at all. Though Sir Claude may deny that his phrase is a pun, if we read what he says against its obvious grain he unwittingly describes with precision the rules that govern his society. Which of the two meanings he "intends" cannot be told for sure.

The narrator had earlier mingled economic imagery and the imagery of a game to define Maisie's growing insight into the people around her. Speaking of her attempt to figure out who is the ally of whom and of her inability to get the "sides" to come out right, the narrator (or Maisie herself) thinks of it as a children's game in which there is always an odd person out: "If it had become now, for that matter, a question of sides, there was at least a certain amount of evidence as to where they all were . . . Here indeed was a slight ambiguity, as papa's being on Mrs. Beale's [side] didn't somehow seem to place him quite on his daughter's. It sounded, as this young lady thought it over, very much like puss-in-the-corner, and she could only wonder if the distribution of parties would lead to a rushing to and fro and a changing of places" (94). The OED cites a description of this game from *The Gentleman's Magazine* of 1738 that fits admirably Maisie's location at the center of a crisscross design with her two parents and her two foster-parents at the corners: "In this play, four Boys or Girls post themselves at the four corners of the room and the fifth in the middle, who keeps himself on the watch to slip into one of the corner places when the present possessors are endeavouring to supplant one another." If Maisie were to succeed in replacing Mrs. Beale as Sir Claude's companion, leaving Mrs. Beale the odd person out, she would have escaped her place at the center where she is the mediator of exchanges from which she does not benefit. She could do this, however, only at the expense of entering the vicious circle. Later Maisie's sense that Mrs. Wix, for all her moral sense, is being corrupted by Mrs. Beale, whom she claimed to despise, is expressed in a somewhat similar figure of a process of substitution gone askew. The first trope appears to be Maisie's, the second the narrator's. "She put it together with a suspicion that, had she ever in her life had a sovereign changed, would have resembled an impression, baffled by the want of arithmetic, that her change was wrong: she groped about in it that she was perhaps playing the passive part in a case of violent substitution" (301).

Maisie escapes from the vicious circle. She cannot fit herself in, even when she tries, as she does when she is tempted to take that train to Paris with Sir Claude. She escapes the vicious circle by the condition she sets for giving up Mrs. Wix, as Sir Claude recognizes. In the final scene of the novel, in an ecstasy of ironic admiration, he affirms that Maisie "made her condition—with such a sense of what it should be! She made the only right one" (356). In what sense is Maisie's offer to give up Mrs. Wix if Sir Claude will give up Mrs. Beale the only right one? On the one hand, it is ideally right, based on an absolute standard of right and wrong. An expression of this in terms of Mrs. Wix's moral standard would say: "It would be good to put an end to the adultery of Sir Claude and Mrs. Beale. Anyone with a moral sense would know that." On the other hand, Maisie's condition—which also involves a betrayal of her obligation to the only person who has faithfully cared for her—affirms her desire to have Sir Claude to herself. It is based on a spasm of something still deeper than a moral sense, her love for Sir Claude. Nevertheless, Maisie goes on affirming her decision even when she knows that Sir Claude will refuse her condition. She acts in knowledge that Sir Claude cannot give up Mrs. Beale, that he will not take her offer of herself alone. She therefore acts in such a way that she ensures her own highest bliss of giving up rather than taking and, at the same time, ensures the bale of the others. What she does is especially bale for Sir Claude. He will remain with Mrs. Beale in full knowledge of the weakness that staying means. He takes the lesser good, or the positively bad, in awareness of the better, the best. Maisie acts with the peculiar self-righteous cruelty, causing great pain while acting in the most exemplary way, that characterizes Isabel, Strether, Maggie, Milly, and the rest of James's major protagonists. Maisie's renunciation, like that of the others, is at the same time an act of ferocious aggressiveness against those around her.

The reader again confronts an undecidability, this time the vicious circle of an alternation between several incompatible readings of what Maisie does, each based on the text. Even if the reader concludes that Maisie by this time knows all about sex and adulterous betrayal, the reader still cannot easily decide how to evaluate what she does on the basis of this knowledge.

This vibration of undecidability, however, is by no means the endpoint of the reading of the novel, nor is it a permanent aporia of interpretation. More remains to be said, with Sir Claude's help. He is reproached by Mrs. Wix for having "nipped" Maisie's growing moral sense "in the bud": "You've killed it when it had begun to live" (354). His response is: "I've not killed anything . . . on the contrary I think I've produced life. I don't know what to call it—I haven't even known how decently to deal with it, to approach it; but, whatever it is, it's the most beautiful thing I've ever met—it's exquisite, it's sacred" (354). The narrator a little later describes him as speaking of Maisie "with a relish as intense now as if some lovely work of art or of nature had suddenly been set down among them" (356).

No doubt Sir Claude is speaking to some degree defensively, to cover his disappointment that he has not been able to persuade Maisie to join him and Mrs. Beale. He is speaking also to cover his guilt for having "once more dodged" (264) his obligations by refusing Maisie's appeal. On the other hand, the terms of Sir Claude's ironic praise of what Maisie has done are significant. They aestheticize and sanctify Maisie in terms just like those James uses in the preface and notebooks to describe the "blessed" rigorous conditions of narration he has set for himself. Maisie, like the book that tells her story, is a "beautiful thing," "exquisite," "sacred," "a lovely work of art or of nature."

Sir Claude's terminology, like James's in the preface, echoes

Kant's description, in the *Kritik der Urteilskraft,* of the work of art as a part of nature that is beyond nature, sacred, therefore a value beyond price, sui generis, a law unto itself. Therefore it cannot be judged by ordinary domestic, economic, ethical, or political standards of value. If Maisie measures those around her by her own unique scale, she herself is unable to be measured by the scales available to Sir Claude and the others. She cannot be incorporated into their vicious circle of "violent substitution" and taking without giving. Sir Claude affirms this: "It wouldn't do—it wouldn't do. We *can't* work her in. It's perfectly true—she's unique. We're not good enough—oh no!" (360).

"Violent substitution": the phrase names not only the ordinary metaphorical transfer whereby a word is carried over from its normal, literal usage to a figurative usage. The phrase also corresponds closely to the definition of catachresis as the "forced and abusive transfer" of a word from its usual meaning to cover a region that has no literal name, as in "eye of a storm." As an unmarried female, on the threshold of adolescence, a young woman, moreover, who has been abandoned by her biological parents, Maisie has no fixed social role or identity. By a process of violent substitution the people around her attempt to "work her in," to give her a place in the vicious circle. But Maisie, like Ottilie in Goethe's *Die Wahlverwandtschaften,* remains a blank, a floating signifier. In the end she refuses to be employed in the game of substitution that would make her a living catachresis. It would do this by putting her in a special place authorizing the substitutions replacing lover by lover among those around her. She might therefore be called an allegory of catachresis, that is, an allegory of the way this figure fails in the end to hide the vacancy it would cover. Since Maisie in her uniqueness has no namable or knowable identity, she cannot be made to play a part in the game.

The reader can now see what Maisie, like James's other protagonists, gets out of giving up all hope of entering into the normal round of sexual or economic giving and taking. And the reader can glimpse the way Maisie's bliss is an oblique allegory of James's bliss in creating her. James's is the Pygmalion-like joy of going beyond the vulgar facts of social reality in late nineteenth-century England and creating a heroine who is ideally sensitive, imaginative, and intelligent, thus making that "beautiful thing," an admirable work of art. In the preface to *Maisie,* speaking not of *Maisie* but of "In the Cage," James calls this transformation a vice. He has "the vice of reading rank subtleties into simple souls and reckless expenditure into thrifty ones." He has an "irrepressible and insatiable, extravagant and immoral, interest in personal character and in the 'nature' of a mind" (xx).

Maisie's bliss is also a version of Pygmalion's joy. If James has fashioned Maisie as a compensatory image, Maisie's incorrigible error throughout her coming to know is the projection onto her parents and their associates of ideal persons. Her characteristic act is not so much coming to know as it is wondering. But wondering, as James makes clear, is not constative but performative, in the sense defined by J. L. Austin and others. It is projective, positional, or impositional, transforming things by acts of language.

This is especially evident in the scene James singles out in the preface for special praise, as the "type-passage . . . for the expression of its beauty" (xiv), namely the poignant episode in which Maisie meets the Captain, the latest in her mother's long line of lovers. She imagines, with a passionate intensity of desire, an ideal relation between her mother and the Captain in which her mother is loved, valued, and protected. Or rather she does not so much imagine this relation as try to speak it into existence by what she says to the Captain and makes him say:

> "Say you love her, Mr. Captain; say it, say it!" she implored.
> Mr. Captain's blue eyes fixed themselves very hard. "Of *course* I love her, damn it, you know!"
> At this she also jumped up; she had fished out somehow her pocket-handkerchief. "So do *I* then. I do, I do, I do!" she passionately asseverated. (153)

What Maisie gradually learns in the course of growing up is that such speech acts create not a real world but an imaginary, linguistic world. She implores the Captain to go on loving her mother: "Then don't do it only for just a little . . . Like all the others" (155). This iterated invocation of an ideal reality does not prevent that liaison from ending like all the others, as she later learns. Maisie's final choice is for the inner world her wonder has created.

When James describes in the preface Maisie's unique power as "the wonderful importance . . . of lending to poorer persons and things, by the mere fact of their being involved with her and by the special scale she creates for them, a precious element of dignity," he is obliquely describing his own procedure of making a beautiful work of art out of unpromising materials. He is also describing Maisie's bliss as the transformation of vulgar persons into ideal figures, prosopopoeias of her own moral ideals. At the climax of the novel, she momentarily imagines an idyllic life with Sir Claude. She will live alone with him "in a little place in the South," leaving Mrs. Beale and Mrs. Wix to live together in "a community of blankness" "in a little place in the North" (343). Later, when she has "already seen that she should have to give him up," her final appeal to Sir Claude to come away alone is defined as "the last flare of her dream" (352).

When in the end Maisie comes to know, as she foresees, "Most," "Everything," "All" (281), what she comes to know is the incompatibility between what the people around her really are and the ideal figures she has by a species of erroneous personification projected onto them. It is in order to protect the bliss of this idealizing activity that she gives up, leaves Sir Claude with Mrs. Beale, and takes the boat back to England with Mrs. Wix, just as Maggie Verver condones her husband's adultery, Milly Theale turns her face to the wall and dies, and Strether goes back alone to Massachusetts, having been true to his principle to get nothing for himself. If Maisie is unique, she decides, acts, and judges on a unique basis and law. Her wonder, governed by this law, transfigures things and people. It gives them connections with the "universal." This accomplished transformation is the value beyond price she gets from her abnegation.

What Maisie preserves, what it seems to her (the reader may guess) worth giving everything up to preserve, is just that separate realm of imaginative consciousness that she had long ago discovered, when she was a young child. This discovery happened in a moment that the narrator defines as nothing less than "literally a moral revolution and accomplished in the depths of her nature" (15). In that moment she found that she could by acting stupid and by keeping her own counsel avoid being the mediator of insulting

messages sent back and forth between her parents: "She had a new
feeling, the feeling of danger; on which a new remedy rose to meet
it, the idea of an inner self or, in other words, of concealment"
(15).

The idea of a concealed and concealing inner self is, in the narrator's notation, directly related to a rudimentary act of childish
personification preparing for the more grownup one I have been
describing—the idealization of her mother, the Captain, and the
rest. As proleptic of that, the moral revolution of her new insight
has the effect of bringing her dolls to life: "The stiff dolls on the
dusky shelves began to move their arms and legs; old forms and
phrases began to have a sense that frightened her" (15). A little later
she is shown treating her French doll, Lisette, in the same way that
her mother treats her, Maisie. Maisie too now keeps puzzling secrets and refuses to answer questions: "Little by little, however, she
understood more, for it befell that she was enlightened by Lisette's
questions, which reproduced the effect of her own upon those for
whom she sat in the very darkness of Lisette. Was she not herself
convulsed by such innocence? . . . She could only pass on her lessons and study to produce on Lisette the impression of having
mysteries in her life, wondering the while whether she succeeded
in the air of shading off, like her mother, into the unknowable"
(34).

The latter part of the novel makes extravagant use of the word
"free." When Maisie's mother abandons Sir Claude for good, he
exults, "I'm free—I'm free!" (230). Mrs. Beale unwittingly echoes
these words when she tells Maisie and Mrs. Wix that Maisie's father has abandoned her (Mrs. Beale) for good: "I'm free, I'm free!"
(290). Mrs. Beale and Sir Claude, however, use their freedom only
to consolidate a new form of bondage, their bond to one another.
When Sir Claude uses the expression twice more, however, in the
final scene, to describe Maisie ("You're free—you're free" [356]; "I
only insist that she's free—she's free" [359]), the word has an ironically different meaning. It means not only that Maisie is free to
choose for herself and to do what she likes. It also describes the
way she has freed herself from the vicious circle or, rather, is intrinsically free by the fact of her isolation within an ideal goodness.
This ideal is defined as a separateness that cannot be worked in, but

its functioning in the real social world is a work of prosopopoeia: the production of ideal personages against which everyone else is judged and found wanting.

The reader of *Maisie* (and of Maisie) now has an answer to the question posed at the beginning of this chapter. Why, for James, is renunciation the highest virtue? Why does renouncing always turn out to be the right thing to do? We know now that the reasons for this are more linguistic than ethical or, rather, that ethical responsibility is itself posed in terms of a universal linguistic predicament. Renunciation for James is not so much a free choice as a linguistic necessity that must be freely chosen and accepted. Renunciation expresses "symbolically" the impossibility of any adequate embodiment of the "universal." It expresses, moreover, the incommensurability between the demand made on the unique individual by the universal moral law and any expression of this demand that would convey it perspicuously to others—so I could, for example, make what Maisie does (or what James does) the known basis for my own doing.

In the moment of her ultimate renunciation, Maisie herself becomes unknowable. This has devastating consequences for the ethical functioning of the author's prosopopoeia and the reader's. If Maisie is truly unique, if she is absolute in the sense of "not tied to the ordinary social round and scale of measurement," if she measures things by her own unique scale, then she is unknowable. What is unique cannot be known or spoken in words. It vanishes from our circuit of knowledge. We cannot work it in. In an essay on Freud's *Dora* Neil Hertz has compared Freud's penetrative psychoanalytic knowing of his patient to James's celebration of what *he* was able to know through Maisie's knowing. Hertz, however, does not stress the importance of the moment when Maisie escapes James's knowing, even though he has made her.[19] In the end, at the moment when she becomes an adult, a fully responsible, knowing, ethical subject, James, or his delegate the narrator, can no longer know what Maisie knew. But this is just the moment when knowledge is most essential if we are to judge rightly what Maisie does, if we are to do her full justice, perhaps take her as a model for our own actions. James, or his narrator, it appears, can only know Maisie with full intimacy so long as she remains a wondering child. Something similar happens in his other novels, for example when Milly's inner life vanishes from direct report by the narrator towards the end of *The Wings of the Dove*. The dramatization of this is Kate's burning of Milly's now never-to-be-read deathbed letter to Densher.

The notation of this crucial failure in knowledge in *What Maisie Knew* is the more or less abrupt disappearance, at the end of the novel, of the narrator's habitual close reporting, in indirect discourse, of what Maisie thought and felt. These notations make a crescendo of admiring inwardness, culminating in the passage about the something still deeper than a moral sense. That close identification of what Maisie knew and what the narrator knows of what Maisie knew gradually fades in the remaining pages into sparser and sparser notations of what Maisie saw of the behavior of Mrs. Beale, Mrs. Wix, and Sir Claude (but any spectator present would have seen the same things). The narrator's knowing finally disappears into the representation of an emotion that is as much Mrs. Wix's as Maisie's, or belongs as a single affect to both at once: "they gave up half the voyage to letting their emotion sink. It sank slowly and imperfectly" (363). Finally, in the last sentence of all, the narrator's power of introspection is no longer operative. The point of view shifts to Mrs. Wix, who is shown seeing Maisie from the outside: "She still had room for wonder at what Maisie knew." Maisie's wonder, the trait James most values her for, has now been displaced to Mrs. Wix. The reader's direct access to Maisie's wonder, if that wonder still exists, has vanished with the vanishing of the narrator's insight into Maisie's mind.

The novel has reached a limit beyond which narration cannot proceed. Narration fulfills in part that universal enterprise of accounting for everything presupposed by the Leibnizian "principle of reason" or, more precisely, the *principium reddendae rationis sufficientis,* the principle that a sufficient reason can be and ought to be rendered for everything.[20] The encounter with something that cannot be narrated puts the universality of that principle in question. The other formulation of the principle of reason, *nihil est sine ratione* (nothing is without reason), can be read in two ways: as a restatement of the claim that everything can be accounted for or as the proposition that one thing cannot be accounted for, namely, "nothing." At just the moment we most need to know what is going on in her mind, Maisie's subjectivity becomes a nonentity that no longer exists as something or someone whose story can be told according to the narrative presuppositions operative here.

At the same moment, another crucial transformation may occur. My reading has presupposed a male gender for the narrator and has seen the narrator as a transformation of James himself. On this basis I have projected onto the novel the drama of a man's attempt to penetrate and master a woman's mind, making the novel analogous in this to Freud's *Dora*. But the vanishing of Maisie's subjectivity may lead the reader to see that he or she (more likely he than she) has been the victim of an ideological projection. The reader has assumed that the preface if not the novel in some way gives direct access to James's selfhood and personality, though this too is an illusion generated by prosopopoetic projection. The reader has in addition imposed a male gender on the narrator as an aspect of that creation of a personality for the narrator I earlier identified. But not one word of the novel fully justifies giving any gender at all to the narrator, however irresistible, especially to a male reader, the assumption may be that the narrator is male. The vanishing of the narrator's access to Maisie's mind and the consequent collapse of the doubled structure of mind knowing mind may lead the reader to recognize that the narrator has all along been an impersonal or neutral power of narration, "neuter" in the sense of *ne . . . uter,* neither one nor the other, neither male nor female. In changing himself into the narrator of *What Maisie Knew* James depersonalized himself and became the narrative voice, "le 'il,' le neutre" (the it, the neutral), that Maurice Blanchot identifies in a celebrated essay.[21] If the male reader assumes that the narrator must be male, an extension or transformation of James himself, this may be because he wants to identify himself with the narrator he has projected and then enjoy in imagination the pleasure of entering the mind and feelings, even the bodily sensations, of a person of the other sex. But if the narrator as the surrogate of the reader invokes Maisie, calls her into being by giving words to her inarticulate or half-articulate wonder, the moment of her disappearance from the narrator's ken abruptly reverses that. The reader comes to recognize that it has been Maisie who has invoked the subjectivity of author, narrator, and reader. They have been invoked not in the sense that Maisie authorizes their existence as mastering male personalities but in the sense that she invokes all three as neutral and impersonal powers of knowing and narrating. The narrator is depersonalized and unsexed by the act of narration, as the reader is by reading, the author by writing.

Another way to describe this triple vanishing into impersonality of Maisie, narrator, and reader is to say that *What Maisie Knew* is postulated on two contradictory technical conditions of narration. One condition arises from James's inveterate and "immoral" interest in other minds and a corresponding addiction to recording from within what he calls, apropos of "In the Cage," "a course of incident complicated by the intervention of winged wit" (xxi), meaning the winged wit of the protagonist. On the other hand, James is constrained by his equally intransigent commitment to the "scenic method," which alone will take him far, "into the flushed, dying day" (N162). The scenic method will take him, that is, to a horizon of death that is allegorized in the moment that Maisie's wondering childhood dies, ending the book. In the last chapter of *Maisie* the commitment to the scenic method wins out over the commitment to the introspection of others. There is, strictly speaking, no room for the latter or for a personified narrator, in a rigorous application of the scenic method.

This shift in the degree and kind of the narrator's access to Maisie is recorded in crucial sentences in the preface. James speaks first of the way Maisie's freshness, her capacity to wonder, is associated with the degree of "resistance" he is able to impute to her: "Successfully to resist (to resist, that is, the strain of observation and the assault of experience) what would that be, on the part of so young a person, but to remain fresh, and still fresh, to have even a freshness to communicate?" James then goes on to name the moment when that resistance ends with the death of her childhood:

the case [is] with Maisie to the end that she treats her friends to the rich little spectacle of objects embalmed in her wonder. She wonders, in other words, to the end, to the death—the death of her childhood, properly speaking; after which (with the inevitable shift, sooner or later, of her point of view) her situation will change and become another affair, subject to other measurements and with a

new centre altogether. The particular reaction that will have led her
to that point, and that it has been of an exquisite interest to study in
her, will have spent itself; there will be another scale, another perspective, another horizon. (xi)

This passage plays on the economic imagery whose importance I
have discussed: "rich," "interest," "spent itself." The narrator and
James find value in the valueless because Maisie's wonder gives
them value. The passage prepares for the use of such figures a little
later in the description of Maisie's wonder as a unique scale that
evaluates others.

The final sentence about *Maisie* in the preface returns to the economic imagery once more to define Maisie's resistance as valuable
just because she had so much to resist. She is valuable, paradoxically, just because she is so outrageously "taxed." Maisie's "case" is
"remarkable exactly by the weight of the tax on it." Her "active,
contributive close-circling wonder . . . provides distinction for
her, provides vitality and variety, through the operation of the
tax—which would have done comparatively little for us hadn't it
been monstrous" (xiv). Since it is James himself who has put this
"monstrous" tax on Maisie, his treatment of her is that strange
species of child abuse of which hostile early readers of *What Maisie
Knew* accused him.

The passage about objects "embalmed" in Maisie's wonder also
plays in a curious way on the notion that death is the hidden proper
name for any lapse in sequence. Maisie's wonder is death-dealing
in the sense that it leads ultimately to an intermittence, the death
of her childhood that is "a foretaste of the experience of death."
This figurative death is also a foretaste of death for author, narrator, and reader. When Maisie grows up she escapes our knowledge
and, in that lapse of sequence, it is as if she has died. This is figured
in the way Maisie's decision to be faithful to Mrs. Wix puts her
into the place left for her by the death of Mrs. Wix's own natural
child, about whom the reader hears much in the early part of the
novel. If Maisie herself after a fashion dies, her wonder has been,
all along, death-dealing. The transformative power that wonder
has, the power to turn Ida, Beale, Sir Claude, and the rest into
"striking figured symbols" of the "universal," is described, almost

casually and in a passing trope, as killing them off. They become no more than "objects embalmed in her wonder."

It may be some instinctive resistance to literature's death-dealing power that makes the notion that a work expresses a universal truth that is at the same time unique, cut off from historical, social, and political determining conditions, seem so scandalous to many. This is especially the case these days, though such resistance is an eternally recurring feature of literary study. At least part of the "new historicism" or of the widespread general "rehistoricizing" of literature today is born of a refusal to recognize what is inaugural in literature, inaugural precisely in its historical effects. This power could be successfully denied, resisted, or ignored if literature could be fully accounted for by its historical contexts. The price for this would be to make literature and the study of literature of little account. If all I learn from the study of literature is that it repeats, reflects, mirrors, or is determined by its historical circumstances, in however complex a way, then it would seem more sensible, a better use of precious time, to study history *tout court*. One danger in the current turn back to history is that it might erroneously be taken to justify giving the historical context of a work without the necessary scrupulous reading of the text that historical context is supposed to explain. This does not mean that a careful establishing of the historical context of a work is not necessary. Far from it. But it does mean that the cry "Always historicize!" cannot be taken as the last word in literary study, if it means a promise that historicizing alone will provide a full and adequate accounting for any work.

In *What Maisie Knew* Mrs. Wix's invocation of the moral sense, on the one hand, and the desire of Sir Claude and Mrs. Beale to make their liaison appear respectable by the pretense that Mrs. Beale is taking care of Maisie, on the other, are explicable as the reflection of ideological features of late Victorian society, as are those divorce laws and sexual conventions I identified at the beginning of this chapter. Mrs. Wix, Sir Claude, and Mrs. Beale are shown in their different ways to be the slaves of social convention. James's late-Kantian notions of the work of art as beyond price are also ideological formations. Even the decision to make Maisie a girl depends on ideological assumptions common in the society to which James belonged and for which he wrote. These include the presupposition that girls are more sensitive, more sexually innocent than boys, and are much more difficult for a male author or narrator to understand. If a culture goes on repeating to itself, "Sticks and snails and puppy-dog tails: that's what little boys are made of. Sugar and spice and everything nice: that's what little girls are made of," boys and girls may actually come to behave as if they were differentiated in this way. What is most terrifying about ideological formations is not that they are errors bred of the confusion of a linguistic with a natural reality, but that they may actually bring to pass the state of affairs they erroneously describe. A false constative proposition becomes an effective performative speech act. The "other," the ideology of gender differences presupposes, is more difficult to penetrate if difference in sex is added to the other "othernesses" of the other person. This means that the male can learn something unknowable in any other way if he can "pierce the veil of feminine mysteries." Freud's *Dora,* as recent feminist critics of Freud have argued, depends on the same ideological assumption. Sir Claude, in *Maisie,* may be obliquely testifying to this assumption's strength by his habit of calling Maisie "old boy" or some other affectionate male name—as if to hide from himself that she is changing before his eyes into a woman who can look at him with more than filial eyes.

Maisie herself, however, escapes from all these cultural assumptions, as does the novel itself (with her help). She resists them, puts them in question by measuring them by her "fragrance of an ideal." By refusing to join the vicious circle she liberates herself from them, thereby perhaps making it possible for the reader of her story to become in some small degree "free." What she does and what she causes others to do by her doing, like the novel itself, cannot be fully accounted for by its relation to the ideology of its surrounding society. This remnant, the inassimilable residue, the "residuum" that is "the *full* ironic truth" about Maisie, is its most precious part, as James claimed.[22]

But do not let what I mean, and claim James meant, by "the universal" be misunderstood. What is universal in *Maisie* is not

some eternal "value" or "theme," but the incommensurability between ascertainable meaning and historical effect when language
intervenes in the materiality of history. "Language" includes the
language of literature, but is not limited to it. My discussion in the
next chapter, of Kleist's "On the Gradual Fabrication of Thoughts
While Speaking," is an attempt to explain more exactly this incommensurability.

ONE LAST SET of questions remains. If the reader brings Maisie
back to life from the words on the page, what then should the
reader do as a result of this? What has he or she already done by
reading? How can the reader render full justice to *What Maisie
Knew*? Exactly to what or to whom does the reader render justice
in performing this act? These questions return to the problem of
the ethics of reading. Just what is the reader's ethical obligation in
this particular case?

The answer, it would seem, is clear. Readers have an ethical responsibility to render justice to the text. We do this on the basis of
the reading. The making public of the reading, in acts of teaching
or of published criticism, is a doing that does other things in its
turn. The act of reading, it seems, should model itself on the author's act, on the narrator's, and on Maisie's own.

All of these acts are themselves at one time or another defined in
the figure of reading. The way Maisie's bliss is bale for the others,
for example, is defined as "the most interesting item to be *read* into
the child's situation" (vi, my italics). Maisie's "rather tormented"
inability to decipher what people are saying and doing around her
is figured as her inability to play games or to read books too advanced for her age:

> By the time she had grown sharper, as the gentlemen who had cri-
> ticised her calves used to say, she found in her mind a collection of
> images and echoes to which meanings were attachable—images and
> echoes kept for her in the childish dusk, the dim closet, the high
> drawers, like games she wasn't yet big enough to play. The great
> strain meanwhile was that of carrying by the right end the things her
> father said about her mother—things mostly indeed that Moddle
> [her nurse], on a glimpse of them, as if they had been complicated

toys or difficult books, took out of her hands and put away in the closet. A wonderful assortment of objects of this kind she was to discover there later, all tumbled up too with the things, shuffled into the same receptacle, that her mother had said about her father. (12)

But if the reader is another Pygmalion, defining Pygmalion's act as a "reading into," it is clear what is unsettling about this model. This may be expressed in several ways. One is to recognize the impossibility of knowing, for author, narrator, protagonist, or reader, whether we are in the presence of an accurate reading or of a reading into, or, indeed, which of these is to be valued over the other. The full ironic truth is latent not in the vulgar facts of the real case, but in the "subject" as James detaches it from its mesh of defining circumstances and plays the torch of his imagination over it. The narrator finds words for Maisie's experience that she does not herself have. This transforms that experience, even if only by a shade of a difference. Maisie's prime faculty, her wonder, is celebrated for its ability to change things and people not in themselves worth our interest into figures of the universal. In all these cases reading is baseless or exceeds its base. It would appear, on the face of it, to be difficult in principle to exempt the reader's act from being another version of the same procedures of "reading into."

Another way to put this difficulty is to say that, after all, as James makes brilliantly clear in the preface to *The Golden Bowl*,[23] what the reader reaches by way of the text, and therefore what he has most obligation to honor, is not the text itself but that to which the text gives the reader access. This is that "universal" of which all the text's figured symbols are allegorical expressions. The word "allegory" here means both the use of personification and the saying of something that otherwise cannot be said at all. If Maisie is singular, if she cannot be fitted in, if she is ultimately unknowable and unspeakable, except by the narrator's silence, she has the inexpressibly valuable gift of turning those around her into personifications of the unspeakable. If the reader repeats this use of personification as catachresis, he or she too is open to the charge of trying to say what cannot be said.

The final way to express the difficulty of rendering justice is to say that the *full* ironic truth, the universal, is the incommensurability between Maisie's wonder, James's imaginative act, the narrator's act of storytelling, and the reader's act of reading, on the one hand, and any straightforward ethical action that will "do good" in the social and political world, on the other. Maisie, like James's other signal protagonists, ultimately renounces participation in the social round. She withdraws in order to protect her moral and imaginative deal, which cannot be made materially operative in the real world. This harsh law would presumably hold in any conceivable society. The fact that Maisie's bliss is bale for others is not a contingent historical fact. It is, according to James, a universal law of human life.

Insofar as Maisie's wonder is the manifestation of a universal moral ideal, it has no direct purchase on the concrete social world of taking without giving. Or, rather, it *has* an effect, but the effect of making bad worse. Or (and this is the final difficulty), since her goodness is ultimately unknowable, it has effects that are unpredictable, ironically askew, never a straightforward matter of cause and effect. Something happens in the real world as a result of her choice, but that happening is performative rather than cognitive. It possesses the inherent uncertainty of all speech acts, since it has to be read to be acted on and to become effective.

This means that what the reader does is a productive "reading into" for which he or she must take responsibility. A reading is not a cognitive reporting of an ascertainable and verifiable interpretation. If that is what is meant by "reading," *What Maisie Knew* is, strictly speaking, unreadable. In spite of this, however, reading happens and can be made public. But the reader can never fully verify the reading or accurately predict the effects of publishing it, though the reading occurs by an ineluctable necessity. When you or I read *What Maisie Knew,* what happens happens. We are by no means free to make *Maisie* mean anything we want. If the vanishing of Maisie from the ken of both narrator and reader depersonifies both, then neither the narrator nor the reader is a freely willing "I" responding to another "I," that is, Maisie, and then choosing to act in one way or another on the basis of what is known about her. The reader's "I" reasserts itself on the other side of a depersonifying lapse in knowledge that is like a foretaste of death. Insofar as Maisie ultimately escapes from the author's, the narrator's, and the reader's knowledge, escapes at just that moment when all three most need to know her from within in order to render a just judgment on what she does, all three are left on their own, as Maisie was. The reader too must decide it by a word of his or her own. This happens in an act of reading that is a doing that does other things in its turn. But it is a doing that is not soundly based on clear and demonstrable knowledge. Moreover, the reader must even take responsibility for the arbitrary positing of the "I" that affirms the doing.

My exploration of the ethics of narrative, in this first example of reading a story, has encountered a triple lapse in sequence that is like a triple foretaste of death. One discontinuity is the uncrossable gap between what the reader knows and what Maisie knows at the point when she crosses the border into adulthood. This unknowability means the reading is based at best only on the priceless knowledge that the reader cannot know. The second intermittence is that between what the reader knows and what he or she makes, the reading. The reading does not quite follow the knowledge. It cannot help but exceed its knowledge and launch out on its own, just as Maisie does in the condition she makes to Sir Claude, though her condition is the only right one. The final break is that between what the reader produces, for example a classroom seminar or a published essay, and the performative effect of that in the real world of students and readers. Something happens, but what that something will be cannot be known beforehand. There is no reason, moreover, to suppose that the act of publishing or teaching will necessarily be exempt from the cruel law that says bliss for the reader and bale for those who read the teaching.

Whether this disquieting ethical law of a possible incongruity in the realm of reading will be exemplified in the further readings in this book, or whether that law will come to be better understood, remains to be seen. But I can assert now, on the basis of my reading, that these various lapses in sequence may all be put under the aegis of Pygmalion's creative gesture. That gesture may be defined as "the invention of the other,"[24] taking "invention" in its double sense of both "create" and "reveal," and taking "the other" in the strong sense of something radically unknowable that is, paradoxically and surprisingly, met in an act of wondering, imagining, or reading. It appears at first that the author, narrator, protagonist, and reader can encounter nothing that they have not, in one way or another, made. But prosopopoeia, as the invention of the other, encounters something unknowable, something, moreover, that is as much obscured as uncovered by being personified.

CHAPTER 3

Just Reading:
Kleist's "Der Findling"

What is the role of theory in teaching, and what ought it to be? According to Heinrich von Kleist in "Über die Allmähliche Verfertigung der Gedanken beim Reden" (On the Gradual Fabrication of Thoughts While Speaking),[1] the role of theory in teaching should be, or has to be, nil. Creative and productive speaking of whatever sort, including teaching, does not take place by the forethought and rational calculation implied by the word "theory." It occurs spontaneously, unpredictably. Teaching, like other forms of speech, is most effective when it is made up on the spot by someone who has no idea where a sentence is going to end when it is begun. A teacher should speak first and think later. The more "theoretical" a teacher is, the more ineffective the teaching will be, just as, to use Kleist's example from another essay, a wrestler who tries to think out his next move will almost certainly lose.

A moment's reflection will show that things are not so simple in this area of thought and action. The current situation, in the study of literature at least and in the United States, is characterized by the almost universal triumph of theory. This is true in spite of the continued active presence of what Paul de Man called "the resistance to theory."[2] On every side we have not only the development of a large number of powerful competing theoretical discourses, hermeneutic, Lacanian, feminist, reader-response, Marxist, Foucaultian, structuralist, deconstructionist, new historicist, and so on, but also the accompanying immense proliferation of courses, curricula, books, handbooks, dissertations, essays, lectures, new journals, symposia, study groups, and institutes that are overtly concerned with theory. This victory of theory has transformed the field of literary study from what it was when I entered it forty years ago. In those happy days we mostly studied primary works in the context of literary history, with some overt attention in our teaching to the basic presuppositions of the so-called New Criticism: the primacy of metaphor, the universality of the principle of organic unity, and so on.

The present-day triumph of theory is no doubt overdetermined. It has many incompatible causes or, it might be better to say, "concomitant factors," in order to avoid begging the question by slipping in the word "causes." The turn to theory is motivated in part by a widespread loss of confidence in the value of primarily studying works in the traditional canon. Also put in doubt has been the traditional justification for the study of the canon. I mean the assumption that such study transmits from the old to the young the fundamental values of our culture, "the best that has been known and thought in the world." Defenses of the canon on these grounds are certainly still being made, but usually in a way that makes their ideological motivation evident. Such defenses no longer go without saying. Our consciousnesses have been raised, no doubt to a considerable degree by the works of theory. We are likely to feel that no choice of books for a syllabus, for example, or no choice of ways to read those books, is politically innocent. Such choices can no longer be justified by appeal to a universal consensus or by appeal to universal standards valid for any time, place, group, institution, or particular classroom.

The triumph of theory is a response to this situation and an attempt to think one's way out of it. The teacher wants to be justified in what he or she does. The appeal to theory is one way of seeking that justification. One of the major functions of literary theory is as a critique of ideology, that is, a critique of the taking of a linguistic reality for a material one. The ideology in this case involves the hidden assumptions of our procedures of teaching and of the general institutionalization of literary study. So theory has become more and more a subject of study for its own sake. But literary theory is of little or no use unless it is "applied," used. It must be active, productive, performative. What theory produces ought to be new readings, in the broadest sense of that word. These read-

ings in their turn will be performative rather than passive or cognitive. They will make something happen. The readings in question would of course include new readings of the works of theory.
I mean "readings" in a strong sense of that word—critical, rhetorical, productive readings as opposed to passive interpretations of
the manifest thematic content of the texts. Theory, like primary
literature, is of no use unless it is read in this sense. Only then will
theory facilitate readings of other texts, readings that, as Derrida
says in "Mochlos," will be radically inaugural in the sense that they
will propose a new "contract" with the university and with the
society or the state that university serves. "For example," says Derrida,

> when I read a sentence from a given text in a seminar (a statement of
> Socrates, a fragment of *Das Kapital* or *Finnegans Wake,* a paragraph
> of *The Conflict of Faculties*) I do not merely fulfill an already existing
> contract; I am also writing, or preparing for signature, a new con-
> tract with the institution, between the institution and the dominant
> forces of society. Here, as in any negotiation—a precontractual ne-
> gotiation always transforms a former contract—here is the moment
> for every imaginable ruse and strategic ploy.[3]

To the degree that modern critical theory is intrinsically performative, political, it is implicitly opposed to the vast enterprise
of assimilative rationalizing that is usually assumed to be the university's chief reason for being. It is not surprising to find that the
university responds to this threat by various strategies, for example by encompassing theory in courses that treat it just as another object of knowledge, no different from the Victorian novel
or Romantic poetry or Renaissance drama (though of course the
reading of the latter should be productive and inaugural too). The
more successfully theory is institutionalized according to certain
agenda, the more successfully it may be rendered harmless. This
danger is not the result of some contingent misunderstanding
coming to theory from the outside. It follows from an intrinsic
cleft within theory itself. This cleavage renews itself within the act
of reading that theory is supposed to anticipate, understand, and
control. Insofar as theory is constative, its function is epistemological: to promote clear-seeing knowledge, as the etymology of the

word "theory" suggests. Insofar as theory has the performative face I have been recognizing in it, its function is to cooperate with reading or to facilitate reading or in fact to be an act of reading that is a productive event in the real world of material history. The two aspects of theory cannot be reconciled, harmonized, or synthesized. They are not logically or dialectically opposed, but asymmetrical. I turn to a reading of Kleist's "Allerneuester Erziehungsplan" (The Very Last Word in Modern Educational Theory) to try to understand this asymmetry better.

Kleist's little essay was first published in two parts in October and November 1810. It appeared in Berlin's first daily newspaper, the *Berliner Abendblätter,* founded and edited by Kleist himself. One of Kleist's masterpieces, the essay on puppet theater, also appeared in the *Berliner Abendblätter.* Censorship problems led to the closing of the newspaper in March 1811. "Allerneuester Erziehungsplan" belongs to the genre of the fictional or parodic letter to the editor. This is somewhat obscured in the English translation, which omits the two words of epistolary address inserted in the German original just before the second paragraph: "Hochgeehrtes Publikum" (Most Esteemed Public). The first paragraph is supposed to be by Kleist the editor. He explains that the letter "illustrates the amusing nature of the suggestions that find their way to our editorial desk" (223). This is then followed by the salutation and then by the letter itself. Like a strange work by Edgar Allan Poe, "A Chapter on Autography," Kleist's jeu d'esprit is a spoof. But like Kleist's irony in general (he is one of the great ironists), or like irony as such, the irony here is exceedingly difficult to pin down. Presumably Kleist had more in mind than making fun of the apparently absurd educational ideas presented in the imaginary letter, but what *did* he have in mind? Or is that the wrong way of asking the question, insofar as it presumes we might appeal back to some putative intention in the mind of Kleist? As always, our only resource is to read the text and see what we can make of it.

Kleist's first target, it may be hypothesized, is Goethe's *Die Wahlverwandtschaften* (Elective Affinities), which had appeared in 1809, a year earlier. Kleist had reason to have it in for the great Goethe, who had bowdlerized Kleist's play *Der zerbrochne Krug*

(The Broken Jug). The play was a fiasco when it was produced, and Kleist blamed Goethe for that. Goethe had in addition disapproved of Kleist's play *Penthesilea* and refused to lend his support to Kleist's journal *Phöbus*. Kleist affirmed that he was determined to "tear the wreath" from Goethe's head.

Elective Affinities is based on a comparison, a "Gleichnisrede" or parabolic analogy, between the natural realm of chemical reactions and the human realm of irresistible erotic attractions. Just as a sulfate displaces a carbonate when sulfuric acid is applied to lime, so Ottilie displaces Charlotte in Edward's affections. The law in question may be expressed in a proportional equation that corresponds to the sort of formula Aristotle used to describe the transfers of metaphor:

> Denken Sie sich ein A, das mit einem B innig verbunden ist, durch viele Mittel und durch manche Gewalt nicht von ihm zu trennen; denken Sie sich ein C, das sich eben so zu einem D verhält; bringen Sie nun die beiden Paare in Berührung: A wird sich zu D, C zu B werfen, ohne dass man sagen kann, wer das andere zuerst verlassen, wer sich mit dem andern zuerst wieder verbunden habe.[4]

> Suppose an A connected so closely with a B, that all sorts of means, even violence, have been made use of to separate them, without effect. Then suppose a C in exactly the same position with respect to D. Bring the two pairs into contact; A will fling himself on D, C on B, without its being possible to say which had first left its first connection, or made the first move toward the second.[5]

Another figure is present in this passage, however, which undermines the apparent primacy of the natural world and thereby undoes the logical orderliness of the workings of the analogy. If the human world is said to be subject to a law whose primary operation is in the natural world, that natural law is expressed in anthropomorphic terms borrowed from the human world: "A will fling himself [werfen sich] on D, C on B." But one element does not literally fling itself on another, as a lover is drawn irresistibly to his beloved. The apparently empirical "scientific nomenclature" (37), such as the term "elective affinities" for the attraction of elements to one another, is in fact a set of prosopopoeias imported from the human realm to cover a blank place in the vocabulary of science and to ascribe volition and animation to what in fact has none. It would be a mistake to assume that Goethe did not know this. *Elective Affinities,* like Kleist's parody of it, is an ironical work through and through, including its title.

Kleist's first target in "The Very Last Word," nevertheless, is the apparently serious use by Goethe in *Elective Affinities* of a scientific analogy to identify the law governing human erotic relationships, a law stronger than the marriage bond. In Kleist's case the ironic undecidability lies in the solemn dumbness of the pedagogue, C. J. Levanus, Konrektor (Assistant Headmaster), who is supposed to have written this letter to the editor. The astute reader, however, will presume that Kleist is using this subterfuge to express ideas of his own. The name "Levanus" may be a clue. It is apparently an allusion to Jean-Paul Richter's work of educational theory, *Levana* (1807). The word may suggest both "someone who raises up" and "light-weight." What is in Goethe's novel an affinity, an irresistible desire to embrace and combine, an erotic law, is for C. J. Levanus the reverse, a law of repulsion:

> Physical science, in one of its newest chapters on the nature of electrical bodies, teaches us that when we bring an electrically neutral body into proximity with, or, to put it more technically, into the "atmosphere" of, an electrically active body, the neutral one is suddenly activated too, and in fact assumes the opposite charge. It is as though nature had a horror of excessive and disproportionate quantity, and when any two bodies come into contact there seems to be an ordained tendency to correct for the unbalance that has been caused by their new relation . . .
>
> This remarkable law can be observed to operate in the moral as well as the physical realm, although, as far as we know, it has hardly received attention until now. A man in a condition of total indifference, for example, as to some issue or other, does not only instantly cease to be so upon contact with someone firmly opinionated in the matter, but his entire being (if we may so express it) modulates into polar opposition: he assumes the term + when the other is −, and − when the other is +. (223)

It is as if Kleist were saying to Goethe, "Anything you can do, I can do better. Two can play at this game, and see what a ridiculously different result one gets by changing the scientific metaphor." In a characteristic strategy that Kleist often deploys within a single work of his own (rather than in ironic opposition to the work of another), the juxtaposition of two different paradigms casts doubt on the whole enterprise of thinking and acting in terms of models based on metaphorical analogies. And yet, as is confirmed by Kleist's references here to Basedow and Campe, Pestalozzi and Zeller, four celebrated pedagogical theorists of the time, he knew something of contemporary theory. His essay suggests that he was aware that such a theory is often no more than the elaborate working out and then institutionalization of a metaphor, for example the comparison of children to flowers or vegetables in the word "kindergarten" or the analogy between children in school and rats in a maze in behaviorist theories.

In Kleist's spoof of Goethe, however, as well as in Goethe's novel, the claim that "this remarkable law can be observed to operate in the moral as well as the physical realm" has already been implicitly prepared (and undercut) by personifications in the description of the inhuman, inanimate physical process. Natural events are named by way of terms that suggest they are human. An example is Kleist's formulation about "the electrical excess with which the positively charged body is, so to speak, diseased" [den Elektrizitätsüberschuss, woran jener, auf gewisse Weise, krank ist] (223; 329). If moral laws are borrowed from nature, they have already been imported there by language and especially by its ubiquitous personifications. Recognition of this in Kleist's "so to speak" undermines the validity of the analogy, since it recognizes that what science gives us is not nature or physical process as such, but a nature that has already been turned tropologically to man's account, accounted for in man's terms.

After this setting forth of the law of contraries, C. J. Levanus proceeds to his clarifying examples. Each one is a little narrative. This puts "The Very Last Word" within the group of short works by Kleist consisting of a series of short narratives exemplifying some difficult, ironic, or paradoxical conceptual point. The group includes "On the Gradual Fabrication of Thoughts While Speaking", "Über das Marionettentheater" (On the Puppet Theater), and "Unwahrscheinliche Wahrhaftigkeiten" (Improbable Realities). But the function of storytelling in these works is not purely cognitive, nor are the works themselves aimed primarily at imparting knowledge. Each in one way or another dramatizes a situation in which storytelling is performative. It leads its auditors not only to know something but also to do something, and it implicitly exhorts its readers to do something too. This sequence represents allegorically the effect on you and me of reading the work. The text itself reminds the reader that stories not only provide knowledge but also have effects in the realm of moral or political action. In "The Very Last Word" the emphasis is on the contrast between the effects of theory in teaching and the effects of narrative in teaching.

A series of stories exemplifies the point Kleist is making: the story of the lady who secures a rendezvous with her lover by suggesting to her husband that he stay at home for a quiet evening with her, the story of the ship's captain who reverses his order to blow up his ship at the first mention of the word "surrender," the story Levanus tells from his own experience about the way his prodigality was in danger of turning his sister into a miser, the story of the horrible prison that makes some of its inmates models of virtue, and so on.

The first thing to note about these anecdotes is that, though they at first seem to lead unequivocally to the conceptual generalization about the law of opposites that C. J. Levanus wants to make, the more the reader thinks about each of them the more enigmatic and odd each seems to be. Each flies off on a tangent of its own and exceeds the concept it is meant to exemplify. All are slightly askew and do not quite fit the paradigm Levanus has set up. If theory, as I have argued, *is* praxis or finds its proper fulfillment in praxis, there is no theory without its accompanying narrative examples. The relation between theory and narrative example is an uneasy one, as unsettling as the relation between the moral law as such, in Kant's thinking about ethics, and the narrative examples of its operation that form (to speak in Kant's own metaphor) the aesthetic bridge from the law to everyday praxis. In teaching, as in any other practical activity, we do not just want to know what to do "in theory." We need to know what to do here and now, in this particular classroom, with these particular students, and in teaching this particular topic or text.

Perhaps the best example in Kleist's essay of the asymmetrical relation between theoretical concept and narrative example is the story of the Portuguese ship's captain. The captain has attempted to do what the essay seems to advocate, to use the law of opposition, "the law that inclines us to throw all our weight of opinion into the opposed position" (224), to achieve the result he wants. Here is Kleist's explanation of how this may be done: "Someone remarks, 'That man over there is fat as a beer barrel.' The truth is, he is of average corpulence. I, however, taking a closer look, do not merely correct the error, but I call upon God Himself to witness that the fellow is skinny as a stick" (224). If this law operates universally, it would follow that in our schools we should not try to teach virtue by good example, but should use the opposite strategy. Therefore, says Levanus, "we are of a mind to establish a sort of School of Vice, or better said, a School of Contrariness, of Virtue through the Vices" [sind wir gesonnen, eine sogenannte *Laster-schule,* oder vielmehr eine *gegensätzische* Schule, eine Schule der *Tugend durch Laster,* zu errichten] (226; 334). The curriculum will include Sacrilege, Bigotry, Insolence, Self-Contempt, Servility, Avarice, Cowardice, Temerity, and Extravagance. The claim is that their opposites will be magically generated by such teaching.

The Portuguese captain has proceeded on just this theory. His ship has been attacked by three Venetian vessels, and he has instructed the fireman to blow up the ship at the first mention of the word "surrender." When further resistance seems futile, the officers call upon the captain to surrender, the fireman starts to put a match to the powder kegs, and the captain responds in just the opposite way from the one he had foreseen. He is horrified by the prospect of blowing up his ship and orders the white flag raised. The law of opposition prevails, but in this case it is an opposition to an opposition that produces the contrary of the result the captain had attempted to preprogram. He wanted to avoid surrender by way of opposition, and he ends up surrendering after all.

Far from leading to predictable results, the narrative example seems to suggest that the law of opposition puts anyone who tries to use it in the endless regression dramatized in the game of odd and even or in the dilemma Freud gives in *Jokes and Their Relation to the Unconscious:* "If you say you're going to Cracow, you want me to believe you're going to Lemberg. But I know that in fact you're going to Cracow. So why are you lying to me?"[6] As soon as a lie is used to assert the truth, it is possible that the lie may really be the truth, that is, a lie to the second power. The example of the ship's captain seems to suggest that Levanus' law of opposition, far from leading to predictable pedagogical results, leads to an endless regression in which you cannot be sure ahead of time whether the plus or the minus, the odd or the even, will happen to win out. Just as, according to Freud, there are no negatives in dreams, so the law of opposition, since it works by figurative analogy, is not the basis of sure prediction. It is a free-floating power that language has to make something happen. You can be sure that *something* will happen when the word "surrender" is uttered, but exactly what cannot be predicted.

The situation gets worse as the essay progresses. A considerable part of its ironic comedy lies not just in the absurdity of a school in which students would take Gluttony 101 or an advanced seminar in Boorishness, nor in the way the narrative examples do not quite prove Levanus' point, but rather in the wild incoherence of Levanus' logic as the essay proceeds. The more he goes on writing the more inconsistent, contradictory, and illogical he gets. Presumably this is meant as a parody of the incoherence, as Kleist saw it, of the educational theory of his day.

After having argued that we should teach virtue by giving courses in vice, Levanus moves on to what are in fact quite different theoretical figures for successful teaching, *Bilden* for *Bildung*. The paradigm of polarity is a deterministic or dialectical law. It appears to be paradoxical but should, so it seems, give rise to a perfectly reasonable, lawful, and predictable theory of education. Teach boorishness and your pupils will automatically have good manners. However, after having argued with a mad remorseless logic, on the basis of the physical fact that a positively charged object automatically generates a negative charge in what is nearby, Levanus goes on to oppose the traditional theory of teaching virtue through good example by way of two quite different arguments.

We are likely to have, he says, "exaggerated notions [Begriffe] about the power of education in the first place" (227). In fact a child is exposed to many other determining influences. And in any case each child is programmed by an innate genetic principle of growth

that overrides all external influence, not only schooling but even
the more powerful influence of a bad parent who "undertakes the
systematic corruption of the child that she nurses at her breast":
"Aber das Kind ist kein Wachs, das sich, in eines Menschen Hän-
den, zu einer beliebigen Gestalkt kneten lässt: es lebt, es ist frei; es
trägt ein unabhängiges und eigentümliches Vermögen der Ent-
wickelung, und das Muster aller innerlichen Gestaltung, in sich"
(A child is not made of wax, which can be kneaded into this or that
desired shape. It lives, it is free, it bears within itself an independent and intrinsic capability for development and the blueprint for
all higher conditions of mind and spirit; 335; 227.) This is an entirely different theory of education from the one implied in the
story of the ship's captain, one closer to that lying behind the image of the kindergarten, or close to that proposed in Rousseau's
Emile. A child is like a seed or a young plant. It already contains
within itself the genetic program (*Muster*) of all its future development. If we just leave it alone it will develop properly, or it will
develop according to its own innate plan even if we do not leave it
alone. Intrinsic nature will win the day.

This shades off at the end of Levanus' letter into yet another
argument, one much less reassuring. Education has an entirely unpredictable effect, and so education according to any one pedagogical theory is as good as education according to any other: "In our
school as in theirs [schools run, that is, according to other theo-
ries], for every one who is destroyed there will be another in
whom virtue and morals will blossom in a robust and hearty way;
the world will remain rather much as it is, and what we have
learned by experience from Pestalozzi and Zeller, and all the other
experts in our modern art of pedagogy, we shall also be able to
claim for ourselves: If it doesn't do much good, it doesn't do much
harm either" (227–228).

Is Levanus just hopelessly mixed up? Did Kleist therefore mean
no more by this text than to make fun by parody of the confusions
and contradictions of pedagogical theorists? Or is it possible that
Kleist is using this opportunity to express positions of his own on
causality, development, and storytelling, positions that, for example, may be posited in a different way in his more celebrated
essays or in his stories and plays? A clue may be given in the fact

that most of Levanus' examples involve someone's reaction to language. I hear the word "fat" and I respond with "skinny as a stick." The ship's captain hears the word "surrender," and something happens that he had not foreseen. He surrenders. The wife says, "Let us spend a quiet evening together," and her husband rushes off to the tavern. In all these cases it is a question of what words or other signs make happen. It is a question, that is, of an act of reading.

Levanus first says that reading operates by the law of contrariness, *Gegensätz,* then that the child grows according to an internal blueprint, or, to put this in terms of reading, that reader response will determine the projected meaning. He then finally affirms that the proferred words or signs will have some effect or other, but an entirely unpredictable one. The incoherence of the three positions Levanus takes suggests that Kleist's real target in this text is not so much the specific error of Goethe's chemical model for human relations in *Elective Affinities* as the more fundamental error of trying to figure a sequence that is fundamentally linguistic in any trope drawn from the phenomenal world. The model of electrically charged bodies or the model of the life form with "an intrinsic capability for development" is as bad as the model of chemical affinities. No such figure is appropriate as a way of talking about a sequence in which words or other signs are put forth and then read. Only the third and final of Levanus's three concepts of what happens in reading is specifically linguistic. We may hypothesize that it is to take precedence over the other two, just as the final example of the fencing bear, in "On the Puppet Theater," takes precedence over the first two examples of the narcissistic boy and the marionettes.

Levanus' examples exceed and contradict the first two of the concepts they are apparently meant to illustrate. What they support is the third concept, the one that says that you can be sure that something will happen when signs are proferred and then read, but that there is no way to predict what that happening will be. Reading, for Kleist, is performative, but what it is going to make happen cannot be known beforehand, either by the law of elective affinities or by the law of electrically charged bodies or by the law of intrinsic growth, though the temptation to try to make sense of what happens in reading by one of these aberrant metaphors is irresistible. To put this in the terms used by Paul de Man at the end of "Shelley Disfigured," the triumph of language, in every area of human life, is so complete that we must say that

> nothing, whether deed, word, thought, or text, ever happens in re-
> lation, positive or negative, to anything that precedes, follows, or
> exists elsewhere, but only as a random event whose power, like the
> power of death, is due to the randomness of its occurrence. It also
> warns us why and how these events then have to be reintegrated in a
> historical and aesthetic system of recuperation that repeats itself re-
> gardless of the exposure of its fallacy.[7]

I began by asking what is the role of theory in teaching. Kleist's brilliant exposure of the fallacious assumption that theory should precede and guide teaching argues for a shift in the focus of our reflections on what happens in the classroom. Teaching is practical, not theoretical. Its results cannot be controlled proleptically by theory. Insofar as theory is part of the clear-seeing, clear-thinking, and clear-naming that is essential in our modern technological and rational society, of which the university is a major institution, theory is unable to foresee or control the effects of reading. This is because teaching is never the occasion of the triumphant application of a rational theory about what will happen when such and such a text is taught in a certain way. Teaching is most comprehensively to be described as an event of reading. The effects of reading, in a given classroom and with a given teacher and given students dwelling at a certain moment in history within a certain specific institutional and social context, can never be known for certain beforehand. Reading is a speech act of a peculiar and definable kind, not an epistemological event to be defined as the passing on of a received and codified knowledge.

If Kleist is right, there should be a shift of attention from theory to reading. This would include the reading of theory and the theory of reading, but it would also mean a close pragmatic, empirical attention to what actually happens in reading. There is no reading that is not theoretical, but the actual act of reading is always to some degree the disconfirmation of theory. The interaction between theory and reading might be defined as a constant infinitesimal calculus in which reading informs and alters theory, along with the other vital and inaugural effects it has.

It will not do, however, to speak of this as an entirely cooperative interaction. Theory and reading, as I have said, remain not so much opposed as asymmetrical. The two are therefore incapable of entering into the kind of productive dialectical give and take suggested by my figure of the infinitesimal calculus. This is true as much of a theory of reading as positional and inaugural as it is of any other theory of reading. By the fact that it is a theory, such a theory is universal, totalizing. Any theory assimilates what is idiosyncratic in the individual act of reading into the general rational accounting for everything by the principle of reason that is presupposed by most literary study.

Reading itself has a double face. On the one side there is its positional uniqueness, its place as the introduction into the human world of the radically other. On the other side, by the fact that it is a reading, it is rational, iterable, capable of being institutionalized, written down as commentary or interpretation, printed in many copies, read by many people in many different circumstances. William Empson's *Seven Types of Ambiguity* is the record of an extraordinarily innovative series of acts of reading, as Empson came week by week to his tutor, I. A. Richards, to present the readings that were the basis of the book. *Seven Types of Ambiguity*, however, has now been assimilated into our culture. It forms part of the narrative of the historical development of modern literary criticism. The readings it records are repeatable, like the laboratory experiments that confirm or disconfirm a scientific theory. Empson's readings are performed again each time his book is read.

Let me return once more to Kleist's little text about the role of theory in teaching. He initially poses psychological and physical theoretical models for what happens in teaching, whereas, as his examples show in spite of themselves, teaching is a linguistic phenomenon not properly described in such terms. Kleist's main target, then, is the illicit use of models drawn from science as a description of what happens in teaching. The sequence of incompatible narrative models is not unlike the sequence in Kleist's "On the Puppet Theater" in that both sequences move toward a climactic story of reading and toward a radical conception of what happens in reading. "The Very Last Word in Modern Educational Theory" ends with an overt recognition that teaching is an act of reading in which language is performative. Teaching is performative not in the sense that a physical force makes something happen that can be calculated beforehand, but in the sense of a linguistic positing that is radically unpredictable in its effects. On the other hand, each act of reading will always be recuperated into some historical, causal, rational, dialectical, or theoretical scheme, according to preconceived assumptions, even if those assumptions involve a theory of reading as incalculably performative and originating, as an example of what Derrida calls "the invention of the other." Only for a brief moment, in a lightning flash, can there be a glimpse of what is originating about each act of reading, before some theory or other descends to put out the light. We must therefore return again and again to perform the act of reading itself, in order to try to catch that moment before it vanishes.

SHOULD I TEACH KLEIST? To whom or to what am I responsible when I ask this question or decide it in one way or the other? To my solitary conscience? To my students? To my institution? To the society my institution serves? To the text itself? With whom or with what is a contract to teach Kleist signed and ratified? At what point in my transactions with Kleist's writings can these questions be asked? Might it not be the case that I would need to have taught Kleist already before I can in any responsible way ask the question, "Should I teach Kleist?" This would mean that I would need already to have committed the error of teaching Kleist before I can have any chance of knowing it is a error.

But if the question can only be decided after the fact, something exceedingly strange will have happened to all the words in my initial question. The "should" will have meaning in relation to a field of responsibility that did not exist before the teaching took place, when it is already too late to act on a decision that I should *not* teach Kleist. The "I," moreover, will no longer be the name of the willing and knowing ego that surveys the field of possible actions and chooses rationally among them in terms of foreseen consequences. The "I," along with the necessity of taking responsibility for its actions, will also have come into existence only after the fact. "Teaching" will no longer be the passing on to students of a knowledge or even of a procedure of reading over which the teacher has mastery. It will be seen as a positing that cannot know what it is doing until that doing has been done. Even "Kleist" will no longer be the name of a body of texts whose meaning the teacher (or anyone else) can know in advance and have responsibility for passing on to others. "Kleist" will rather be the name of an unknown entity that can only be known, if at all, by means of a leap in the dark. The teacher (the future anterior "I") can only find out who or what Kleist is through the act of teaching him. Any teacher would like to avoid walking into the trap set up by these reversals of our ordinary ideas of pedagogical responsibility. This takes me back to my initial question. I would really like to know if I should teach Kleist. Or at least I would like to know why it is I cannot know—I would like to "comprehend the incomprehensibility" of the question, as Kant says we can do in the case of our inability to comprehend the unconditional necessity of the moral imperative.[8]

The choice of Kleist is of course not arbitrary. It is not only motivated, but overdetermined. Kleist's story "Der Findling" provides another splendid example of a variation on the Pygmalion story. I shall later attempt to read that story in the light of the question of whether I should teach Kleist. But all of Kleist's work—plays, stories, anecdotes, journalistic sketches—focuses in one way or another on the question of civil, moral, religious, and interpretative judgment and on the rendering of justice. This includes the obligation imposed on the reader of Kleist's works to render justice to those works. Kleist's work centers on the question of the law, in the broadest sense of that term: moral law, civil law, religious law, aesthetic law, the law of causality. One can be sure that any work by Kleist will be about the "should" and so implicitly raise questions about whether I should teach the work.

Kleist is supposed to have been disastrously "influenced" by his reading of Kant. Reading Kant brought on his so-called Kant crisis, about which he wrote in a letter of March 22, 1801, to his fiancée Wilhelmine von Zenge: "Mein einziges, mein höchstes Ziel ist gesunken, und ich habe nun keines mehr" (My one, my highest goal has sunk from sight, and I have no other; 634; 95). One might guess, remembering again what Kant says about comprehending incomprehensibility, that Kleist was forced by his reading of Kant to substitute for his previous highest goal of self-education (*Bil-*

dung in the specific sense of the collecting of eternal truths that can be carried into the higher realm of life after death[9]) the new goal of explaining in all he wrote why it is that these goals are gone. Or, rather, he was reduced to inventing and recording narratives that manifest the impossibility of knowing whether one has reached the truth in a given case and is therefore in a position to render true judgment. This would mean that Kleist's writings are narrative ex-empla of the *impossibility* of comprehending the incomprehensibility of our ethical situation. To put this in the terms of Kleist's example in the letter to Wilhelmine: The world appears green. This may be because we are wearing green glasses. But the world may really be green. There is no way to tell, since there is no way to take off the glasses. "We can never be certain that what we call Truth is really Truth, or whether it does not merely appear so to us. If the latter, then the Truth that we acquire here is *not* Truth after our death, and it is all a vain striving for a possession that may never follow us into the grave [und alles Bestreben, ein Eigentum sich zu erwerben, das uns auch in das Grab folgt, ist vergeblich]" (95; 634).

But was it just that reading Kant should have had such a negative effect on Kleist? Was Kleist a good reader of Kant? Is his Kant the same Kant I have elsewhere taken, more or less as everyone does, as the spokesman for belief in an unconditional moral law, and whom Derrida reads as having faith that philosophy can adjudicate the conflict of faculties in the university, adjudicate the question of who should teach what? This might be phrased as another form of my initial question: "Should Kleist have read Kant?"

Nietzsche, in a passage in "Schopenhauer as Educator," one of the "untimely meditations," does not exactly say that Kleist should not have read Kant, but he does say that a serious reading of Kant will always produce something like its effect on Kleist, namely a corrosive, destructive skepticism. Nietzsche says that Kant scholars would have to be revolutionized before the Kantian revolution can take place, and he sees this as unlikely, since most readers of Kant do not read him seriously.[10] I shall return later to the issue of what it might mean to think of an act of reading or teaching as revolutionizing either teacher or student. Now the question is the following: Is Nietzsche describing either Kant or Kleist correctly?

If so, it would appear that my questions are answered already. I ought to teach neither Kant nor Kleist if I can know for sure that the effect of doing this will be a gnawing and disintegrating relativism, an undermining despair of all truth. But I need to go with circumspection here, not take Nietzsche's word for it, and see for myself what happens when I read Kleist (or Kant, for that matter).

LET ME TURN, then, straight to Kleist's "On the Gradual Fabrication of Thoughts While Speaking." This is one of Kleist's many "kleine Schriften." It was written in 1805 or 1806 while he was living with his half-sister Ulrike in Königsberg. "Little" though it is, it is longer than many of Kleist's anecdotes, essays, and imaginary letters. Like others of Kleist's well-known short works, this essay is made up not of a single enigmatic story or situation but of a series of short narrative examples that are supposed to converge to prove a conceptual point, though they do not seem quite congruent with one another. Nor do they demonstrate with absolute clarity the point they are supposed to prove. They provide rather, as is the case with Kleist's writings generally, somewhat disturbing food for thought.

As in the case of all the little works by Kleist, it is difficult to be sure just how seriously to take this one or how to go about taking it seriously. The work is ironical through and through, which should not be taken to mean that it is not serious. To say that it is ironical, however, is not much help, beyond identifying one of the areas where the work of reading must take place. Ironical in what way exactly? Where is the irony to be located? In the conceptual formulation itself? In the incongruity between that and the narratives that are supposed to exemplify it? In the creation of the voice of an imaginary speaker who is by no means certainly to be taken as Kleist speaking straightforwardly in his own person? Or somewhere else, for example in some kind of discrepancy within language rather than in what language names?

But suppose the essay itself is to be taken as an example of the gradual fabrication of thoughts while speaking? What will happen then to the question of whether this is Kleist speaking straightforwardly as himself? Kleist's sister, or at any rate the speaker's sister, is mentioned in the first anecdotal example, and that matches the biographical facts. The essay, moreover, is dedicated to Kleist's close friend, Rühle von Lilienstern, and the first sentence addresses him directly as "mein lieber, sinnreicher Freund" (my dear and very clever friend; 391; 218). Perhaps the essay is not ironical at all, but absolutely straight. That question must, for the moment, remain open.

The focus of the essay seems to be somewhere in the region occupied by Paul Valéry's "Sur la méthode de Leonardo da Vinci" and Jacques Derrida's "Psyché: L'invention de l'autre." All three works, that is, concern themselves with the actual moment-to-moment activity of thinking, speaking, or writing, the question of how you get from here to there while doing these things. All three works define thinking, writing, and speaking as radically innovative or improvisatory, "inventive" in one of the senses of this word. For all three you do not know where you are going by thinking, writing, or speaking until you get there. For all three these activities are extrapolations reaching out into the void to create the goal they will attain rather than interpolations filling in the path between an origin and a predetermined goal. Nevertheless, by a strange kind of magic, it appears when you reach the goal that it has been there all along waiting to be discovered. Invention creates the field within which the thought already exists, waiting to be thought and expressed in language, just as the Declaration of Independence created the supposedly preexisting people who were the necessary justification for the declaration of independence.[11]

But I am most interested here in what Kleist's essay implies for the question of the responsibility of the teacher. This requires taking Kleist seriously and applying to the teaching situation what he says about the gradual fabrication of thoughts while speaking. I have spoken so far as if thinking, writing, and speaking were for Kleist parallel activities. In fact, his target is the presupposition that thought precedes and commands speaking. His strategy is to affirm a paradoxical reversal of the usual assumption about the line of cause and effect. We tend to assume that first we think and then we express those thoughts in spoken language. In another briefer essay, "Von der Überlegung: Eine Paradoxe" (On Thinking Things Over: A Paradox), Kleist argues that we should act first, as a wrestler does in a match, and think things over in retrospect. If this is a paradox, it is one relatively easy to accept as true. One remembers the story of the centipede who lost the ability to walk when he asked himself which foot to put forward first.

More difficult to accept is the argument that the same thing goes not for a physical activity like wrestling but for a mental activity like speaking. Speaking seems to presuppose *Überlegung* or thinking things over as the very condition of its existence. Surely no one would want to be taught by a teacher who did not know what she was going to say before she opened her mouth to speak. Nevertheless, Kleist argues that to say we think first and then speak is a false metalepsis, a reversal of the true order of cause and effect. As he says, paraphrasing the French aphorism and justifying my claim that Kleist's "little writings" are food for thought, if "l'appétit vient en mangeant," if appetite comes while we are eating, "l'idée vient en parlant," the idea comes while we are speaking (319; 218). Just how does this occur?

Kleist gives six examples, each a miniature narrative: an anecdote about the way he solves mathematical problems by talking them over with his sister, who knows nothing about mathematics; the story of how Molière composed plays by consulting his maidservant, who presumably knew nothing about composing plays;[12] the story of Mirabeau's defiance of the emissary from the king, in a speech that initiated the French revolution; a fable by La Fontaine, "Les animaux malades de la peste," in which the fox saves himself by an improvised speech; the counterexample of the shy person who suddenly bursts into unintelligible speech in a social gathering, just because he has thought over too carefully what he is going to say; and finally the pedagogical example of the oral examination in which students are asked to make up answers on the spot to questions like "What is the state? or What is property?" (222).

The astute reader will notice that those hypothetical examination questions are by no means random. They are not only fundamental questions in political science generally, for example in Rousseau (whose work Kleist much admired). They are also the questions raised by the examples in Kleist's essay. Mirabeau's speech initiating the French revolution, like all revolutionary moments, raises in an acute form the question, "What is the state?" And all the examples Kleist gives involve the question of property, of the proper, of propriety. Can a discovery or a speech act be said to belong to the person who makes it if it is performed by accident? Can a state be said to have been properly founded, and therefore be a proper guarantee of the ownership of property, if it comes into existence by accident? Does a knowledge properly belong to us as a possession (*Eigentum*) if the thought that expresses it is created by our unpremeditated speech rather than the other way around? "Denn nicht *wir* wissen," says Kleist, "es ist allererst ein gewisser *Zustand* unsrer, welcher weiss" (For it is not *we* who "know," it is rather a certain *condition,* in which we happen to be, that "knows"; 323; 222).

Though Kleist's last example of the oral examination might appear to be the one most relevant to my topic of the responsibility of the teacher, the role of speaker here is assigned to the student, not the teacher. But I claim that an understanding of what Kleist is saying here is best attained by taking all six of his examples as emblems of teaching. In all six examples there is a speaker and an audience of one or more. This might seem to correspond to the situation of the teacher face to face with her students and to argue that teaching is an intersubjective act or a dialogical one, in which the teacher is inspired by the presence of the students to eloquent insights she did not have before she started talking. This is so only in a paradoxical sense for Kleist. The listener, far from being the correspondent in a living dialogue, is what might be called the straight man or the dummy (in the sense of the dummy in bridge) who knows nothing and learns nothing. In fact his ignorance and neutrality are necessary to the function he performs.

There are present in each story Kleist tells not two elements but three: the reader, the dummy who facilitates that reading by an apparent neutrality, and some text to be read, taking *text* here in its broad sense of a set of signs urgently requiring interpretation, the mathematical problem to be solved in the first example, the germ story of the play to be written in the case of Molière's discussions with his maidservant, the political situation when the king has dissolved the estates in the case of Mirabeau, the speech of the lion and the fox's response in La Fontaine's fable, the preexisting thought in the example of the shy man who suddenly speaks in a social gathering, and the questions "What is the state?" and "What is property" in the case of the oral examination.

I have suggested that the readings in each of Kleist's examples are parallel to the spontaneous moves the wrestler makes to floor his opponent. They are performative acts in which words make something happen. I have said that these acts occur "by accident." "Accident" in fact is not quite the right word, since these acts are linguistic events that escape from the opposition between accident and necessity, just as they escape from the opposition between free and involuntary acts. It would be better to say that these are acts of random linguistic proposing that are governed not by thought or by will but, in a disquieting form of noncausal causality, by preexisting grammatical and syntactical forms. These forms are matrices that are meaningless in themselves, since they are no more than impersonal forms of linguistic articulation. The speaking "I" does not choose them. They choose me or choose the forms my speech must take, though they by no means determine the semantic meaning those forms turn out in retrospect to have. They are an indeterminate form of determination. A virtually limitless set of semantic meanings can be expressed in a given syntactical and grammatical shape. Nevertheless, the shape of language has the power to bring into existence expressions that are not only semantically meaningful but have a terrible power, when they are read in their turn, to bring something physically violent to pass in the real world, for example to "cause" the French revolution and the Terror, in the case of Mirabeau's speech, or to "cause" the monstrously unjust tearing to pieces of the innocent donkey, in the case of the fox's speech in La Fontaine. They cause it in the sense of appearing to justify it, but that is only through the reading of what in itself initially had no meaning.[13]

In each case the syntactical unit in question is the sentence, or what Kleist calls the "period" (219), that is, the minimal grammatical unit necessary to express a complete thought. In the case of Mirabeau's speech, the word "period" must be taken to refer to a longer rhetorical unit extending over several sentences, bound together by semantic repetition and by connectors like "but" or "and." In each case the speaker has no idea when he begins his period how he is going to end it: "Ich glaube, dass mancher grosse Redner, in dem Augenblick, da er den Mund aufmachte, noch nichte wusste, was er sagen würde. Aber die Überzeugung, dass er die ihm nötige Gedankenfülle schon aus den Umständen, und der daraus resultierenden Erregung seines Gemüts schöpfen würde, machte ihn dreist genug, den Anfang, auf gutes Glück hin, zu setzen" (I am convinced that many a great speaker, in that moment of opening his mouth to speak, has been unsure of what he was about to say. But trusting the circumstances to provide both the right line of ideas and the necessary mental stimulation, he is encouraged to risk a beginning; 320; 219).

The translation at the end here is a little loose, where it most needs to be strictly accurate. A more literal translation would say "makes him confident enough to set down (or posit: *setzen*) the beginning, trusting to good luck." Another related word, "Fortsetzung," drawn from a large number of German compounds ("durchsetzen," sift, accomplish, "entsetzen," relieve, dismiss, "versetzen," transfer, remove, "übersetzen," transport, translate), appears in a parenthetical sentence at the end of the essay: "(Die Fortsetzung folgt)" (The continuation follows, or, colloquially, To be continued). This is omitted altogether in the English translation. Presumably the translator thought that, since Kleist's essay was not in fact followed by anything, the parenthetical promise could be omitted. But the unfulfilled promise is an important part of the text, since the issue it raises is the question of what sequel, *Fortsetzung*, there can be after an inaugurating positing, *Setzung*, that is random and arbitrary, cut off from both before and after. What continuation can follow such a beginning?

After the initial positing of a syntactically incomplete fragment, says Kleist, without any idea in the speaker's mind of where the sentence is going to end, the thought is gradually "fabricated." It is fabricated not so much by the situation or by the speaker's feelings, as Kleist's formulations here and there somewhat reassuringly encourage the reader to believe, but by his need to complete the grammar and syntax of the sentence he has blindly begun, as the examples actually demonstrate.

In the case of finding the solution to an algebraic problem by talking it out to his sister, who does not know what he is talking about, Kleist describes how he invents in the midst of speaking ways to postpone the completion of the sentence until the insight comes that allows him to finish the sentence and solve the problem at the same time: "die Erkenntnis, zu meinem Erstaunen, mit der

Periode fertig ist" (my full thought, to my astonishment, is completed with the period). If he finishes the sentence too soon, the solution will be lost, since it is the sentence structure that is gradually fabricating his thoughts while he is speaking: "Ich mische unartikulierte Töne ein, ziehe die Verbindungswörter in die Länge, gebrauche auch wohl eine Apposition, wo sie nicht nötig wäre, und bediene mich anderer, die Rede ausdehnender, Kunstgriffe, zur Fabrikation meiner Idee auf der Werkstätte der Vernunft, die gehörige Zeit zu gewinnen" (I mumble inarticulately, drawl out my conjunctions, use unnecessary appositions, and avail myself of all other dilatory tricks to gain the time required for fabricating my idea in the workshop of Reason; 320; 218–219). This sentence, especially in the original German, is an example of what it names, especially the last clauses, where an adjective hangs in the air, separated from its noun by an interpolated clause ("anderer, die Rede ausdehnender, Kunstgriffe"), and, as is of course possible in German, the final verb is postponed through a series of suspensive clauses: "zur Fabrikation meiner Idee auf der Werkstätte der Vernunft, die gehörige Zeit zu gewinnen." From a semantic point of view, on the other hand, the final image of the fabrication of ideas in the workshop of Reason both suggests a reasonable activity of the deliberating mind and, at the same time, implies a mechanical fabrication taking place of its own accord and in its own good time, outside the realm of the speaker's conscious control, if he just draws out his sentence long enough to let the fabrication take place.

In the case of Mirabeau's speech before the emissary from the king, Kleist emphasizes the comic uncertainty of Mirabeau, who has no idea when he begins that his speech will end by creating the new French nation and a new parliamentary assembly to represent them. The new state, with its citizens and their representatives, its laws and privileges, did not exist at the beginning of the speech. By the end of the speech it does exist, or at any rate it is spoken of as if it had existed before Mirabeau began speaking. It has been brought into existence neither by Mirabeau's deliberate forethought nor by his conscious intention, but by the arbitrary positing power of his need to complete the grammatical and rhetorical patterns he initiated out of the obligation to say *something* in re-

sponse to the king's master of ceremonies. Here is Kleist's dramatization of the way Mirabeau made up his answer on the spot:

> "Yes," answered Mirabeau, "we have heard the King's command
> . . ." I am certain that he made this affable start [diesem humanen
> Anfang] without the faintest prescience of the bayonet thrust with
> which he was to conclude.
> "Yes, Monsieur," he repeats, "we have heard it . . ." Clearly he
> still has no idea of what he is about.
> "But by what right," he continues, whereupon a fresh source of
> stupendous ideas opens up to him [geht ihm ein Quell ungeheurer
> Vorstellungen auf], "do you proclaim commands to us? We are the
> representatives of the Nation!" This is exactly what he needs, and
> leaping to the pinnacle of audacity, he cries, "The Nation *issues* com-
> mands. It does not *receive* them. And to make myself absolutely
> clear to you"—only now does he hit on the words that express the
> total opposition for which his soul stands armed—"you may tell
> your king that we will not leave our places except at the point of the
> bayonet." (320–321; 219)

The example from La Fontaine is a brilliant comic analogue to
Mirabeau's speech. Kleist subjects the fox's speech to the same
kind of analysis he uses for Mirabeau's. The fox also has no idea
what he is going to say when he starts talking. He knows only that
he must flatter the lion, who has admitted to killing a sheep or two,
under the pressures of hunger, a sheepdog also, and perhaps even
the shepherd. But the fox must at the same time persuade his auditors that he is no worse than the lion and that neither he nor the
lion is the one who ought to be sacrificed:

> "Sire," says the Fox, who must deflect the fury from himself, "you
> are too generous. Your noble zeal carries you away. Of what impor-
> tance is the slaughter of a sheep? Or a dog, that most undignified of
> brutes? And "quant au berger," he continues, coming to the crux,
> "on peut dire . . ."—albeit he knows not what—"qu'il méritoit
> tout mal . . ."—a lucky stroke, but now he is momentarily per-
> plexed—" . . . étant . . . "—a bad phrase, but a time-winning
> one—" . . . de ces gens-là . . ."—and now he at last finds the
> thought which plucks him from his quandary—"qui sur les ani-
> maux se font un chimèrique empire." [14]
> And then he proves how it is the donkey, that bloodthirsty one
> (ravager of herbs and grasses), who most deserves to die, where-
> upon the others fall on him and tear him to pieces. (322; 220–221)

All six of Kleist's stories are versions of the same paradigm. In each, a complex speech act involving several distinct stages occurs. Each, as I have said, is a reading. The reader is in a shrewd situation made up of an array of signs demanding speech or from which he can extricate himself only through speech. In Mirabeau's case what is "read" is, according to Kleist, not just the speech of the king's emissary demanding that the estates disband, but those minimal signs of condescension and disdain that show him what social situation will be perpetuated if he does not say something in defiance: "Perhaps, after all, it was only the twitch of an upper lip [das Zucken einer Oberlippe], or the ambiguous fingering of a wrist frill [ein zweideutiges Spiel an der Manschette], that precipitated the overthrow of the old order in France" (321; 220).

Kleist is famous for the violence and lightning-like rapidity with which decisive actions occur in his stories. The violence here is not of action but of speech, or rather of the speech act, the speech that acts. Mirabeau's speech is spoken of as a "thunderbolt" and a "bayonet thrust." The speech is, however, the thunderbolt and the bayonet thrust of an arbitrary act of power performed by a piece of language that comes out of nowhere to fulfill the need to put words in the blank places in a syntactical pattern.

The instantaneous suddenness of this speech act, the impossibility of reducing its occurrence to the polarities of chance and necessity, means that it occurs outside time or cannot properly be reassimilated into a temporal sequence. It cannot reasonably be made part of the line of a historical narrative extending before and after.

Nevertheless, if the performative speech act is outside the temporality of retrospectively constructed historical time, at the same time it has a temporality of its own. Within the suspended and extended moment of the gradual fabrication of thoughts while speaking, a specifically linguistic time is generated. This temporality reaches out toward a not yet foreseen future to come back to the beginning in the moment of a triumphant completion of the thought. The period takes time to complete. During that time the forward march of historical or narrative time is suspended. Only when the "period" is finished, only when the string of words generated by the gradual fabrication of thoughts has come to an end and makes sense, can it be turned back on retrospectively. Only then has the thought been expressed in a code that allows it to be repeated, iterated, say by being printed, therefore capable of entering history again each time it is read. In this turning back the sentence is "read" for its referential or performative import, and then acted on in one way or another. Or, rather, the reading itself is an act, not so much a speech act as a reading act. This reading act constitutes the reassimilation of the linguistically codified thought into historical and narrative time. An example is the moment when Mirabeau, after his speech of defiance is over and the emissary has gone, proposes "that they constitute themselves the National Assembly and declare themselves inviolable in that capacity" (220).

The word "period" names not only the sentence or other syntactically complete unit of words. It also names a space of time, as when we speak of the Romantic period. "Period" is also the name of the mark of punctuation that signals the end of a sentence (the period marks the end of a period). But the linguistic temporality generated by the period during which thoughts are gradually fabricated while speaking is not simply the free and unpredictable completion by the speaker of a grammatical pattern initiated at random, out of the desperate need to say *something*. Nor would it be correct to say that the pattern, once initiated, dictates or determines the thought. A given grammatical pattern is not only capable of being filled in by a virtually limitless number of different semantic expressions. It is also at every turn capable of being given a new turn, or added to even when it appears to be finished, for example by the introduction of a subordinate clause, prepositional phrase, or parenthetical expression, or through the indefinite extension that the insertion of a conjunction, "but," "and," "or," will allow. Through the adroit manipulation of connectives or modifiers, the syntactical unit can be kept open for as long as it takes to complete the thought. In fact it could hypothetically be kept open forever.

Moreover, the gradual process of linguistic fabrication is, while it is going on, in the examples Kleist gives, rhythmically punctuated by "attempts" or "tests" (*Versuchen*) coming from the outside, to appropriate Kleist's word as a name for these interventions. The interventions come from that apparently neutral dummy. The dummy thereby plays an essential role in the gradual fabrication of thoughts while speaking, though it is by no means the dialogical function of actually contributing to the content of the thought. Rhythm, punctuation or articulation, threat of interruption: these are the three aspects of the interventions from without, interventions from the other. These, along with the linguistic verve of the speaker, cooperate or interfere with one another to generate the temporality of the impositional speech act.

Let me try to explain these aspects, as they are exemplified in two of Kleist's examples, the way he solves mathematical problems and Mirabeau's speech. In the first situation, says Kleist, "Nothing on such occasions can have a more salutary effect than a casual gesture from my sister as if to interrupt, for my intellect, already sorely exercised, becomes all the more agitated at this external threat to tear it away from the speech which is guiding it [durch diesen Versuch von aussen, ihm die Rede, in deren Besitz es sich befindet, zu entreissen], and like a great general when circumstances marshal against him, I am suddenly a degree more capable of my objective" (320; 219). In the other case, I take it that when Kleist says, "Perhaps, after all, it was only the twitch of an upper lip, or the ambiguous fingering of a wrist frill, that precipitated the overthrow of the old order in France" (220), he means to describe reactions by the king's emissary that occur during the course of Mirabeau's speech. These are threats to him and to the completion of his thought while he is in the act of speaking.

The threat of interruption is double. On the one hand there is the danger that the period will be broken off before it is complete. This would lead to the permanent loss of the thought whose completion depends on the continued élan of the speaker. On the other hand the danger is that the interruption will lead to the premature completion of the sentence, cutting off the thought whose unformulated contours would now exceed the bounds of the completed period. In that way too the thought would be lost.

Nevertheless, these threats of interruption play a fundamental role in the fabrication of the thought. A series of syllables without rhythmical emphasis and without the articulations signaled in written language by spaces and by marks of punctuation—dashes, commas, colons, semicolons, underlinings, capitalizations, quotation marks, the period at the end—is meaningless. A series of words in a foreign language pronounced with approximate correctness but with the wrong rhythmical emphasis often conveys nothing at all when addressed to a native speaker of that language. Moreover, alteration of the punctuation of a sentence, alteration of the signals that indicate the proper rhythmical cadence of the sentence, can change the meaning drastically. One example: "It's about time they turned their attention to history, politics, ethics." "It's about *time*—they turned their attention to history, politics, ethics."[15] The two sentences are opposite in meaning. One says it is timely and good to attend to politics; the other says it is an error, an inattention.

The rhythmical emphases of an oral sentence, like the marks of punctuation in a piece of written language, are without semantic meaning in themselves. A dash is without referential significance. You do not enunciate it when you read the sentence aloud. The rhythm of a spoken sentence does not alter the semantic content of the words taken separately. Such elements indicate joints, hinges, articulations, spaces, or pauses, the nonsignifying and nonphenomenal syntactical aspects of language without which language could not make sense. As is indicated by Kleist's mimings of the gradual process whereby Mirabeau's speech and the fox's speech are completed, the attempts at interruption from without play the paradoxical role of providing the rhythmical pauses, emphases, and articulations that mean nothing in themselves but are nevertheless necessary to the fabrication of the thought. The paradox lies in the fact that the threats of interruption, like marks of punctuation, at once have nothing to do with signification and have everything to do with it.

Yet it will not do to assert that these threats of interruption are entirely positive in their effect. If they articulate, they also disarticulate. If they give the sequence of words the cadence necessary to meaning, at the same time they are antirhythmical caesuras, breaks, or suspensions. These disarticulations are the traces within the linguistically generated thought, when it is complete, of the contingencies and discontinuities that are hidden and forgotten when the achieved "period" is turned back on retrospectively, given a logical meaning, and assimilated into one or another historical narrative.

The completed period is a strange kind of anacoluthon. It is strange because it does not include changes in person, number, or tense that make the sentence grammatically inconsistent, a "failure in following," as the word "anacoluthon" etymologically means. At the same time, however, the period contains all along its trajectory moments when its forward movement was interrupted and then started again, taking perhaps an entirely unforeseen direction in constative meaning and in performative force. The period appears perfectly grammatical, but it is an encrypted anacoluthon. It has barely discernible fissures where the contingencies of its original process of formation may be discerned by a sharp-eyed observer.

Kleist's essay is about time. It is also about history, politics, ethics. If Mirabeau's speech, or the fox's, is taken as an allegory of the act of reading or teaching, the escape of impositional speech acts from historical or temporal sequence would mean that reading or teaching is made up of a series of creative moments, little black holes in the midst of the temporal flow. But unlike black holes, which are said to absorb everything around them into themselves, these moments have efficacy to make other things happen in their turn. How does something escape from these black holes?

It happens through the retrospective reading of the completed sentence or period. Once the speech has been made, it can be turned back on and be seen to make semantic sense, to have referential validity as a reading of the signs making up the situation. As such, the speech now enters political or historical time. It was abstracted from time during the moments it was being made, since it had not yet been recuperated through any technique of historicization. Now, after the fact, it becomes possible to make the speech an element in a narrative, though this occurs only through forgetting, ignoring, or erasing the traces still remaining within it of the absurd contingencies that generated it. Nevertheless, the narrative achieved by this act of forgetful reading may illustrate a larger conceptual hypothesis. Examples of this would include Kleist's retelling of the Mirabeau story as one of a series of anecdotes intended to persuade the reader of the truth of his hypothesis about the gradual fabrication of thoughts while speaking. It would also include my retelling of the story here.

Each such speech, moreover, once it is retrospectively read, contains directions for political or institutional action. Once the speech is made, the one who has made it has to take responsibility for it. This means taking responsibility for the political or institutional changes the reading of it implies, as well as for the "I" who is created by the speech. The Mirabeau who counts as an actor on the stage of world history came into existence as he made his speech. It was one of the unforeseen concomitants of his speech act. But the same thing is true for the speakers in Kleist's other examples. In each case the newborn "I" must now take responsibility for what he has done. This obligation is as much incurred in an act of teaching as in an act of political insubordination such as Mirabeau's thunderbolt. This, I take it, is what Derrida is saying in the passage already quoted from "Mochlos, or the Conflict of Faculties." Kleist's "On the Gradual Fabrication" asserts that reading or teaching takes place by the sort of fundamentally improvisatory response to a text that can find its appropriate allegory in Mirabeau's speech or the fox's. The teacher's response is both determined and not determined by the possibilities of meaning in the text. Or it is neither determined nor not determined but, as "Mochlos" says, constructs in its turn one or more models of community. This happens, however, only when it is read, after the fact of its original lightning-like or random imposition when it was written. The reading is another such impositional act. The reader is never passively subservient to the injunction "Read me, and then institutionalize the results of your reading!" A reading enjoins certain political or institutional changes, for which the reader must take responsibility.

When Mirabeau begins his speech, there is no French nation and the estates are not its representatives. The nation, its representatives, its rights and duties, especially the right to issue commands rather than receive them—all come into existence in the course of the speech. The cogency and power of Mirabeau's speech rests on the referential force of the terms he uses, on his ability to speak in the name of the French nation and as one of its legal representatives. But this is absurd. A piece of language cannot logically be both performative and constative at the same time, both create the entities to which it refers and at the same time refer to them as preexisting entities on the basis of which it makes sense. Mirabeau's speech in itself is a series of nonreferential words, "Nation," "representatives," "*issues* commands," "your King" (as opposed to "our king"), and so on, put in the places where the grammar requires something if Mirabeau is to complete the period he so affably begins. Its grammar and diction are "correct," that is, examples of possible sentences in the French language. Since it makes retrospective sense, Mirabeau's speech can enter history by creating the entities it names. It enters history as, to use Derrida's word, the proposal of a "contract" that demands an elaborate political and social institutionalization.

But this institutionalization can take place only through forgetting that the speech itself was the random imposition of a set of words that had no referential sense when they were uttered. This forgetting is an act of violence as great as the first. In Kleist's retelling of the story of Mirabeau's speech, the forgetting occurs after the departure of the king's emissary, when Mirabeau cools down, ceases to act as a lightning bolt of linguistic imposition, and reenters, as suddenly as he had left it, the realm of rational calculation and the taking of responsibility for the meaning of what he has said. "We read," writes Kleist in a passage I have already quoted in part, "that Mirabeau stood up as soon as the Master of Ceremonies had gone, and proposed that they constitute themselves the National Assembly and declare themselves inviolable [unverletzlich] in that capacity. For having in the manner of a Kleistian Bottle discharged himself, he had once again become neutral, and suddenly abandoning his defiant attitude began to consider the continuing danger from the Royal Tribunal and the necessity for extreme caution" (E 220).[16] Mirabeau, in short, instantly forgets the absurdity of the speech he has made. He and his colleagues proceed in a rational way to implement the presuppositions of the speech in all the ways that create the new French regime, with its system of law, its constitution, its power to coin and print money, to raise armies, to execute criminals and enemies, and all the rest of the powers and duties of a sovereign state.

That this institutionalization, the ratification of the terms of the proposed contract implicit in a reading of what Mirabeau has said, is used to justify acts of extreme physical violence, the Terror, just as the fox's speech leads to the (justified) tearing to pieces of the bloodthirsty donkey, ravager of herbs and grasses, is not at all reassuring. This is especially true if we take these anecdotes as allegorical representations of what is likely to be involved in that "new contract with the institution, between the institution and the dominant forces of society," that "Mochlos" says is involved in something so apparently innocuous as the reading of a sentence in a given text in a seminar.

It is possible now to make a generalized description of what Kleist's essay implies for the responsibilities of the teacher. Teaching, like analogous speech acts that include declarations of independence, is an element in a series of acts of violence, each one the forgetting or erasure of the one before. These acts enter the materiality of history. Moreover, they must be carefully distinguished from one another. The text read by the teacher was itself originally an act of violent linguistic imposition, a case of the fabrication of thoughts while speaking or writing. This must be forgotten by the teacher, who reads the text as a discourse of achieved semantic and referential meaning. She also reads it as enjoining the reader or teacher to institutionalize the study of that text in a certain way. But the teacher's reading is a second act of linguistic impositional violence. Her own discourse, again after the fact and retrospectively, takes on rational meaning and enters history as enjoining or mandating in its turn a new contract with the institution and with society. All teaching is political, not just in the tame sense that it has political implications or expresses political opinions directly or indirectly, but in the more radical and disquieting sense that it has political power. The teacher, in short, must take responsibility for what she has said, even though what she has said was said blindly and only takes on meaning and the power to imply a new institutional organization, a new society, through the forgetting of this fact, in the way Kleist describes. The ratification of this new contract and the practical carrying out of its terms, finally, involves a third act of violence—the social violence of one sort or another that will be entailed in carrying out the conditions of the new contract, for example, changes in curricula, in departmental structures, or in the legitimizing of canons, with their various social consequences.

I return finally to my initial question, "Should I teach Kleist?"

The answer is that, if Kleist is right, I cannot *not* teach Kleist. It's about time we should teach Kleist. It's about time—we should teach Kleist. Whatever I teach I shall be caught up in the process Kleist describes and shall be reenacting or repeating a new version of the process (in both senses) that Kleist calls the gradual fabrication of thoughts while speaking.

How can a reader do justice to Kleist's "Der Findling" (The Foundling)? How can we read it justly or just read it? There is no doubt that the acts of reading and of rendering justice, doing it right in two ways, are vigorously thematized in "Der Findling," as in Kleist's other stories. What the reader is in the act of doing is also being done by the characters in the story. If, but only if, the reader can read justly what Kleist is saying about reading and doing justice, he or she can justifiably transfer the results of that reading as a judgment on the activity at that moment being performed.

Though Kleist's essays do contain some essential narrative elements, those texts make a more or less straightforward conceptual or theoretical argument. "Der Findling," on the other hand, is pretty much pure narrative, with little conceptual explanation of the story. Kleist's stories are famous for the laconic reserve with which violent and strange events are narrated. This style has been compared to a bureaucratic report, to chronicle history, or (by Friedrich Gundolf) to "legal and official German of the Baroque period following the Reformation."[17] It seems as if just reading would be helped by an accurate placing of the style. However that may be, "theory" in the sense of abstract presuppositions will not help much in reading such a story. This is true even of Kleist's own theories developed elsewhere, though puzzled readers will seek all the help they can get. In the end I just have to read the story for myself and try to pass judgment on what happens when I do that. The judgment will be, as I have been arguing, a doing that will do other things in its turn, in the real historical and material world "outside the story."

"Der Findling" is a good example of the famous lightning-like violence with which things occur in Kleist's stories. There are no less than seven deaths in the story, including all the principal characters. Most of these deaths occur, and all are reported, with brutal abruptness, as are other events in the story: "his son, the eleven-year-old Paolo, catching the infection from Nicolo, died within three days" (232); "[Colino] clasped her hand affectionately one last time and died" (235); "as if struck by an invisible lightning bolt at the sight of him, [Elvira] fell headlong from the stool to the inlaid floor" (236); "Nicolo's wife, Constanza, was brought to bed with child and died, together with the infant she had borne" (237); "Nicolo stood up thunderstruck" (245); "before he was able to utter a word, he collapsed unconscious on the bed" (245); "Just the day before, Piachi had buried the unfortunate Elvira, who had died from the effects of a high fever brought on by the episode" (246); "with the strength that rage lent him, [Piachi] threw Nicolo . . . to the floor and dashed his brains out against the wall" (246); "unaccompanied by any priest, [Piachi] was hanged, very quietly, in the Piazza del Populo" (247).

In spite of the fact that, as one early journal review said of "Die Marquise von O . . . ," "even to summarize the plot is to ostracize oneself from polite society" (20), the almost irresistible response to reading one of Kleist's stories seems to be to summarize the plot. The preface by Thomas Mann and the introduction by the translator of the English version, Martin Greenberg, mostly do just that. It seems as if the meaning of each story must lie in the sequence of events, or as if the chief effect of Kleist's stories is a strong compulsion to repeat that sequence once more, passing the story on to others: "You won't believe this, but just let me tell you what happens in Kleist's 'Der Findling.'" All of Kleist's stories are what he called one of his short works: "Unwahrscheinliche Wahrhaftigkeiten" (Improbable Veracities). The reader goes over and over the events trying to figure out how things could have happened this way.

The double bind of this situation is vigorously expressed by Sosia in Kleist's play after Molière, *Amphitryon*. Sosia is speaking of his encounter with a double of himself. It is another example of those plausible mistaken identities that punctuate Kleist's work:

Ins Tollhaus weis ich den, der sagen kann,
Dass er von dieser Sache was begreift.
Es ist gehauen nicht und nicht gestochen,
Ein Vorfall, koboldartig, wie ein Märchen,
Und dennoch *ist* es, wie das Sonnenlicht. (1.268)

I'd send off to the madhouse any man
Who claims to understand a bit of this.
There simply is no rhyme or reason to it,
It's wizardry, as in a fairy tale,
And yet it's there, like sunlight, all the same.[18]

Everything, we all tend to assume, has its reason, its cause. Therefore it can be ultimately understood by the reason. If not, the universality of the principle of reason is put in doubt. On the other hand, whoever claims to understand such an unreasonable sequence of events is mad. Only the unreasonable can understand and explain the genuinely unreasonable. Still it *is:* "Und dennoch *ist* es." It is there in the sunlight for anyone to see. Or rather it is *like* sunshine, the irresistible force of light that brings things out of obscurity. With Kleist's stories, either to explain or not to explain is madness. Either way you have had it, as far as keeping sane goes. Readers of Kleist seek a reasonable explanation in order to keep their reason.

What principles of explanation does the text of "Der Findling" (as opposed to the plot as summarizable in other words) propose for events so apparently unreasonable? Can the reader find in the words Kleist wrote any laws, rational or irrational, that may govern these violent events? One explanation with textual support would be to say that the events come about through a hideous series of accidents, things possible but unlikely. The story would thereby go against one of Aristotle's basic laws of good plot construction: that it should consist of the probable. As Kleist's strange stories accumulate in our minds, we come to have a horrible suspicion that they may be exemplary, that it may be normal for things in the real world to happen as a series of "improbable veracities." And when we come to think about it, *Oedipus the King* is not so likely either. The unlawful law of human life may be that things happen by sheer unreasonable accidents that have disastrous effects in the social world.

"It so happen[s]" (231) that the pestilence has broken out in Ragusa when Piachi just happens to have taken his son by an earlier marriage, Paolo, along with him on a business trip there, and it just happens that Paolo catches the fever and dies, while Nicolo, the foundling, source of the infection, recovers and Piachi does not catch it. It just happens that Colino is "struck on the head by a falling stone" (235) when he is rushing into the burning house to save the young Elvira. Nicolo has "chosen quite by chance" (236) to wear the costume of a Genoese knight, so that his similarity to the dead Colino strikes Elvira like a lightning bolt when she happens to see him. It just happens that Nicolo not only looks like Colino but has a name that is an anagrammatic rearrangement of the little ivory letters lying on the table that spell "Colino." It just happens that Colino is the nickname for Nicolo. It just happens that Piachi comes back home unexpectedly as Nicolo is about to commit his sexual assault on Elvira, his foster mother. Everything in the story happens by absurd happenstance, when "es fügte sich" (as luck would have it; 208; 240). In the incongruence between human desires and intentions, on the one hand, and on the other a physical world in which things happen as they happen, the reader finds the reason of this unreason.

An explanation of this sort is incomplete. Not only do other contradictory factors enter in, but such a mode of explanation still leaves the mind and its spontaneous commitment to the principle of reason dissatisfied. Such an explanation identifies not so much the reason of the story's unreason as one source of its unreason, the unreason of its unreason.

Now and then the narrator, for all his laconic restraint, proposes another explanation, a theological one. It is extremely difficult to know whether these details are ironic or not, that is, whether they are the ironic miming of the clichés about "Providence" and "God's will" that everyone in a nominally Christian culture is likely to repeat without thinking. Kleist's relation to religious belief was extremely complex and ambiguous. He was fascinated by the question of how God's justice might manifest itself in this world. This is fundamental, for example, in "Michael Kohlhaas" and in "Der Zweikampf" (The Duel), pointedly so in "Der Griffel Gottes" (God's Stylus).[19]

In any case, elements leading to a theological reading are present in the text of "Der Findling." The reader searching the words to find some explanation for what happens is likely to notice them. Then a decision must be made about how seriously to take them, or about how to take them seriously, how to read them rightly. When Piachi asks whether he may take Nicolo, the foundling, along home with him, as replacement for the real son who has died from the pestilence caught from Nicolo, he is told that Nicolo is "Gottes Sohn . . . und niemand ihn vermissen würde" (a son of God whom nobody would miss"; (200; 233). Nicolo has no ascertainable earthly parents. He is more directly related to God than those with earthly parents are, and therefore more Christlike. Nevertheless, like Heathcliff in *Wuthering Heights,* he enters abruptly into Piachi's family to disrupt it fatally, as indeed Christ did in enjoining us to leave father and mother to follow him.[20]

There are other theological clues. Later in the story, in the flashback account of the adolescent trauma that has darkened Elvira's life, the narrator says that Colino dies "durch eine unbegreifliche Schickung des Himmels" (by an unfathomable decree of heaven; 203; 235). Later still, Piachi's return to catch Nicolo in his perfidious assault on Elvira's virtue is said to be caused not by luck or by chance, but by "die Nemesis, die dem Frevel auf dem Fuss folgt" (the Nemesis that treads hard on the heels of a wicked deed"; 213; 245). This Nemesis has "decreed" the return of Piachi. Here a Greek explanation mingles incongruously with the Christian one. In the last episode of the story Piachi is condemned by the Papal States for his murder of Nicolo and ultimately hanged by the pope's own orders, even though he has refused the absolution that by papal law must precede execution. About this episode there will be more to say, but it is another moment in the story that raises the question of God's intervention in the human world.

The theological explanation directly contradicts the explanation by sheer physical chance or happenstance. Two incompatible responses to the need for a rational or causal explanation exist in the story, but explanation by two incompatible causes is irrational. What the reader wants is something single and reasonable. Driven by this need, we are forced to discount these textual details, to go behind them to seek in the behavior of the characters as accounted for in the text some deeper principle of explanation.

ONE BASIC, even instinctive, principle of reading narratives is the assumption that what recurs must be important. Two procedures of interpreting the world and then acting on that interpretation (fatally, it always seems) govern the behavior of the characters in

"Der Findling." What is most unsettling about our witnessing of the horrible results of interpreting and acting in these ways is that they so obviously duplicate similar acts of interpretation by the narrator and by the reader that are necessary either to tell the story or to make sense of reading it. One is a process of substitution in which similarities are misread as identities. The other is the projection of a causal sequence on what may be only a random series. Both of these errors are not so much phenomenal as linguistic. Let me show how these two ways of reading determine what happens in "Der Findling," though "determine" is not quite the right word for a cause that always works in unpredictable and devious ways. These ways are turned or tropological, like Mirabeau's speech that "caused" the French revolution.

The story opens with the episode in which Piachi adopts Nicolo as a replacement for Paolo: "Piachi swung the boy up into the carriage in one motion and took him along to Rome in his son's place . . . In Rome, Piachi introduced the boy to Elvira, his virtuous young wife, and gave her a short recital of what had taken place; although she could not keep from bursting into tears at the thought of Paolo, her little stepson, whom she had dearly loved, she nevertheless embraced Nicolo, as stiff and strange as he stood before her, showed him to the bed in which Paolo used to sleep, and made him a gift of all the dead boy's clothes" (233). Just as in *Wuthering Heights* Heathcliff's usurping power is indicated by the fact that he is given the name of a brother of Cathy's who died in infancy, so Nicolo substitutes for Paolo by the replacement of the first syllable of Paolo's name, "Nic" for "Pa." Neither Piachi nor Elvira (nor the narrator) is shown to be aware of this ominous fact, nor even shown to be aware of how strange it is that they so quickly and spontaneously take this stranger as a substitute for the dead son.

As a foundling, a son of God whom nobody would miss, Nicolo has no legitimate family place. This means that, like a linguistic shifter or like a wild card in a game, he can be placed in a wide variety of domestic or linguistic places. He is, so to speak, a "placeholder." But this also means that Nicolo never really has the identity that goes with any place in which he is put, any more than a wild card can be limited to the one role it temporarily plays. He subverts and distorts that role. He can, moreover, shift at any moment to another place within the family structure, as he does when he tries to assault Elvira, aspiring to the place of the father. Nicolo eventually appropriates Piachi's possessions. Piachi makes the disastrous mistake of adopting him as a legal replacement for the dead son and signs over to him all his property. Nicolo brings devastation into Piachi's household, ultimately causing the death of all, including himself. It is a devastation brought about by the taking of a similarity for an identity or by the attempt to make a similarity into a virtual identity, to put one male child into the place of another with a somewhat similar name.

Of the "Findling," the child without identifiable parents who is "found" and so appears to be free to be given a new social and family identity without risk, it can be said, reversing the old rhyme: "Losers keepers; finders weepers." Piachi loses everything by finding Nicolo and then by taking him as a substitute for Paolo. He would have been far luckier to have lost him after the first encounter. But the first event, the accidental finding, becomes a decisive cause in the social world only when it is read in a certain way by Piachi and Elvira. It is the reading, not the finding, that does the damage.

The same thing can be said of other decisive elements in the story. Though Elvira has married Piachi and is a dutiful and virtuous wife, her real love remains fixed on the dead Colino, the heroic Genoese knight who was mortally injured in the act of saving her life. Or, rather, her real love has been transferred to the substitute for the dead Colino, the life-sized portrait of him she keeps hidden in a niche in her bedroom behind a red silk curtain and before which she kneels, "in an attitude of ecstasy," "whisper[ing] lovingly the word: 'Colino'" (239). Elvira suffers from that form of compulsive and spontaneous prosopopoeia that takes the form of the ghostly return of the dead as a result of incomplete or unsuccessful mourning. Colino may reappear at any time. Indeed he remains above ground in the form of his portrait, a factitious substitute.

This substitutive fixation on the portrait prepares for the episode in which Elvira is struck unconscious, as if by a lightning bolt, when she sees Nicolo dressed in the costume of a Genoese knight, "die er zufällig gewählt hatte" (which he had chosen quite by chance; (204; 236). Later the perfidious Nicolo dresses again in the costume, puts himself before a black backcloth in place of the portrait, and steps out from it when she opens the red curtain. He deliberately plans to take wicked advantage of Elvira's mistaking of the one man for the other because they happen to look alike. Like Piachi, Elvira has made the disastrous error of reading an accidental similarity as an identity. Whatever the chance happenings, all would have been well if she had not done that. Her misreading leads ultimately to her death, however innocent and loving, however virtuous, she is.

The errors in reading by Piachi and Elvira are repeated in a different way by Nicolo. When he sees the violent effect his appearance as a Genoese knight has on Elvira and when he notices, "zufällig, in der Tat, selbst" (quite by accident) that the ivory letters spelling his name can be rearranged anagrammatically to spell "Colino" and that Elvira blushes and weeps at glimpsing this name, he makes the fatal mistake of assuming that it is really he whom Elvira loves (210–211; 242–243). It is of course not he but the dead Colino, or rather Colino's memory as preserved in the portrait, for whom her love is reserved: "Nicolo, who had watched all this out of the corner of his eye, now felt no doubt at all that it was his own name which lay hidden for her under the transposed letters, and his mad hopes reached the peak of confidence when she stood up, put her work down, and vanished into her bedroom" (243). If Elvira has twice taken a simulacrum for the original, first the portrait and then Nicolo in place of the portrait, Nicolo, who is the second simulacrum, reads himself by mistake as the original.

The episode of the accidental game of anagrams is a real and not a figurative act of reading. It is the model for all the other episodes in which "signs," significant appearances and not letters as such, are misread. Nicolo's disappointment when he discovers his mistake leads him, in "shame, lust, and the thirst for revenge" (244), to dress again as the Genoese knight in order to manipulate Elvira's mistake, "feeling sure that even after she came to her senses she would offer no resistance to the phantasmal, apparently supernatural apparition [seiner phantastichen, dem Ansehen nach überirdischen Erscheinung]" (212; 245).

One of the most disquieting implications of Nicolo's doubling in reverse of Elvira's mistake is the way it indicates that the ethical disposition of the reader makes no difference. Elvira is virtuous, gentle, and loving. Nicolo is as bad as they come. Both make the same error in interpretation. These errors may be defined as ethical in the sense that they are things done in the interpersonal world that do other things in their turn, in this case lethal things. Ethics seems for Kleist to be a linguistic rather than a subjective region of human behavior. However good or bad we are, when we are presented with a series of letters or a set of signs that are ordered by similarity, we *must* read. Or rather we must misread, and the results are likely to be fatal. But the cause of this fatal necessity of misreading remains to be identified.

The final version in "Der Findling" of this law of necessary misreading is the most subtle, the most difficult to recognize as like the others, and the hardest to read. Reading it, however, will take the reader closer to understanding why what happens must happen as it does.

In the rapid series of events at the end of "Der Findling," the government of the Papal States confirms Nicolo in his dispossession of Piachi at the same moment that Elvira dies of the effects of a high fever brought on by Nicolo's assault. "Durch diesen doppelten Schmerz gereizt" (maddened by this double grief), Piachi dashes Nicolo's brains out against the wall. When he is found, he is "holding Nicolo between his knees and stuffing the decree down his throat" (214; 246). Condemned to be hanged, Piachi refuses the absolution that is the legal prerequisite for execution. As Piachi says, Nicolo will not be in heaven but in hell. Piachi wants to go down there so he can "take up my revenge again, which I could only satisfy partly here!" (247). Each day Piachi is taken to the scaffold, where he refuses absolution and is taken back to his cell. He must be hanged, but he cannot be hanged unless he willingly accepts absolution. This perpetual feedback situation leads the pope ultimately to break the double bind by committing the monstrous injustice of having Piachi hanged without absolution and without the attendance of a priest, though this condemns him to damnation.

What is the reader to make of this ending? Is it no more than a melodramatic and shockingly violent Kleistian ending? Is its function no more than to demonstrate that Piachi has been driven mad by what has happened to him, or can more be said of it? A beginning with this "more" may be made by noting that the papal courts have made possible the double bind in which Piachi puts the pope. They have done this by a curious injustice and logical flaw inherent in "a law forbidding a criminal to be executed without his first receiving absolution" (246). This sounds humane enough, but it is an example of the difficulty of reading clearly God's judgment on earthly events. As a result there is a potential or perhaps even necessary injustice involved in any attempt to make oneself the emissary, intermediary, or interpreter of God's judgment.

Examples of this are present in "Michael Kohlhaas" and "The Duel." These two stories take place in the north, in a region governed primarily by the Protestant law of Luther's Germany. "Der Findling," on the other hand, is placed in the south, in Roman Catholic Italy and, more particularly, in the Papal States, where civil and ecclesiastical law are the same. The opposition between north and south, Protestant and Catholic, played an important role in the aesthetic ideology of European romanticism and in its political and cultural aftermaths in the nineteenth and twentieth centuries. This is even true, as Philippe Lacoue-Labarthe has shown, in that most catastrophic form of aesthetic ideology, Nazism.[21] Kleist's attitude toward Catholicism was a complex mixture of fascination and distaste, as shown by a reading of "Das Erdbeben in Chili" (The Earthquake in Chile) and "Die heilige Cäcilie oder die Gewalt der Musik (Eine Legende)" (Saint Cecilia or the Power of Music, A Legend). "Der Findling" takes its place among such works. The setting of its events in Rome is essential to the story, not accidental or anecdotal.

In the Rome of "Der Findling" papal law ensures that justice is done. The murderer is hanged, but he will go to heaven anyway. Authorities that are both civil and ecclesiastical must protect themselves from the crime of deliberately sending a man to eternal damnation. Their highest obligation is to save souls. Yet this apparently humane law is in fact unjust. If the priestly absolution works, if it is an efficacious speech act passing God's power on to man through his earthly representative, then the criminal has been absolved of his crime. He has been "untied" from his guilt, as the etymology of the word "absolution" suggests. He is now guiltless, as white as snow. To hang an innocent man is as much a crime as the one the murderer originally committed. In fact it is the same crime. Once more, as happens generally in Kleist's writings, the act of judgment repeats the crime it is meant to punish. By refusing absolution Piachi springs the trap the authorities have inadvertently set for themselves. They cannot hang him without sending him to hell. This the pope finally does.

Piachi's determination to continue his revenge on Nicolo in hell reveals more clearly than the other episodes what is at stake in all the examples of the fatal misreading of similarities as identities. I began by noting that "Der Findling" is punctuated by death after death, until at the end all the main characters lie dead. Death is perhaps the most radical name, though still only one figurative name among others, for the intermittences that break the continuity of human life all along the line. Of those blank places nothing can be known directly. They can be named only in trope. The misreading of a similarity as an identity is a way of filling in that gap. The mistake gives the chasm of death a face, a figure, a name, and a spurious intelligibility. Piachi and Elvira take Nicolo as a substitute for the dead Paolo. Elvira takes the portrait of Colino as a replacement for the dead Colino.

But these substitutive mistakes are not just any sort of misreading, nor are they the filling of the blank of death with just any sort of figure. They project into the gap a fictive person. They are therefore examples of Pygmalion's error, the projecting and then taking literally of a personification. In "Der Findling" prosopopoeia takes its most radical form: the bringing to life not of the absent or the inanimate but the dead. Prosopopoeia is a way of compensating for the ultimate loss of death. Into that blank, of which nothing can be known or said literally, this figure projects a human face.

Piachi's mad idea that he can continue his revenge on Nicolo in hell is the final example of this tropological error. When Piachi adopts Nicolo, he is already too old to have children by Elvira. Nicolo is his only chance to continue his lineage. Like many men, like King Lear or like Pygmalion himself, Piachi wants to use his power, including sexual power, and at the same time keep it. He wants to extend his masculine power beyond death by delegating it, while at the same time narcissistically keeping it in a closed circuit in which the same reflects the same. Like Lear and Pygmalion, Piachi discovers that the other is truly other and so exceeds his control. It is impossible to have it both ways. Insofar as Galatea is no more than the ivory simulacrum of a woman, manufactured by Pygmalion, he controls her wholly and she is the reflection of his power. But what good is an ivory woman? Pygmalion wants a woman who can respond to his caresses. When Galatea comes alive, however, she necessarily escapes his control.

In the version of this story in "Der Findling," Nicolo is a kind of prosthesis for Piachi's lost virility, even a kind of substitute phallus, as several details in the story suggest. When Piachi presents Nicolo to Elvira he stands erect before her, "fremd und steif" (strange and stiff; 201; 233). One of the things Piachi does not like about the young Nicolo is his precocious sexuality. He was seduced at the age of fifteen by the bishop's concubine. And then Nicolo assaults Elvira, attempting to take the place of his foster father.

The way Nicolo replaces Piachi's lost masculine power is given emblematically in the description of Piachi's murder of Nicolo. Not content with dashing out Nicolo's brains, Piachi holds the dead body of Nicolo between his knees and stuffs the decree down his throat. Piachi's gesture is so insane and so repulsive that the reader may repress it and make no attempt to read it, but it can be read. Piachi puts the body of Nicolo in the place of his organ of generation and then attempts to fill a gap or orifice in that body, sign of something missing, sign of a kind of castration, with the decree issued by the papal authorities confirming his dispossession by Nicolo. If he could put the decree back where it came from, ultimately the mouth of Nicolo, he might be able to close the circuit, fill the void, and regain his own masculine wholeness. But of course he cannot do that.

As he himself says, Piachi fails in his attempt to use the murder of Nicolo as an act of successful revenge. His madness, like all insanity, has its weird logic, but what Piachi wants and needs is impossible to have. He wants not a dead Nicolo as the fulfillment of his revenge for what Nicolo has done to him but rather some satisfactory replacement for what he has lost—his son, his paternal power and authority, the chance to carry on his line. No substitute can make up for the death of Paolo or for the death of his virility. The gesture of prosopopoeia, taking Nicolo as a replacement for Paolo, is the projection of a human figure into the emptiness of ultimate loss. This gesture is eternally unsatisfactory. It contains the seeds of its own undoing and must continually be done again. This is indicated by the way Piachi puts into the wholly unknowable place he will go after his death a hell populated by a Nicolo on whom he can continue his revenge. If Piachi is mad, his madness is only a more extreme form of the madness of prosopopoeia that has been exhibited in a more "sane" form by himself earlier in the story, as well as by Elvira and Nicolo. And the reader necessarily repeats this madness.

THE TWO TOPICS of reading a narrative and rendering justice are intrinsically related to the question of causality. This is true in a particular way for Kleist, but it is also a general fact about reading narratives and making sense of them. A story is readable because it can be organized as a causal chain. A judge and jury pass judgment on a criminal because they are persuaded he acted against the law. It is not by accident or mere homonymy that a judicial "case" is also called a "cause."

A fundamental device of Kleist's stories is to present a series of events in which straightforward causality is suspended or put in question, while at the same time the reader's deeply ingrained habits as an interpreter of stories lead him or her to see the events as a causal chain. The reader's predicament is represented in "Der Findling" by the predicament of the characters, including the legal authorities. Reader, characters, and the judiciary all pass judgment by imposing unjustly a plausible but mistaken causal sequentiality on a series of events that happened quite otherwise. More disturbingly, it was perhaps a random series that could not be justly interpreted according to any causal explanation whatsoever, even though the human mind cannot resist trying to do that. The reader in the act of reading the story repeats the injustice that is dramatized within it. This occurs even though there are violent crimes enough in the story, crimes that cry out for justice.

This rendering of justice is at the same time an act of reading, as indicated by the frequency with which the circulation of actual pieces of writing—letters, notes, legal documents, decrees, and so forth—enters into Kleist's stories as essential elements in the chain of events. But reading must also be taken here in the more general sense of "reading the signs correctly," for example identifying a person by her face, clothes, or voice. An example is the way the data in "The Duel," including the data of written documents, seem to indicate beyond the shadow of a doubt that Littegarde must be guilty of adultery. In fact she is innocent, and her place has been taken by her maid, in another case of substitution and mistaken identity. Any of Kleist's stories would provide examples of this. And it is not just that, as Paul de Man observes, in Kleist's works "the verdict repeats the crime it condemns."[22] The reader, in "innocently" trying to understand the story, performs the injustice once more.

How and why does this happen? Can it be avoided by some procedure of mental hygiene? The effects of misreading are so catastrophic in the stories Kleist tells that the reader would do anything within reason to avoid becoming the next link in a chain of misreadings.

Here we must return to the famous hypothetical effect on Kleist of his reading of Kant. To do so is to succumb, with some help from Kleist's own autointerpretation, to the lure of a causal construction. We say, "Kleist read Kant. This caused a crisis, a turning, a break, a decisive moment, in his life and writings from which he (and they) never recovered." But it is not known for certain whether Kleist read Kant at all or only read about "the recent socalled Kantian philosophy" or, if he did read Kant, what parts of Kant he read, how he read them, and exactly what aspects of Kant were so devastating. It is also possible to read the "Kant crisis" letter as a prelude to the break with Wilhelmine, a disingenuous way of excusing his decision to leave her behind and go to Paris. "Dear Wilhelmine," he says in effect, "I have learned about Kant, and I'm in terrible shape. My highest goal is sunk from sight. I can't work. I've got to travel. Don't worry, I still love you, but I won't be back before Christmas." Here almost all is speculation. Yet it is the plausible causal story about Kleist's Kant crisis that is the basic "idée reçue" about Kant. It is what we all tend to repeat, like so many Bouvards and Pécuchets, whenever the name "Kleist" is uttered—"Kleist: undone by Kant crisis," like "Pyramids: how did they build them?"

Andrzej Warminski, in a brilliant article building on the one by Jacobs cited above, has said almost all that can be said about Kleist and Kant.[23] Although Kleist's remark about seeing the world through green glasses, without being able to remove the glasses and find out whether the world is really green, puts the emphasis on perception in the present, the evidence of Kleist's obsessive concern in his work with illusory causal narrative chains supports Warminski's suggestion that it was perhaps the "second analogy" in *The Critique of Pure Reason* that most troubled Kleist. In a letter of March 28 to Wilhelmine, Kleist says, "But I have only used the eyes as an *explanatory example* [als eines *erklärenden* Beispiels] in my letter, since I might not allow myself the abstract language [die trockne Sprache] of philosophy" (638; 98–99). Kant's second analogy affirms the unavoidable necessity of "seeing" the world according to causal sequences, even though these links may be fictitious and the product of a tropological compulsion. The necessity named in the second analogy might well be analogized or exemplified for someone untrained in philosophy as the necessity of seeing the world as green if you have unremovable green glasses.

In what sense does the question of causality always involve the question of justice? Doing justice is present in three different ways in "Der Findling" and in Kleist's work generally. His stories often involve cases or causes in law in which justice is or is not done by civil authorities. But human justice always involves, for Kleist, divine justice, the question of God's just or unjust dealing with the world, the question ultimately of whether God intervenes in the human world at all in ways that can be discerned and measured. The reader's act, finally, is a judging or doing justice to the words of the story. Our situation as readers is allegorically expressed, that is, "said otherwise," by the situation of the characters in the story, including those impersonal authorities who must hand down a judgment. Examples are the decree giving Piachi's possessions to Nicolo or, in "Michael Kohlhaas," the judgment condemning Kohlhaas to be executed for taking divine and civil justice into his own hands. The characters too must read, justly or unjustly.

Doing justice is both an epistemological and an ethical event.

For Kleist, as for Kant, doing justice always involves the question of causality. This is so not only in the sense that in order to judge a person guilty of a crime it is necessary to establish the fact that he did it, but in the more radical sense that for Kleist as well as for Kant there is no experience whatsoever that is not governed by the second analogy. There can be no experience, no event, no perception that does not include a spontaneous assignment of cause. Understanding in terms of causality is itself an event, a happening. The event in the outside world with its putative causes is doubled by another event in which I see that exterior event as caused. Perception or experience itself involves judgment, rendering justice to something that exists in one way or another as a text to be read. For this reason, ethical judgment cannot be separated from epistemological judgment. To see at all is to see something as caused, therefore to be able to lay the blame somewhere, to say "This happened because of that" or "The sun rose because the earth revolved" or, in reading "The Marquise of O . . . ," when the truth is finally revealed: "The Marquise of O . . . became pregnant because she was raped while unconscious by Count F. . . ." Another way to put this is to say that there is no experience without an implicit narrative. A causal sequence is always an implicit narrative organized around the assumption that what comes later is caused by what comes before, "post hoc, propter hoc." If any series of random and disconnected events is presented to me, I tend to see it as a causal chain. Or rather, if Kant and Kleist are right, I *must* see it as a causal chain: "I render my subjective synthesis of apprehension objective only by reference to a rule in accordance with which the appearances [Erscheinungen] in their succession, that is, as they happen [geschehen], are determined by the preceding state. The experience of an event [of anything as *happening*] is itself possible only on this assumption [Voraussetzung]."[24]

But in what sense, exactly, is perception according to causality a fundamentally *linguistic* event? Much hangs on justifying this claim. Here is more of what Kant says about the second analogy, in the standard translation by Norman Kemp Smith. The passage is singled out and discussed by Warminski: "Understanding is required for all experiences and for its possibility. Its primary contribution [consists] . . . in making the representation of an object possible at all. This it does by carrying the time-order over into the appearances and their existence" (225–226). What Kant really wrote in the last sentence cited is: "Dieses geschiehet nun dadurch, dass er die Zeitordnung auf die Erscheinungen und deren Dasein überträgt" (234). This is more literally translated by Warminski as: "This happens through this, that it carries over the time-order into the appearances and their existence."[25] Even Warminski leaves out the *nun,* so that an even more scrupulously literal translation might read: "Now this happens through this." The "now," if it refers primarily to the sequence of the argument, has at least a muted reference to the way the happening being described always occurs in the present of "die Erscheinung," the shining forth or glistening of appearances that demand to be seen, now.

What's the difference between Smith's translation and Warminski's or mine? Kant's own words emphasize the tautological spontaneity with which "Verstand" (understanding) works. Smith's "This it does" ascribes a spectral intention to understanding. The phrase is a shadowy prosopopoeia. Kant's "Dieses geschiehet nun dadurch" makes the operation of understanding an irresistible happening or event. It happens because it happens, spontaneously, not because anyone or anything chooses that it should happen. The perception of causality is not in the ordinary sense a matter of causality, therefore not a matter in which ethical responsibility can be assigned, though it is presupposed in all ethical judgment: "This happens through this." What happens is that, in any perception or representation of an object, the understanding "carries over" the time-order into the appearances as an inextricable part of their existence.

The time-order is read as causal by the second analogy, whereby we represent each thing that appears, each "Erscheinung," as caused by what precedes it. Metonymical contingency, the accident that two things are side by side in time, is seen as a causal compulsion. The assignment of cause is an inextricable part of the representation to ourselves of what is out there to be perceived. Each thing we see is seen to be what it is because it has been caused by something that came before.

But in what sense is this a matter of language, and what difference does it make whether or not it is? The term "second analogy" gives the clue. It is second because it is discussed in *The Critique of Pure Reason* after its presupposition, the first analogy, which is the assertion that "in all change of appearances substance is permanent" (212). These are called "analogies" because Kant is arguing that the understanding, the faculty by which we make sense of the phenomenal realm of perception and representation, the real physical world out there, works by analogy to the transcendental laws of apperception in the noumenal realm, the realm of pure reason. This realm is quite separate from the phenomenal world. Nevertheless, we unavoidably see the phenomenal world by analogy to the realm of pure reason.

All analogy, however, is a matter of language, as the etymology of the word "analogy" suggests. There are no intrinsic similarities in nature. Each thing is unique. The operation of smoothing over and making similar or equal goes by way of naming, as in the concept "man" or "maple leaf," or even in the subsumption of a contradictory and discontinuous manifold under the proper name "Nicolo," "Elvira," or "Piachi." To see one of these smoothed-over things or people as "like" another one is a second linguistic operation involving the shifting or carrying over of names from one region to another, as when we say "The ship plows the waves." This does not substitute the plow for the ship but the agricultural word "plows" for some nautical term like "cruises." One concept replaces another in an act of metaphorical transference or carrying over, what Kant calls "Übertragung."

In the case of Kant's explanation of the way the understanding sees each object or event as caused, analogy, that is, metaphor or some other figure, operates in several different ways at once. It functions in the imposition of what is a linguistic structure on what is seen as an objective or purely phenomenal one, as when Kant says we cannot experience the object or event except in terms of the time-order of causality that is carried over by the understanding into appearances. It might be better to say that this operation is a catachresis, not a metaphor, since no nonfigurative literal perception is available for which the metaphorical one is substituted. We cannot take off the green glasses that force us to see each event as caused by what preceded it.

But the time-order itself, the pattern we carry over into the representation of objects and events, is itself already metaphorical. It has the structure of a classic metaphorical proportion as defined by Aristotle: A is to B as C is to D. The ship is to the waves as the plow is to the earth. Only, as Kant says, in an important distinction, the analogy in this case not mathematical but philosophical. The relation between philosophical analogy and mathematical analogy is itself analogical.

This introduces yet a third metaphorical transfer into the structure. In a philosophical analogy, the relation may be known if not the cause itself, whereas a mathematical analogy gives you an exact number for X. In a philosophical analogy we say: as A causes B, so X (whatever it is) causes D. Though X cannot ever be identified as such, we can know that X is related to D in the same way that A is related to B, since the principle that each event must have a cause operates universally. The concept of causality is in fact another form of the principle of reason itself. If one Latin word for the Greek word "logos" is "ratio," another Latin equivalent for a different semantic region of "logos" is "causa." To say "each thing has a cause," or "each thing has its reason," is to say in either case a different form of the same thing. The understanding perceives the phenomenal world according to the concepts of pure reason, but in the case of the second analogy the concept in question is itself already an analogy.

This elaborate structure of transferences is governed by metaphor itself. As Warminski puts it, all these metaphors are metaphors of metaphor. This means that it might be just as true to say that the concepts of pure reason are a result of the carrying over into the noumenal realm of the way things are perceived in the phenomenal world as the other way around.

Such a reversible pattern is extremely difficult to think about clearly, since it is an attempt to see around or outside language by means of language. There is always some initial invisible metaphor required to think about the other metaphors. The concept is modeled by what it is the model of. Still it is possible to glimpse the curious doubling back on itself of the operation of the second analogy whereby the internal structure is metaphorical (as A caused B, so there must be an X to cause D), but the relation of that structure to other structures is also metaphorical. It is carried over in the sense that the real object out there is experienced as like the internal event in the realm of "pure reason" of thinking according to a causal matrix, but this thinking is modeled on the way things are perceived in the phenomenal world, itself metaphorical. Either side is a metaphor of a metaphor, in an endless circling governed by metaphor itself.

A figure other than metaphor, however, one not discussed by Warminski, is obscurely at work in Kant's analysis. This is prosopopoeia. This figure is implicit not so much in Kant's abstract formulations as in the examples he uses to illustrate the operation of the second analogy. As can be seen in the scrupulous impersonality of Kant's formulation (as opposed to Smith's translation, with its surreptitious personification), Kant emphasizes the way the servitude of the understanding to the second analogy just happens, without any conscious or personal intent. Nevertheless, what the second analogy forces the understanding to see, at least according to Kant's examples, is something that implies personal agency. Kant's examples are not purely natural, such as the sun rising. They involve human artifacts and their motion, as in the example of the boat moving on the river: "For instance, I see a ship move down stream. My perception [Wahrnehmung] of its lower position follows upon the perception of its position higher up in the stream, and it is impossible [unmöglich] that in the apprehension of this appearance [in der Apprehension dieser Erscheinung] the ship should first be perceived lower down in the stream and afterwards higher up" (229; 221). On the one hand, water flows downhill and carries with it whatever is floating on its surface. A boat must be first upstream and then downstream. On the other hand, the boat might be moved by some manmade device against the stream or more rapidly downstream than the current flows. It is by no means impossible that a boat might be first downstream and then upstream. The example blurs the distinction between natural causes and human agency. It obscurely invites the reader to personify causality and to think of it as the result of a willed intention. This happens in spite of the fact that Kant's conceptual formulations define the perception of causality as an impersonal "happening." For Kant the perception of events as caused also involves implicitly the corresponding projection of some human presence on what is in fact inanimate. As Warminski observes, Kleist's "Unwahrsch-einliche Wahrhaftigkeiten" include anecdotes about boats and riv-ers in which what is "impossible" for Kant is shown to be possible, an improbable veracity.[26]

Kant meets the issue of prosopopoeia face to face (to use the figure) in his opuscule, "Von einem neuerdings erhobenen vorneh-men Ton in der Philosophie" (Of an Overlordly Tone Adopted Recently in Philosophy). Here the issue is not the personification of the impersonal transcendental law of causality but something closely analogous, the seeing of the impersonal moral law as a veiled Isis. Here is the passage:

> The veiled goddess before which we on both sides bend our knees is the moral law in us in its invulnerable majesty. We clearly perceive its voice, and we understand very clearly its commandments. But in hearing it we doubt whether it comes from man and whether it originates from the all-powerfulness of his very own reason, or whether it emanates from some other being, whose nature is un-known to man and who speaks to him through his own proper rea-son. At bottom we would perhaps do better to exempt ourselves entirely from this research, for it is simply speculative, and what (objectively) devolves upon us to do remains the same, let one found it on one or the other principle. The only difference is that the didac-tic procedure of leading the moral law in us back to distinct concepts according to a logical method is alone properly *philosophical*, whereas the procedure consisting in personifying this law and in making of the reason that morally commands a veiled Isis (even when we attribute no other properties to it than those the first method discovers in it) is an *esthetic* manner of representing [eine *ästhetische* Vorstellungsart] exactly the same object. It is indeed per-mitted to rely on this manner, since one has already started by lead-ing the principles back to their pure state, in order to give life to this idea thanks to a sensible, though only analogical, presentation [Dar-stellung], not however without always running some risk of falling into an exalted vision, which is the death of all philosophy.[27]

For Kant, the personification of the moral law as a veiled Isis is merely "an *esthetic* manner of representing" something beyond all figuration and especially beyond personification. It might be better to say "an *esthetic* manner of 'positing' or 'posing,'" to retain the notion of placement embedded in the German words "Vorstel-

lung" and "Darstellung." The moral law is not a person. But we
can use such personifications as long as we begin with the naked
concept and as long as we understand that the personification is a
merely sensible, analogical, and aesthetic presentation of something that is unavailable to the senses, not able to be grasped by
any trope, something that remains invisible behind the veil of all
aesthetic representations. It is aesthetic in the sense of having to do
with appearance, showing forth, "Erscheinung." To take the prosopopoeia literally is an exalted vision that is the death of all philosophy because it is a mode of idolatry. Such idolatry would give
the merely aesthetic priority over philosophy, rather than the other
way around. Such an idolatrous exaltation would claim insight
through the veil, whereas Kant defines the human situation as the
necessity of remaining in doubt, not about the categorical claim on
us of the moral law, but about the source of the moral law. Of that
source we can know nothing except that it speaks authoritatively,
with absolute sovereignty. The moral law is an "unknown X," not
a thing or a thought or a word, especially not a person, but not
nothing either.[28]

The presence of personifications in the examples Kant uses in his
discussions of the categorical imperative,[29] of symbolic thinking,
and of the second analogy indicate that prosopopoeia is not added
to something that has the clarity of philosophical reason, bare of
all figures, already taken back to first principles. The personification of the moral law as a veiled goddess, or of God as a person, or
of causality as the result of some humanlike intention, is fundamental, original, and ineffaceable. It cannot be erased or suspended
by a return to clear, philosophical, reasonable, nonfigurative first
principles. Another way to put this is to say that Kant's use of the
word "analogie" in the passage just quoted indicates the circularity
of his reasoning and the primordial priority of the figure of prosopopoeia. The phenomenal world, open to understanding, is perceived by analogy with the noumenal world of the principles of
pure reason, but these principles are represented, aesthetically, by
analogy with appearances in the phenomenal realm, especially by
analogy with persons. The demand made on us by the moral law,
the necessity of thinking of God anthropomorphically, or the necessity of positing causes for what we see always involves some

form of personification. The central presupposition of this book is that this is also true of the claims made on the reader by works of fiction. Their "themes" cannot be detached from the narratives that personify those themes. Prosopopoeia is not adventitious, but essential.

HOWEVER MUCH EFFACED or muted the question of prosopopoeia may be in Kant's thinking about causality and the moral law, there can be no doubt that the central topic of Kleist's work is the human tendency to project personal agency and concatenation on what may be a random sequence. I have said that it is difficult to see clearly how Kant's second analogy works, since we must use it to think of it. Kleist tells stories that give the reader an admirable opportunity to catch the second analogy at work in determining the way things are seen. Prosopopoeia, Pygmalion's mistake, is perhaps the most disastrous version of the second analogy. Here the second analogy works by way of the projection of a person and human intent where there is none.

On the theological level, what may be a purely natural anomaly or accident is read (literally read in Kleist's work) as the intervention of God's judgment in the human world. In "God's Stylus" a wicked woman leaves money to have a monument with a laudatory inscription erected in her memory after her death. A lightning bolt destroys most of the inscription, leaving only the letters that spell the words, "sie ist gerichtet!" (she is judged!). This is apparent evidence of God's intervention to correct the injustice (263; 278). In "The Duel" a grotesque sequence brings it about that the one who is apparently mortally wounded survives the duel fought to determine by divine judgment the heroine's guilt or innocence, while his antagonist who is only scratched dies a lingering death from blood poisoning. God's judgment is plausibly enough read as pointing one way, whereas the true guilt is revealed only in God's good time. The reader of the story may be led to question the possibility of reading God's judgment at all. But the emperor, in the last sentence of Kleist's story, is led not to give up the whole absurd practice of "holy trial by combat," but to modify the law slightly to allow for some sly wilfullness in the way God chooses to speak through such duels. The projection by prosopopoeia of a

God of judgment who speaks through earthly events is left intact, though with a disquieting legal recognition that it may not be all that easy to read what the stylus of God writes: "no sooner had he returned to Worms . . . than he had the statutes governing the holy trial by combat, wherever it was assumed that guilt was immediately revealed, amended to read: '. . . if it should be the will of God'" (318).

The projection of a concatenation assigning human agency to a random sequence also operates in the purely human dimension of Kleist's stories. The emblem of this procedure is the scene of the anagrammatic letters in "Der Findling." Arranged one way, the letters I, O, O, L, C, N, which just happen to be there, spell COLINO; arranged in another way they spell NICOLO. Nicolo makes the disastrous mistake of reading a secret meaning into this contingent fact: "As Nicolo now picked up the letters, which had been lying on the table for several days, and, with his arm resting on the table top, idly toyed with them, his mind full of gloomy reflections, he discovered—quite by accident for even he was surprised as never before in his life—the combination that spelled the name Colino. Nicolo, who had never known his name possessed this anagrammatic property, was again filled with wild hopes, and darted a hesitant, covert glance at Elvira sitting next to him. The correspondence he had discovered between the two names seemed to him more than a coincidence" (242). But of course it *is* just a coincidence.

All of the cases of mistaken identity in "Der Findling" can be read as versions of this mistake in reading: Piachi's replacement of Paolo by Nicolo, Elvira's loving worship of the portrait of the dead Colino, her mistaken reading of the costumed Nicolo as Colino back from the dead, Piachi's peopling of the unknown void of the life after death with a Nicolo on whom revenge can still be taken. In each case an accidental sequence or spurious similarity is read as causal and therefore reasonable. What is projected is a person who remains continuous through time and who can even survive the definitive hiatus of death, just as certain letters follow one another until they spell NICOLO and make something readable.

But, it might be argued, Kleist's stories reveal in the end the truth behind these mistakes in reading. To this it must be answered, "yes and no." The truth the stories reveal is the devastation that can be caused by mistakes in reading. On the one hand the stories multiply possible ways of putting the presented data together according to the time-order. Several such possible orders are present, in spectral superimposition. The letters that spell "Nicolo" can be rearranged to spell "Colino" or into a series of nonsensical letters. At the same time, Kleist's stories break the causal links they imply by the abruptness of absurd occurrences, each unconnected to what has just come before, each happening with lightning rapidity and contingency. For a moment we glimpse the possibility that the events are not causally connected at all, nor connected by the continuity of the personages through time. As part of the same insight, however, we see that we are compelled to confer sense on contiguous events by seeing them as causally connected and, moreover, as governed by the intentions of some person.

To see this is to see the injustice, the unjustified, arbitrary, and violent nature of the act of reading that we must nevertheless perform. But our insight does not keep us from doing it again. Presented with a random series of letters that happen to spell "sie ist gerichtet," we cannot avoid reading them. I am at this moment doing something of the sort by providing my reading of "Der Findling" and of Kleist's narratives generally. As soon as we learn to read, we cannot *not* read whatever is presented to us to read, but for Kleist all reading is an unjustified imposition, not a triumphant seeing of what is really there.

For Kleist, everything hangs together, but it hangs together as a series of factitious similarities that are inevitably misread as identities, with disastrous results. "Der Findling" is the narration of one such series. But knowing, theoretically, what we can learn from "Der Findling" does not keep us from a recuperation of order and meaning that is another version of the story's unjustified conferring of sense on the data of history, personal life, and literature. We cannot avoid imposing some set of connections, like a phantasmal spiderweb, over events that just happen as they happen. The events within Kleist's stories and the event of reading them are exemplary of this necessity.

These acts, moreover, are ethical doings that have the most concrete material effects. Those who perform such acts must take responsibility for these effects, though they are the result of a series of misreadings for which those who do them are not, in one sense of the word, responsible, since they could not do otherwise. But ignorance of the law is no excuse, nor is the knowledge that we cannot help breaking the law. Nor can we be exculpated by saying "I did not mean to do it," though Kleist's stories show us that the results of prosopopoetic misreading can be, literally, lethal. We did it, and must take responsibility for our deed. The most unsettling feature of Kleist's notoriously unsettling stories is the way they implicate the reader in the injustice they expose. In order to understand the story, the reader must become guilty of a version of the error condemned in story.

CHAPTER 4

Who Is He?
Melville's "Bartleby the Scrivener"

"Bartleby the Scrivener" (first published in *Putnam's Magazine,* 1853) may not seem to fit in this book. The trope of prosopopoeia is nowhere overtly a topic in the story, and there are no apparent examples of the Pygmalion motif. Both the trope and the motif, however, are obscurely present. Moreover, the ethical question is brought to the foreground where any reader may see it. At a crucial point in the story the narrator speaks to himself, or tells the reader he spoke to himself:

> What shall I do? I now said to myself, buttoning up my coat to the last button. What shall I do? what ought I to do? what does conscience say I *should* do with this man, or rather ghost? Rid myself of him, I must; go, he shall. But how?[1]

The passage formulates the question of ethical responsibility in one, but only one, of its most salient modes. It asks the question of my responsibility to act in one way or another toward my neighbor. "Shall," in its first-person form, becomes "ought" becomes "should" becomes "must" becomes "shall" again, but now in its third-person imperative form, in a rising scale of obligation that is mimed in the sequential buttoning of the coat "to the last button."

This sequence forms itself around a classic moment in ethical decision. The narrator appeals to his conscience. He listens to the still small voice of the other within who will solve his problem by telling him what he *should* or *must* do. The trouble here, as at the other moments of the narrator's dealings with Bartleby, is that conscience does not seem to have anything to say, certainly not anything useful or categorical. The still small voice does not speak loud enough to be heard. The outcome of the narrator's colloquy with himself is not any decisive action in direct relation to Bartleby. It is an attempt to evade responsibility, to escape relation to him: "No more then. Since he will not quit me, I must quit him. I will change my offices; I will move elsewhere" (664). The trouble is that any action, even the most passive, is a response to Bartleby and a taking of responsibility toward him, even *for* him. Try as he may, the narrator cannot escape that responsibility—but then he cannot fulfill it either.

It will be seen already that "Bartleby the Scrivener" is not so much the story of Bartleby as it is the story of the narrator's ethical relation, or failure of ethical relation, to Bartleby. This is not so in the usual sense in which one speaks of a displacement from the protagonist to the narrator in stories of a certain narrative structure. An example is the assertion that Conrad's *Heart of Darkness* and *Lord Jim* are really about Marlow. Or it might even be argued that *Middlemarch* is really about the narrator, "George Eliot." No, in this case, the reason for the displacement from eponymous protagonist to storyteller is that, as the narrator begins his narration by saying, the story of Bartleby cannot in any case, or by any means, be told: "While of other law-copyists I might write the complete life, of Bartleby nothing of that sort can be done" (635). "Bartleby the Scrivener" is the story of the failure of the narrator to tell the complete story of Bartleby. It is also the story of the corollary of this failure: the narrator therefore cannot determine his ethical responsibility toward Bartleby and act on it. The moral or message of "Bartleby," if there is one, seems to be the following: I cannot determine what my ethical obligation to my neighbor is, and then act on that obligation, unless I can identify him by telling his story. Storytelling and ethics are, here too, inextricably related.

Just why is it that Bartleby's story cannot be told? Melville's narrator specifies exactly what is necessary to make possible that sort of storytelling called "biography." The story then shows how those requisites are missing in Bartleby's case. It is necessary to know the origin and end of the life in question, along with everything between, in order to narrate the trajectory of the life as a rounded and organic whole. It is necessary, moreover, to know and understand the personality of the person whose biography is being recounted. The biographer must, so to speak, be able to stand face to face with the one whose life he is recounting and see into his soul, in the transparency of a pure "I-thou" relation. It is necessary, that is, to be able to answer the question, "In mercy's name, who is he?"

The two requirements are in fact the same. Only if the biographer has full knowledge of the person's whole life, from beginning to end, can she be said to "know" him or her and therefore be in a position to pass that knowledge on to the readers of the biography. That it is a character in the story, a lawyer whose premises Bartleby will not leave, who formulates the question of personal identity is not insignificant: "In mercy's name, who is he?" To know someone is to be able to name him, but naming, at least in a nominally Christian culture, is always implicitly on oath or "in God's name," as in the original giving of a proper name in baptism. A proper name is validated by the name of the highest metaphysical entity, here named in synecdochic euphemism by one of his attributes, mercy. All true naming is in God's name or in mercy's name. We name our neighbors in the name of the God of mercy. This God we dare not name directly in common speech, for fear of blasphemy, though he is the guarantee of all true naming and of all true identification of persons.

But to name someone truly, to know who he is and therefore to know what our obligation to him is, we must be able to tell his story from beginning to end, as when I must sketch out my life in the witness box as a preface to answering questions or making a deposition. The definition of a complete story, that it should have origin, end, and underlying ground, is metaphysical through and through. The same thing may be said of the notion of "person" and of the notion of knowing that person, making him manifest, by naming him. The requirement of the identification of the person, in mercy's name, and the requirement of a complete story of that person's life are the same.

Narration is the attempt to respond to the metaphysical injunction in the compulsion to biography and autobiography. This is the obligation to bring people into the space of immediate presence where they may be seen and known. The demand for biography or autobiography is the obligation to keep people in the open through writing. Such writing makes them enter the general archives where all that we know is stored and kept available. Biography and autobiography are parts of the general work of making present and keeping present, the work of exposure.

The conjunction of storytelling and responsibility toward others approaches from a new direction the dependence of ethical responsibility on storytelling and the dependence of storytelling on personification, as well as the dependence of personification on storytelling. In this case personification means the valid intuition of a personality behind the appearances that another person presents to the world through time. How can I act responsibly toward a neighbor whose personality I do not know or whose story I do not know, or could not at least in principle come to know?

In the case of Bartleby, none of these requisites of biography is fulfilled. "Bartleby the Scrivener," it might be said, is the story of why it is impossible to tell the story of Bartleby. The narrator begins his story (after identifying himself: "I am a rather elderly man") by saying that he has known many scriveners or law-copyists in his lifetime and "could relate divers histories" of them. Of Bartleby alone the story cannot be told. Even after he has told, after a fashion, the story of Bartleby, the narrator at the end of the text returns to his ignorance of Bartleby: "But ere parting with the reader, let me say, that if this little narrative has sufficiently interested him, to awaken curiosity as to who Bartleby was, and what manner of life he led prior to the present narrator's making his acquaintance, I can only reply, that in such curiosity I fully share, but am wholly unable to gratify it" (671).

Nevertheless, driven by some obscure compulsion or sense of obligation, the narrator chooses to tell the story of Bartleby. He does this in spite of the fact that he begins by telling the reader that it is impossible to do so properly. "Bartleby the Scrivener," it may be, is more the narrator's story by displacement than it is the story of Bartleby, and more an oblique confession than a biography, though it may be difficult to tell what crime it is the narrator has to confess, or whether his confession is efficacious as a means of exculpation. Here is the narrator's initial explanation of his relation to the life of Bartleby:

> But I waive the biographies of all other scriveners for a few passages in the life of Bartleby, who was a scrivener the strangest I ever saw or heard of. While of other law-copyists I might write the complete life, of Bartleby nothing of that sort can be done. I believe that no materials exist for a full and satisfactory biography of this man. It is an irreparable loss to literature. Bartleby was one of those beings of whom nothing is ascertainable, except from the original sources, and in his case those are very small. What my own astonished eyes saw of Bartleby, *that* is all I know of him, except, indeed, one vague report which will appear in the sequel. (635)

This passage is exceedingly odd, in a number of ways. The first sentence seems to suggest a peculiar kind of equation, at least in the valuation of the narrator. The narrator has begun by saying that scriveners as a group are a "somewhat singular set of men." Bartleby is the most singular of all. He is so strange in fact that a few passages from his life are equal to the whole biographies of all the other scriveners the narrator has known. Though the narrator would like to tell the biographies of all of them, he waives that privilege in order to tell the fragmentary bits he knows about Bartleby. It is a good thing that a few bits from Bartleby's life are worth so much, since Bartleby is so anomalous that only disconnected passages from his life can be known and told.

Why is this? The biographies of other scriveners, so it seems, could be told on the basis of second-hand information, but of Bartleby nothing is ascertainable, except from the original sources. "Original sources": the phrase would ordinarily mean written documents, letters or diaries, as opposed to secondary sources, such as the testimony of contemporaries. As the reader learns later, the last thing in the world one would expect to find anywhere would be letters or diaries written by Bartleby. He is not the letter-writing sort. He is rather the place where all letters written by others stop. It turns out that the narrator does not mean "written documents" by "original sources." He means ocular proof. The only original source for trustworthy knowledge of Bartleby is the testimony of the eyes: "What my own astonished eyes saw of Bar-

tleby, *that* is all I know of him." Seeing is believing. The result is
that no "full and satisfactory biography of this man" is possible.
What a full and satisfactory biography is, we know. It goes from
beginning to end and fills in all the gaps between to make a shapely
narrative whole by which a person may be fully known. Of Bartleby's life only a few disconnected passages can be given.

The paradox is that this strange situation disqualifies the reader
of "Bartleby the Scrivener" from having any knowledge of Bartleby at all, since the reader has no knowledge of him in the only
way he can be known, by visual evidence. We know him only by
hearsay. We know what the narrator tells us, by secondary report.
In Bartleby's case, so the reader is told, that is no use at all.

The narrator tells the reader, finally, that the impossibility of
writing a full life of Bartleby is "an irreparable loss to literature."
Why it is irreparable, we know. There is no way whatsoever to fill
the gap. Bartleby's full life remains a permanent blank place in literature. The word "literature" here must presumably be taken in
its old-fashioned sense of letters generally. It does not mean fiction
or poetry, but the written record of what really happened: history,
biography, memoirs, and so on, the general project of bringing
into the open. The impossibility of writing a full biography of
Bartleby is an irreparable loss to literature not just because he was
the strangest of a singular group of men, but for a deeper and more
disquieting reason. This impossibility means a permanent gap in
fulfilling the general responsibility of literature for a full accounting in language for everything that has happened in the real historical world. If something or someone escapes in principle from this
general possibility of being accounted for, as the narrator says is
the case with Bartleby, then the whole project is endangered. It
means there are some things or people that cannot be written,
some things that escape the all-including recording power of literature.

WHAT FORBIDS TELLING Bartleby's story in the ordinary way,
with beginning, middle, end, and organizing sense? The text of
the story gives the answer. In order to read this explanation it will
be necessary to do what the story itself does, that is, to make a
detour from Bartleby back to the narrator: "Ere introducing the

scrivener, as he first appeared to me, it is fit I make some mention of myself, my *employés,* my business, my chambers, and general surroundings; because some such description is indispensable to an adequate understanding of the chief character about to be presented" (635). The best explanation of why is it not only "fit" but "indispensable" might be to say that what I have said so far about the requisites of a full and satisfactory biography has been a little formulaic. Of course a good biography will be complete and shapely! The text itself, especially in what the narrator says about himself and his employees, gives the reader a series of models of proper narrative, proper thinking, and proper doing that will make such commonplaces more specific. Everything in this admirably compact and economical text *works.* Each detail adds something to the reader's understanding of what it is that Bartleby endangers, what he brings to a stop.

The narrator is a lawyer who combines in his practice secure grounding, on the one hand, and mobility on the other. Or, rather, from his fixed place he supervises and facilitates the mobility of money and property. "I am," he says, "one of those unambitious lawyers who . . . in the cool tranquillity of a snug retreat, do a snug business among rich men's bonds and mortgages and title-deeds. All who know me, consider me an eminently *safe* man . . . my first grand point [is] prudence; my next method" (635–636). Prudence goes with snug enclosure. The narrator never puts himself or his clients in danger, until he makes the disastrous mistake of hiring Bartleby. What the narrator means by "snug" is indicated in a small detail in the passage quoted at the beginning: "What shall I do? I now said to myself, buttoning up my coat to the last button." What the narrator's coats are like the reader knows from the description of an old one he gives to one of his employees: "a padded gray coat, of a most comfortable warmth, and which buttoned straight up from the knee to the neck" (640). If the narrator is a snug man in a snug retreat, he is also a buttoned-up man, buttoned up in himself, more likely to take council with himself ("What shall I do? I now said to myself") than to expose himself to others, though his writing down of what he knows about Bartleby is a serious form of unbuttoning. It is an exposure of what has gone on in his conversations with himself.

If the narrator's snugness is a form of safe buttoning up, "method," a word that etymologically means "according to the path or way," goes with the narrator's ability to transfer property and money from here to there, from one person to another. The narrator's "original business," as he tells the reader, was "that of a conveyancer and title hunter, and drawer-up of recondite documents of all sorts" (641). The narrator, from his snug retreat, "conveys" property and money, especially property, from one place to another or from one owner to another. The word "conveyancer," says the OED, was an old term for "a dexterous thief."[2] The narrator's conveyancing takes place by way of documents properly composed and properly executed in the proper number of copies, each exactly like all the others. Copies are needed because the conveying in question depends on having the move validated at both ends, so to speak, and recorded in the middle. Such conveyance, to be efficacious, depends on the law of the excluded middle. Either you own it or I do, a matter of black and white. Hence, in those days before the word processor and the copying machine, scriveners were needed to perform the arduous work of copying and checking the documents the lawyer prepares. These documents must be exactly correct in all their copies in order to perform their function, which is to transfer property from one owner to another or to execute a bond or a mortgage, a promise to pay so much interest along with principal over such and such a time. Such a promise, like a property deed, is a speech act. A conveyance is not primarily constative, though it may contain a description of the property in question. A conveyance is properly performative, if it is written right. It is a way of doing things with words. The lawyer-narrator does not so much put and keep things in their proper places as oversee the legal transfer of property and money from one place to another, from one owner to another. The mobility of property is his business.

More recently, the narrator tells the reader, he has been appointed to a new position, that of Master in Chancery. The Court of Chancery, in the United States as in the England of Dickens' *Bleak House,* is assigned the responsibility of resolving disputed claims, where that law of the excluded middle is in doubt. Such disputed claims are "referred" to the Master in Chancery, who becomes the center of a great activity of conveying from here to there. The narrator speaks of times "when a Reference was going on, and the room full of lawyers and witnesses and business was driving fast" (663). "Reference," according to the OED, is a term for "the act or expedient of referring or submitting a matter, esp. a dispute or controversy, to some person or authority for consideration, decision, or settlement (in legal use *spec.* to the Masters in Ordinary of the Court of Chancery)."

The word "reference" has much resonance these days, when there is dispute over the referential force of words generally or works of literature in particular. "Reference" is also part of the family of *fer* words—the Latin root means "carry"—which includes "transfer," "difference," and "deference" as well as the "prefer" of Bartleby's "I would prefer not to." In the case of the narrator's work as a Master in Chancery, a "reference" is part of the general mobility of property and money that is performed by language in the form of properly written and copied legal documents. The disputed case is referred to the Master in Chancery, displaced from where it was and moved into his office. This office then becomes a scene of much moving to and fro of lawyers, clerks, and copyists, except for Bartleby, who remains immobile. Melville is faithful to local legal and social history when he has the narrator complain that the office of Master of Chancery is now abolished in the state of New York. The narrator says nothing about why this was done, but laments his loss of much income for doing little: "It was not a very arduous office, but very pleasantly remunerative" (636). In the moving around of property, there is a skimming off along the way—the property arrives at its destination somewhat diminished.[3]

More can be said about the narrator's social placement and the habit of mind that goes with it. There is a parallel between the endlessly deferred circulation of property of his vocation and a peculiarity of his speech. "I do not speak it in vanity," he says, "but simply record the fact, that I was not unemployed in my profession by the late John Jacob Astor; a name which, I admit, I love to repeat, for it hath a rounded and orbicular sound to it, and rings like unto bullion. I will freely add, that I was not insensible to the late John Jacob Astor's good opinion" (636). Later he says that

Nippers, one of his copyists, was "not unknown on the steps of the Tombs" (639). The locutions in "not un-" or "not in-" are miniature bits of dialectical reasoning, in which the initial negative is negated in turn to make a synthetic positive, in a happy mobility or round-robin within language not unlike the movement of property the narrator supervises from his snug retreat.

John Jacob Astor was of course a notorious conveyancer, a robber baron who made himself extravagantly rich with deals that approach the meaning of conveyance as theft. His alliterative name turns back on itself in a rounded or orbicular way not unlike the narrator's "not un-" or "not in-," and not unlike the tautological circulation of money in the commercial society the narrator serves. Money is rounded and orbicular not just in the sense that coins are circular, but in the sense that money returns back on itself, as everything becomes valued by money. Money makes a total orbicular system that *rings*. In this it is analogous to the rounded whole that a proper narrative or biography would make. There would be no problem writing the biography of John Jacob Astor. His very name, rounded and orbicular, promises a satisfying wholeness to his life story.

It is difficult to decide just what to call this image, or motif, or system, or program for action and thought that recurs as a kind of normative pattern in all the narrator says. It might be thought of as a matrix into which everything fits or can be made to fit. It takes hold of everything—language, money, property, people, institutions. It then divides all these entities into binary oppositions and makes them go round and round in a perpetual dialectical sublation.

This matrix even seems to have determined the layout of the narrator's offices or at least what he chooses to say about them. The subtitle of "Bartleby the Scrivener" is "A Story of Wall-Street." We know what Wall Street signifies as the name for the center of financial exchange. But the name itself is odd, combining as it does a street or path from here to there, as in "method," with the motif of obstacle or stoppage in "wall." A Wall Street is an embodied oxymoron. The named combines in itself the two motifs of mobility and fixity that organize "Bartleby the Scrivener." No doubt it is only an accident that the great center of legal and

financial activity in the United States is called "Wall Street," but
the name seems uncannily appropriate as a general name for the
place where money and property flow back and forth as on a great
financial boulevard, while at the same time being the place where
the buck may stop, hit the wall. More particularly, the name "Wall
Street" is a perfect encapsulating figure for the opposition between
dialectical and narrative mobility, on the one hand, and dead fixity,
on the other, the impasse face to face with the wall. This opposition organizes, or perhaps it would be better to say, *dis*organizes,
"Bartleby the Scrivener."

The motif of the wall appears in other ways in the story. The
narrator tells the reader that his law chambers were "upstairs at
No. – Wall-street. At one end they looked upon the white wall of
the interior of a spacious sky-light shaft, penetrating the building
from top to bottom . . . [At the other end] my windows commanded an unobstructed view of a lofty brick wall, black by age
and everlasting shade . . . Owing to the great height of the surrounding buildings, and my chambers being on the second floor,
the interval between this wall and mine not a little resembled a
huge square cistern" (636). White wall against black wall: as the
narrator paces from one end of his chambers to the other he encounters a physical embodiment of the oppositional way of thinking that determines both his way of life and his way of narrating
the impossibility of narrating the story of Bartleby. Though he can
move freely from one end of his chambers to the other, he is
blocked at each end by a wall. He lives in a wall street.

When Bartleby is supposed to be working for the narrator, he
often stands for hours looking out of a third window at another
wall. This third wall is neither black nor white but neutral: "I
placed his desk close up to a small side-window in that part of the
room, a window which originally had afforded a lateral view of
certain grimy back-yards and bricks, but which, owing to subsequent erections, commanded at present no view at all, though it
gave some light. Within three feet of the panes was a wall, and the
light came down from far above, between two lofty buildings, as
from a very small opening in a dome" (642). "The next day I noticed that Bartleby did nothing but stand at his window in his
dead-wall revery" (656). "And so I found him there [in the

Tombs], standing all alone in the quietest of the yards, his face towards a high wall" (669). Though the two ends of the social scale, the narrator in his prosperity, someone not unknown to John Jacob Astor, and Bartleby in the Tombs, seem as far apart as black and white, their situations seem strangely similar. Both are walled in, imprisoned in one form or another of a wall street, a way that leads to an impasse. Bartleby in fact, as I shall show, is far freer from the constraints that wall the narrator in, for all his "prudence" and "method."

The narrator's habitual way of narrating appears again in what he tells the reader about the two copyists and the office boy who were his employees before the advent of Bartleby. These pages might seem to be more or less irrelevant to the main story, put in to fill it out and give it verisimilitude by a description of the other inhabitants of No. – Wall-street. In fact the paragraphs about Turkey, Nippers, and Ginger Nut give the reader an extended example of the way the narrator would like to be related to other people generally and to Bartleby in particular. He wants to be able to tell a rounded and orbicular story about anyone, as the law can be made to apply to all cases. One of his instinctive moves in relation to other people, so it seems, is to control and understand them through narration. Such narration is another mode of conveyance. It conveys what and who they are to the reader. The whole of "Bartleby the Scrivener" might be defined as an unsuccessful attempt to control and command Bartleby in this way.

With Turkey, Nippers, and Ginger Nut, however, the narrator is conspicuously successful. Their names are more than accidental labels. As the narrator tells the reader, the names are sobriquets they have imposed on one another as metaphorical symbols of their natures. In this case, as in a familiar concept of metaphor as the basic trope of poetry, figures tell the truth. They are a splendidly economical means of representing reality. Turkey, Nippers, and Ginger Nut, says the narrator, "may seem like names, the like of which are not usually found in the Directory. In truth they were nicknames, mutually conferred upon each other by my three clerks, and were deemed expressive of their respective persons or characters" (637).

Since these characters can be known, a shapely narrative can be made of them in their relation to one another. Turkey, the narrator tells us, is sober in the morning but drunk in the afternoon, while Nippers suffers from indigestion and nervous irritability mainly in the morning. Ginger Nut, the office boy, lives mostly on nuts. He also supplies apples and the cake called Ginger Nut to Turkey and Nippers. The three of them together can be described as an archetypal story, the narrative in which the course of man's life follows the diurnal course of the sun. Of Turkey the narrator says: "In the morning, one might say, his face was of a fine florid hue, but after twelve o'clock, meridian—his dinner hour—it blazed like a grate full of Christmas coals; and continued blazing—but, as it were, with a gradual wane—till 6 o'clock P.M. or thereabouts, after which I saw no more of the proprietor of the face, which gaining its meridian with the sun, seemed to set with it, to rise, culminate, and decline the following day, with the like regularity and undiminished glory" (637). If Turkey's day rises and sets with the sun, his afternoon irascibility is beautifully and economically balanced by Nippers' temper. Nippers is milder in the afternoon, less sharply nippy, since his indigestion is better. This occurs by a reciprocal law of nature that makes it possible to make sense of both Turkey and Nippers. It is possible to tell their stories, to take possession of them through narration. "It was fortunate for me," says the narrator, "that, owing to its peculiar cause—indigestion—the irritability and consequent nervousness of Nippers, were mainly observable in the morning, while in the afternoon he was comparatively mild. So that Turkey's paroxysms only coming on about twelve o'clock, I never had to do with their eccentricities at one time. Their fits relieved each other like guards. When Nippers' was on, Turkey's was off; and *vice versa*. This was a good natural arrangement under the circumstances" (640–641).

The narrator's description of himself and his employees indirectly tells the reader the requisites of a proper biography of Bartleby. It also shows, more directly, what personal, social, economic, and political order Bartleby enters. In this society wage slaves and their disabilities are immediately present to employers.

BARTLEBY APPEARS on the threshold, "motionless," "pallidly neat, pitiably respectable, incurably forlorn" (642), in answer to the narrator's advertisement for another copyist. He needs a new worker because his appointment as Master in Chancery has brought him more business. Bartleby's entrance suspends the narrator's power over those around him, both his ability to command them through narration and his control over them as their employer. This interruption is analogous to the way the appearance of the Reverend Hooper wearing his black veil, in Hawthorne's story, threatens the community harmony of the good people of Milford.[4]

Bartleby exerts his power over the narrator through a peculiar combination of words: "I would prefer not to." These words, along with Bartleby's passionless passivity in uttering them, wholly unman and disarm the narrator.[5] The conditional "would" lacks the specification of the terms of the condition that would limit the meaning of the sentence. "I would . . ." if: what? He does not say.

"Prefer" has a wide range of meanings in the OED, but most involve some hypothetical putting forward of one thing over another, not the positive action of "transfer" but the neutral approbation of something or someone, its tentative putting forward to see what happens, so to speak. The word "prefer" can mean: (1) to put forward or advance in status, rank, or fortune; to promote (to a position or office of dignity); (2) to forward, advance, promote (a result); (3) to put or set in front or before; (4) to put, place, or set something before someone for acceptance; to hold out, proffer, offer; (5) to lay a matter formally before someone for approval; to bring forward a bill, prayer, indictment; (6) to refer, attribute, ascribe; (7) to set or hold one thing before others in esteem; to like better (now the chief sense); (8) to be preferable to, surpass, excel.

It is easy to see how this range of meanings vibrates between active and passive senses, without ever quite being either. The preferred may either be better or be put forward as better. Many of the meanings of "prefer" involve not the physical action of putting something forward but some use of performative language to proffer or promote something or someone, as in "preferred stock," "preferential treatment," or "preferment at court." To say "I prefer grapes to apples" is neither active nor passive. It does not change either the apples or the grapes, unlike that realm of speech acts where "I pronounce you man and wife" changes the bride and groom into a married couple. In contrast to "refer," "transfer," "offer," and "confer," where the *fer* names a real act of carrying over, "prefer" is a weak member of this family of words. It tentatively holds out, proffers, or offers to put one thing above another.

That there is something uncanny about the word "prefer" is shown by the way the narrator, Nippers, and Turkey catch the word, like a disease, mock it, play with it, and unconsciously adopt the trick of using it. "Somehow," says the narrator, "of late I had got into the way of involuntarily using this word 'prefer' upon all sorts of not exactly suitable occasions" (655), and Nippers and Turkey both use the word inadvertently: "Oh certainly, sir, if you prefer that I should," says Turkey, and "Nippers at his desk caught a glimpse of me, and asked whether I should prefer to have a certain paper copied on blue paper or white." "He did not in the least roguishly accent the word prefer. It was plain that it involuntarily rolled from his tongue. I thought to my self, surely I must get rid of a demented man, who already has in some degree turned the tongues, if not the heads of myself and clerks" (656).

Even this neutral or passive-active motionless motion in the word "prefer," which can turn the tongue of the man who happens to hear it, is disabled of such force as it has by the incomplete conditional in Bartleby's "would," by the negative in "not," which says not that Bartleby would prefer to do this or that, but that he would prefer not to do . . . whatever his employer has asked him to do. The final word, "to," is the beginning of a prepositional phrase left hanging in the air, presumably by the elision of the words that would complete it: "to . . . do what you have just asked me to do." "I would prefer not to": he does not say he will and he does not say he won't.

And what of Bartleby's first word, "I"? "I" have shown that there is doubt that the question "who is he?" can be answered in reference to Bartleby. By what authority, then, in the name of what ego or subjectivity, does Bartleby get his authority to speak in such a sinister and subversive way the "I" that is a necessary part of all performative utterances, even when it remains merely implicit, as when I sign my name? What "I" beyond all limited, circumscribed, and therefore efficacious "I's" speaks through Bartleby as the bringing to a halt of all felicitously operative "I's"? To what demand does he respond in uttering those words? The right reading of "Bartleby the Scrivener" depends on answering these questions right or on showing that they are unanswerable.

The effect on the narrator and on his whole busy work of this simple sentence, even the first time it is uttered, is devastating. It brings everything to a sudden stop. Though the narrator's business continues, it is punctuated thereafter by moments of hiatus whenever Bartleby utters his "I would prefer not to." Why does Bartleby's expression of what the narrator calls "passive resistance"— "Nothing," he says, "so aggravates an earnest person as a passive resistance" (646)—function so well to bring things to a stop?

One answer is purely logical. As opposed to positive statements or negative statements or even to the sort of positive negatives to which the narrator is prone ("I was not unemployed"), what Bartlebay says resists dialectical sublation. The phrase is neither black nor white. There is nothing you can do with it. It is like an endless loop in a process of reasoning. The disruptive energy of this extraordinary group of everyday words is limitless. A shorthand way of describing that power is to say that Bartleby's sentence cannot be assimilated to any dialectical or oppositional way of thinking. You can neither deny it nor accept it. It is neither constative nor performative, or perhaps it might be better to say that it is an exceedingly disquieting form of performative. It is a use of words to make something happen, but what it makes happen is to bring about the impossibility of making anything happen with words. It performs the blockage of all those forms of performative language by which the narrator lives and makes his living. It also neutralizes his power of narration. Bartleby's "I would prefer not to" is like Bartleby's middle window looking out on the dead wall of indeterminate color.

Bartleby's formula is a way of doing things with words, but what it performs is the stoppage of all performative utterances or inscriptions, for example of those "conveyances" that the narrator produces professionally and that Bartleby copies. Though Bartleby later on extends his "I would prefer not to" to copying and to all the other duties for which he has been employed, at first he is perfectly willing to copy: "As if long famishing for something to copy, he seemed to gorge himself on my documents. There was no pause for digestion" (642). His first utterance of his "I would prefer not to" comes, significantly, when he is first asked to check or verify something he has copied. The performative efficacy of the documents, their ability to transfer property and money from here to there, from one owner to another, requires that they exist in several copies each exactly correct and each exactly like all the others: "It is, of course, an indispensable part of a scrivener's business to verify the accuracy of his copy, word by word" (642). An unverified copy is a dead letter. It is of no more use than a blank sheet of paper. By refusing to proofread what he has copied, Bartleby renders all his work of copying null and void. He might as well have been copying gobbledegook, like that habitué of the British Library who used to sit copying nonsense scribbles with scrupulous care from one notebook to another.

A proper name with a mistake in it seems especially to disable a document from performing its function of conveyance. On the title page of my copy of the Library of America volume that contains *The Piazza Tales*, the name Melville is misspelled "Meville," in large capitals. It is a striking misprint. No doubt it occurred by the same logic that makes, according to Poe in "The Purloined Letter," the big words written across a map all but invisible. But the effect of having a volume labeled "Herman Meville" is strangely to cast doubt on the authenticity of the whole, as though Melville had made a mistake in signing his name to it or as though some impostor had signed. Is the volume really by Melville? Or is it by some other author named "Meville"? How many other mistakes does the volume contain? The name on the title page of a book is in a sense the verification of the whole. In this case that label is a misprint, a *coquille,* as the French say, a dead letter. Bartleby's refusal to check what he has copied may mean that the narrator's documents will be strewn with such disabling dead letters.

I have said that Bartleby's passive resistance to checking what he has copied renders it "dead letter." The reference of course is to the penultimate paragraph of "Bartleby," in which the narrator gives the reader at last the "one vague report" (635) that is all he knows of Bartleby except what his astonished eyes saw and his astonished ears heard. This "little item of rumor" (671) may be true or false, but it is all the narrator knows of Bartleby's life before his pallid figure appeared at the door. "The response was this: that Bartleby had been a subordinate clerk in the Dead Letter Office at Washington, from which he had been suddenly removed by a change in the administration" (672). As most readers of the story have noted, and as the narrator himself says, this is an admirably suggestive and moving bit of information. A dead letter is a letter that for one reason or another does not reach its destination. The address is wrong, or the addressee has moved without a forwarding address. Or the addressee is dead. In any case the letter is dead in the sense that it does not accomplish its purpose, which was to transmit its message from here to there. A dead letter is like an inefficacious speech act. More precisely, it is like one of those documents Bartleby has copied but now refuses to verify. A living letter, on the other hand, like an efficacious document of conveyance, is animated with purpose and meaning. It does something. One might say that a dead letter is simply a letter in the sense that we speak of the "materiality of the letter." The letter killeth, but the spirit giveth life. The biblical opposition between letter and spirit hovers somewhere around in the phrase "dead letter."

The narrator, by a kind of pun or slippage between two meanings of "dead," assumes in his examples that all the letters Bartleby worked with in the dead-letter office were dead because their intended recipients were dead. But of course a letter may find its way to the dead-letter office for all sorts of other reasons. Still, the ultimate absence of the addressee in the land of the dead, where no letters can be sent or received, is the paradigmatic case of the situation that renders a letter dead. Anyone who has ever written a letter to someone who turned out to be dead will know what an uncanny experience it is to get the letter back marked "addressee deceased." If prosopopoeia in one of its meanings is the ascription of a face, a voice, or a name to the dead, a letter sent to a dead person is a strange kind of prosopopoeia. It is an inadvertent address to the dead or an invocation of the dead that implicitly presupposes an answer. To receive a letter from someone now dead is another matter. Is not the text of "Bartleby the Scrivener" such a letter from the grave, whether we think of it as a communication from the narrator, whose first words are "I am a rather elderly man," or as a communication from Herman Melville? In any case, the narrator in the penultimate paragraph of the story focuses eloquently on what is moving about a letter that becomes dead because its intended recipient is dead, and on how appropriate it is that Bartleby should have worked among such letters:

> Dead letters! does it not sound like dead men? Conceive a man by nature and misfortune prone to a pallid hopelessness, can any business seem more fitted to heighten it than that of continually handling these dead letters, and assorting them for the flames? For by the cart-load they are annually burned. Sometimes from out the folded paper the pale clerk takes a ring:—the finger it was meant for, perhaps, moulders in the grave; a bank-note sent in swiftest charity:—he whom it would relieve, nor eats nor hungers any more; pardon for those who died despairing; hope for those who died unhoping; good tidings for those who died stifled by unrelieved calamities. On errands of life, these letters speed to death. (672)

The reader should not misunderstand the way this final clue allows an understanding of Bartleby's nature and of his effect on the narrator. To think of Bartleby as exercising by "I would prefer not to" a power to make the live letter dead would be to return to thinking in terms of binary opposites. Such thinking can easily be assimilated into the dialectic of either/or by which the narrator lives and works. Bartleby's expression of a preference not to verify the accuracy of his copies turns them into dead letter not in the sense of mere letter as opposed to spirit or in the sense of unsignificant marks as opposed to significant ones. He makes what he has copied into something more ominous and uncanny. He makes them into words that have meaning but have been drained of their efficacy and made into the ghosts of themselves. They have been etiolated, whitened, neutralized—neither words nor nonwords.

This power to neutralize words appears in a different way in Bartleby's gift for absurd literalism. This displaces the most ordinary words from their usual active meaning and makes them something ghostly. Bartleby's use of "prefer" leads the narrator's employees to use the word in all sorts of inappropriate contexts. It becomes a kind of oral misprint or slip of the tongue in their speech. Just as the name Bartleby has, unlike the names Turkey, Nippers, and Ginger Nut, no metaphorical or allegorical resonance whatsoever, at least none that I can identify, but is a pure proper name if there ever was one, so he has a gift for making absolutely literal remarks that seem just slightly off the point. When the narrator goes back to confront Bartleby in his old offices, where he is causing disturbance by "haunting the halls and stairways," he asks Bartleby what he is doing there. "Sitting upon the banister," says Bartleby (666). And when the narrator visits Bartleby in the Tombs, where he has been imprisoned for vagrancy, Bartleby stands with his face toward a high wall and refuses to look at the narrator. "I know you," he says, "and I want nothing to say to you" (669). An odd locution! Presumably he means "I do not want to say anything to you," but that is not what he says. "Want," like "prefer," hovers in the neutral space between passive and active meanings. When the narrator tries to console Bartleby by telling him he has sky and grass in the prison courtyard, Bartleby answers, "I know where I am" (669). This gift for literal remarks, like his "I would prefer not to," puts a stop to further conversation or interchange of words between people.

THE EFFECT OF Bartleby's words on the narrator's sense of himself is as devastating as their effect on the practice of his profession. He is rendered at once immobile and mobile or, it might be better to say, he is put in a neutral state in which immobility and mobility come to the same thing, since motion is no longer directed to a goal. Movement is turned into a way of staying in the same place.

On the one hand, the narrator is frozen in place: "I sat awhile in perfect silence, rallying my stunned faculties" (643); "For a few moments I was turned into a pillar of salt, standing at the head of my seated column of clerks" (644); "I was thunderstruck. For an instant I stood like the man who, pipe in mouth, was killed one cloudless afternoon long ago in Virginia, by summer lightning; at his own warm open window he was killed, and he remained leaning out there upon the dreamy afternoon, till some one touched him, when he fell" (659).

On the other hand, the narrator is compelled to a pointless mobility by Bartleby's immobility. He cannot move Bartleby from his premises. It seems a logical absurdity to call in the police and have so stationary a man removed as a vagrant: "a vagrant, is he? What! he a vagrant, a wanderer, who refuses to budge? It is because he will *not* be a vagrant, then, that you seek to count him *as* a vagrant. That is too absurd" (664). The narrator therefore decides to move himself to new offices. Later, when he is held accountable for the fact that Bartleby still haunts his old offices, he tries to escape by a curious kind of mobile quiescence:

> I now strove to be entirely care-free and quiescent; and my conscience justified me in the attempt; though indeed it was not so successful as I could have wished. So fearful was I of being hunted out by the incensed landlord and his exasperated tenants, that, surrendering my business to Nippers, for a few days I drove about the upper part of the town and through the suburbs, in my rockaway; crossed over to Jersey City and Hoboken, and paid fugitive visits to Manhattanville and Astoria. In fact I almost lived in my rockaway for the time. (668)

If it is an absurdity to call in the police to arrest the immobile Bartleby for vagrancy, the narrator himself is made into a vagrant by Bartleby. He wanders pointlessly from one place to another in a kind of fugitive movement in place that is wonderfully expressed by the name of his conveyance.

A "rockaway" was the ordinary name for a certain kind of carriage. The word combines movement in place, "rock," with actual movement across the ground, "away." This combination admirably corresponds to the narrator's sad state. Whether he is motionless or mobile, motionless-mobile with a momentarily arrested energy when he is turned into a pillar of salt or paralyzed as if struck by lightning, or, on the other hand, mobile-motionless with a vagrancy that has no goal and goes nowhere, the narrator is rendered impotent by Bartleby: "Indeed, it was his wonderful mildness chiefly, which not only disarmed me, but unmanned me, as it were. For I consider that one, for the time, is a sort of unmanned when he tranquilly permits his hired clerk to dictate to him, and order him away from his own premises" (650). The sentence is itself unmanned by being deprived of the noun that would be modified by the adjectival "unmanned": "is a sort of unmanned" does not make sense. This grammatical impotence corresponds to the narrator's unmanned state, which is both implicitly sexual and at the same time social and political. The narrator has been deprived of the masculine authority necessary to control other men.

At the same time, this associate of John Jacob Astor is not fulfilling his responsibility to keep the working classes subordinated and doing the work they have been hired to do.

The narrator has the most urgent need to contain Bartleby, to reduce and encompass him, to *read* him, so that he can get on with his work and repossess his own integrity. The narrator's need can be seen as the presence within the text of an allegory of the reader's own need to dominate the story by interpreting it. This need is abundantly manifest in the scores of essays published on the story. I began by saying that there is a displacement of focus from Bartleby to the narrator and that the narrator's problem is a question of ethical responsibility: What should he do? What ought he to do? What does his conscience tell him he must do?

The narrator tries or considers a series of strategies for dealing with Bartleby. Much of the black comedy of the tale consists in the narrator's report of his frantic attempts to do something about Bartleby, this "cadaverous" presence, this "incubus" or "ghost" who "haunts" his office like an "apparition," and who "like a very ghost, agreeably to the laws of magical invocation, at the third summons," appears when the narrator calls him by name.

The narrator at one point, when he first discovers that Bartleby is secretly living in the law offices, even has a proleptic vision of Bartleby as a corpse. That vision is of course fulfilled when Bartleby dies at the end of the story:

> For the first time in my life a feeling of overpowering stinging melancholy seized me. Before, I had never experienced aught but a not-unpleasing sadness. The bond of a common humanity now drew me irresistibly to gloom. A fraternal melancholy! For both I and Bartleby were sons of Adam . . . These sad fancyings—chimeras, doubtless, of a sick and silly brain—led on to other and more special thoughts, concerning the eccentricities of Bartleby. Presentiments of strange discoveries hovered round me. The scrivener's pale form appeared to me laid out, among uncaring strangers, in its shivering winding sheet. (651–652)

The attempt to deal with Bartleby by seeing him as an example of mankind generally, therefore as like oneself and as understandable as oneself, is echoed in some of the criticism of "Bartleby." This strategy returns in the last sentence of the story: "Ah Bartleby! Ah humanity!" The double exclamation sounds as if to say the one thing is to say the other, as if Bartleby were a valid synecdoche for all of mankind. But this comforting assimilation is in blank contradiction to the chain of clues that say Bartleby is not so much mortal, like the rest of us, as already dead. He is a ghost come back from some realm beyond the grave to haunt the living and to interrupt all those everyday activities of our common humanity.

The strategies tried out or considered by the narrator to deal with this walking corpse, to lay the ghost or exorcise it, to do something about him, with him, in response to him, are a repertoire of the various ways available at that moment in history for making sense of human life. First they are ways of placing others, one's neighbors, of assimilating them into common humanity and thereby identifying one's responsibility toward them. How can I know how to act toward someone if I cannot see that person as in some sense like myself? At the same time, the narrator's strategies are implicitly different ways of interpreting the course of individual or collective history. They make it possible to tell a story or to create a shapely narrative out of Bartleby's life. In addition, they are procedures for assimilating people into a process of dialectical reasoning and thereby making it possible to account for them.

What is most extraordinary about the narrator's strategies for dealing with Bartleby is their multiplicity and their incoherence. Insofar as they reflect the resources available to Melville or the resources he thought were available, they suggest that the culture of Melville's day, far from being a single monolithic discourse of ordering, was an astonishing heterogeneity of incompatible ways of making sense of life. Charity; the presumption that either free will or predestination governs what happens; assuming a premise; making a bet; paying him off or bribing him to leave; bringing in the police; interpreting him as *luny* or as a forger; taking him home, getting him a place, ordering him out, denying relationship or responsibility altogether, moving out himself; finding out his history so he can place him—all these strategies are tried by the narrator. All fail.

The narrator's first instinct is to dismiss Bartleby instantly as an employee who has refused to obey a reasonable order. But Bartleby has not, after all, refused to obey. He has simply said that he would prefer not to. And this remark has been made in so even-tempered and dispassionate a manner that it cannot be responded to as an act of defiance or aggression. There is in fact nothing human about it. Bartleby's "I would prefer not to" is as impersonal as if it had been uttered by a statue or a being from beyond this world, a ghost or a cadaver:

> I looked at him steadfastly. His face was leanly composed; his gray eye dimly calm. Not a wrinkle of agitation rippled him. Had there been the least uneasiness, anger, impatience or impertinence in his manner; in other words, had there been any thing ordinarily human about him, doubtless I should have violently dismissed him from the premises. But as it was, I should have as soon thought of turning my pale plaster-of-paris bust of Cicero out of doors . . . This is very strange, thought I. What had one best do? (643–644)

Since direct action is clearly inappropriate, some other strategy must be tried. The rest of the story is primarily the report of methods for doing something about Bartleby. Diverse as these are, they are all ways to do nothing, ways of deferring action, ways of pretending that nothing has really happened to endanger the ordinary way of doing things. If Bartleby's "I would prefer not to" is a syncope, like a missed heartbeat, in the ongoing march of business, history, reasoning, and narrativity, if it is a blank place that endangers the enterprise of conveying, in all its dimensions, the narrator's instinct is to pretend that nothing has happened: "But my business hurried me. I concluded to forget the matter for the present, reserving it for my future leisure" (644). Later, after the second episode of iterations of "I would prefer not to," he says: "But once more business hurried me. I determined again to postpone the consideration of this dilemma to my future leisure" (646).

It is essential to the hiatus created by Bartleby's strange utterance that it can, may, and must be repeated. It is iterable, and it is iterated. The comedy of "Bartleby the Scrivener" lies in the narrator's attempts to respond to Bartleby's indefatigable repetition of his characteristic locution in a way that will at once pretend it has not happened, reassimilate it into the flow of reason and business, and at the same time allow the further deferral of decisive action.

The narrator alternates between leaving Bartleby alone and telling himself that treating him charitably is meritorious, on the one hand, and, on the other, allowing his exasperation to get the better of his judgment, giving Bartleby an order, and getting passively resisted once more. The narrator tells himself that he can earn "a delicious self-approval" by endeavoring "charitably to construe to his imagination what proves impossible to be solved by his judgment": "To befriend Bartleby; to humor him in his strange wilfulness, will cost me little or nothing, while I lay up in my soul what will eventually prove a sweet morsel for my conscience" (647). Later, when Bartleby has been especially exasperating and they are alone together in the office, the narrator remembers the sad story of the murder of Adams by Colt in the solitary office of the latter. He is saved from a similar act by remembering the divine injunction to "love one another": "no man that ever I heard of, ever committed a diabolical murder for sweet charity's sake" (661). But the narrator also feels "additional incentives tempting me to my fate" (648), the fate of being baffled, paralyzed, and stymied again by hearing Bartleby say "I would prefer not to": "The passiveness of Bartleby sometimes irritated me. I felt strangely goaded on to encounter him in new opposition, to elicit some angry spark from him answerable to my own" (647).

Of course neither of these techniques works. How can one feel and act charitably toward someone about whom one knows nothing? The divine injunction is to love your neighbor, but Bartleby is a ghost, a walking dead man, a living statue, a kind of zombie possessed by who knows what malicious spirit. The idea of befriending or of loving Bartleby as one loves one's neighbor is absurd. But dealing with him harshly and ordering him to do his duty as hired help does not work either. He neither refuses nor agrees to do what he he asked to do. His power lies in this neutrality, in the impossibility of arousing any anger in him in response to one's own anger: "But indeed I might as well have essayed to strike fire with my knuckles against a bit of Windsor soap" (647).

Since neither of the direct responses works, the narrator tries more indirect methods. He decides to ask Bartleby "certain calm questions . . . touching his history, &c," and then, depending on whether he is willing to answer, paying him off and firing him or, on the other hand, paying him enough to go back home "to his native place" (653). If he can learn about Bartleby's past life, then he can tell his story and know who he is, thereby assimilating him into the ordinary human community. Bartleby of course gives his usual answer to these requests, and the narrator is once more back where he started, stuck with Bartleby, unable to go forward or back.

By this time Bartleby has refused not only to verify copies but even to copy documents in the first place. He stands in the narrator's office all day staring at the wall outside his window. The narrator tries ordering Bartleby to leave the office after six days have passed. When Bartleby remains, he tries to bribe him to go, leaving thirty-two dollars on the table (quite a bit of money in those days), telling him to lock the door when he leaves, and going home himself in the expectation that Bartleby will be gone the next morning. Or, rather, the narrator does not have an "expectation" but makes an "assumption." As he passes the hours after he has left Bartleby, the narrator sets his own assumption against Bartleby's preference. The words name two different ways of being related to the future. Bartleby's "I would prefer not to" is a gesture toward an infinitely postponed future. It is the deferral of any present action, either positive or negative, in the name of a future that can never come and that can never be verified as such, since it is no more than a preference. An assumption, on the other hand, like all the narrator's ordinary professional life, is a mode of thinking and acting that is safely within history, narrative, and rational speculation. An assumption forms a prior ground presupposing a certain prospective fulfillment of that assumption. An assumption joins past, present, and future together in an organic, logical whole, like a good narrative.

The pages describing the battle between assumption and preference are among the most brilliantly comic in this extended black comedy. They identify the mode of thinking and living within which the narrator, his culture as a whole, and no doubt most readers of Melville's day and our own continue to dwell, as well as the radical threat to this mode posed by Bartleby and his "I would prefer not to." Or rather, since Bartleby's phrase and even his way of life are perfectly ordinary or possible ones, it might be better to say that Bartleby personifies a permanent threat haunting from within our ordinary way of speaking, thinking, and living. Bartleby may be figured as a ghost, but the threat he represents does not come from outside the everyday world of society, business, and ordinary language. Bartleby makes every assumption vulnerable to a permanently disabling suspension:

> The beauty of my procedure seemed to consist in its perfect quietness. There was no vulgar bullying, no bravado of any sort, no choleric hectoring, and striding to and fro across the apartment, jerking out vehement commands for Bartleby to bundle himself off with his beggarly traps. Nothing of the kind. Without loudly bidding Bartleby depart—as an inferior genius might have done—I *assumed* the ground that depart he must; and upon that assumption built all I had to say. The more I thought over my procedure, the more I was charmed with it. Nevertheless, next morning, upon awakening, I had my doubts,—I had somehow slept off the fumes of vanity . . . My procedure seemed as sagacious as ever,—but only in theory. How it would prove in practice—there was the rub. It was truly a beautiful thought to have assumed Bartleby's departure; but, after all, that assumption was simply my own, and none of Bartleby's. The great point was, not whether I had assumed that he would quit me, but whether he would prefer so to do. He was more a man of preferences than assumptions. (658–659)

Theory is here set against practice. An assumption is purely theoretical, in the sense of being verbal, not real. Rather than being grounded securely in something outside language, assumption presupposes a certain course of events and then waits for them to occur. A preference, on the other hand, is real, practical, material. It is already embedded in the concrete world where language is efficacious in making something happen or, in Bartleby's case, in effectively preventing anything from happening. Insofar as the narrator's procedure of assumption is consonant with his professional practice of conveyancing, it reveals the passing of property back and forth to be a mere legal fiction, fencing with air.

The insubstantiality of assumption is revealed by its association with another procedure for dealing with Bartleby, the wager or calculation of probabilities. As he walks to his office the next morning to see whether his assumption is correct, "arguing the probabilities *pro* and *con,*" the narrator overhears a man say, "I'll take odds he doesn't," and though the remark bears no relation to Bartleby he instinctively answers, "Doesn't go?—done! . . . put up your money" (659). The bet, like the assumption, is a speech act that attempts to take possession of the future with words. In both cases a primitive belief in the magical efficacy of words lies behind the linguistic move: "I'll bet he does" or "I assume he will." A bet or an assumption, however hypothetical or speculative, is anchored in the extralinguistic world in the sense that it is ultimately verifiable. Either he does go or he does not. It is an either/ or opposition, like ownership: either you own it or I do. It is not so much that Bartleby's preference (he remains in the office of course) causes the narrator to lose his bet or falsifies his assumption as that it postpones indefinitely the moment when either outcome can be verified. Bartleby does not say "I refuse to go" or "I won't go." He says "I . . . would . . . prefer . . . not . . . to," and all the narrator's assumptions cannot avoid colliding with that strange combination of solidity and insubstantiality, present in the pale form of Bartleby standing in his office, "like the last column of some ruined temple":

> What was to be done? or, if nothing could be done, was there any thing further that I could *assume* in the matter? Yes, as before I had prospectively assumed that Bartleby would depart, so now I might retrospectively assume that departed he was. In the legitimate carrying out of this assumption, I might enter my office in a great hurry, and pretending not to see Bartleby at all, walk straight against him as if he were air. Such a proceeding would in a singular degree have the appearance of a home-thrust. It was hardly possible that Bartleby could withstand such an application of the doctrine of assumptions. But upon second thoughts the success of the plan seemed rather dubious. (660)

After the failure of all these strategies for getting rid of Bartleby, the narrator tries another. In part through charity but in part through the notion that it is his fate to have Bartleby permanently in his chambers, he decides to try to live with Bartleby, to take him as a permanent fixture in his office. The narrator looks into two quite different books that deny man free will in determining his life, "Edwards on the Will" and "Priestly on Necessity." For Jonathan Edwards man does not have free will because everything he does is predestined by God. For Joseph Priestly, on the other hand, man is bound within the chains of a universal material necessity.

Everything happens through physical causality, and therefore everything happens as it must happen, as it has been certain through all time to happen. In either case Bartleby's presence in the narrator's rooms is something predestined:

> Gradually I slid into the persuasion that these troubles of mine touching the scrivener, had been all predestined from eternity, and Bartleby was billeted upon me for some mysterious purpose of an all-wise Providence, which it was not for a mere mortal like me to fathom. Yes, Bartleby, stay there behind your screen, thought I; I shall persecute you no more; you are harmless and noiseless as any of these old chairs; in short, I never feel so private as when I know you are here. At last I see it, I feel it; I penetrate to the predestinated purpose of my life. I am content. Others may have loftier parts to enact; but my mission in this world, Bartleby, is to furnish you with office-room for such period as you may see fit to remain. (662)

This strategy fails too, when the narrator's clients and associates let him know that Bartleby's presence in his offices is scandalizing his professional reputation. It is then that the narrator, who is nothing if not logical, conceives his strangest way of dealing with Bartleby. Since Bartleby will not budge, he himself will leave. The immobility of Bartleby turns the narrator into a nomad: "No more then. Since he will not quit me, I must quit him. I will change my offices; I will move elsewhere" (664).

When the new tenants and the landlord of his old premises come to charge the narrator with responsibility for the nuisance Bartleby is causing, "haunting the building generally, sitting upon the banisters of the stairs by day, and sleeping in the entry by night" (666), the narrator tries first a new strategy of saying he is in no way related to Bartleby or responsible for him. But it is no use: "I was the last person known to have anything to do with him, and they held me to the terrible account" (666).

The narrator then meets Bartleby once more face to face. He offers to set him up in a respectable position, as a clerk in a dry-goods store, a bartender, a bill collector, or a companion for young gentlemen traveling to Europe. To all these ludicrous suggestions Bartleby replies that he is not particular, but he would prefer to remain "stationary" (667). The narrator then, and finally, offers to take Bartleby home with him, like a stray cat, and give him refuge there. This meets with the same reply. The narrator flees the building and becomes truly a vagrant, wandering for days here and there in his rockaway.

The narrator's life and work seem to have been permanently broken by the irruption of Bartleby. It is not he but his old landlord who deals effectively with the situation. He has Bartleby "removed to the Tombs as a vagrant" (668). This is just what the more intellectually consequent narrator has not been able to bring himself to do, not just because Bartleby is not, strictly speaking, a vagrant and not just because doing such violence to Bartleby would disobey the law of charity, but because he cannot respond with violence to a resistance that has been purely passive and has thereby "disarmed" or "unmanned" any decisive action: "Turn the man out by an actual thrusting I could not; to drive him away by calling him hard names would not do; calling in the police was an unpleasant idea . . . You will not thrust him, the poor, pale, passive mortal,—you will not thrust such a helpless creature out of your door? you will not dishonor yourself by such cruelty? No, I will not, I cannot do that" (660, 664)

Even after the police have been called in and society has placed Bartleby where he belongs, the narrator continues to be haunted by a sense of unfulfilled responsibility. He visits him in the Tombs, the prison so called because it was in the Egyptian Revival style of architecture, but also no doubt in response to a deeper sense of kinship between incarceration and death: "The Egyptian character of the masonry weighed upon me with its gloom. But a soft imprisoned turf grew under foot. The heart of the eternal pyramids, it seemed, wherein, by some strange magic, through the clefts, grass-seed, dropped by birds, had sprung" (671). Bartleby is appropriately placed in the Tombs since, if the prison courtyard where Bartleby dies is green life in the midst of death, Bartleby has been death in the midst of life. In the Tombs the narrator makes his last unsuccessful attempt to deal with Bartleby in a rational manner, to reincorporate him into ordinary life. He "narrates" to the prison authorities, as he says, "all I knew" about Bartleby, telling them Bartleby does not really belong there but must stay "till something less harsh might be done—though indeed I hardly knew what" (669). He yields at last to the accounting for Bartleby that had been used by Ginger Nut: "I think, sir, he's a little *luny*" (645). The narrator now tells the "grub-man" in the prison, Mr. Cutlets, "I think he is a little deranged" (670). One powerful means society has for dealing with someone who does not fit any ordinary social category is to declare him insane.

Mr. Cutlets has his own curious and by no means insignificant way of placing Bartleby. He thinks Bartleby must be a forger. "Deranged? deranged is it? Well now, upon my word, I thought that friend of yourn was a gentleman forger; they are always pale and genteel-like, them forgers. I can't help pity 'em—can't help it, sir. Did you know Monroe Edwards?" To which the narrator answers, "No, I was never socially acquainted with any forgers" (670). In a way Mr. Cutlets has got Bartleby right, since forgery involves the exact copying of someone else's handwriting in order to make a false document that functions performatively as if it were genuine. Bartleby is a species of forger in reverse. He copies documents all right, but he does this in such a way as to deprive them of their power to make anything happen. On the other hand, when the narrator has copied documents checked, corrected, and made functional, he is himself performing an act of forgery. He may not be socially acquainted with any forgers, but he is in a manner of speaking one himself.

The arrangement he makes with Mr. Cutlets to feed Bartleby in prison is the narrator's last attempt to reincorporate Bartleby into society. There is much emphasis on eating in the story, on what the narrator's different employees eat and drink and on how little Bartleby eats, apparently nothing at all in prison: "'I prefer not to dine to-day,' said Bartleby, turning away. 'It would disagree with me; I am unused to dinners.' So saying he slowly moved to the other side of the inclosure, and took up a position fronting the dead-wall" (670). Eating is one of the basic ways to share our common humanity. This Bartleby refuses, or rather he says he would prefer not to share in the ritual of eating. To refuse that is in the end deadly. Bartleby's death makes him what he has been all along, a bit of death in the midst of life.

It is entirely appropriate that the narrator's account of Bartleby should end with Bartleby's death, not because any biography should end with the death of the biographee but because in death Bartleby becomes what he has always already been. As I have said, his "I would prefer not to" is strangely oriented toward the future. It opens the future, but a future of perpetual not-yet. It can only come as death, and death is that which can never be present. There, at the end, the narrator finds the corpse of Bartleby, "strangely huddled at the base of the wall, his knees drawn up, and lying on his side, his head touching the cold stones" (671). In an earlier version, the "Bartleby" fragment in the Melville family papers in the Gansevoort-Lansing Collection at the New York Public Library, Bartleby is found by the narrator lying in a white-washed room with his head against a tombstone: "It was clean, well-lighted and scrupulously white washed. The head-stone was standing up against the wall, and stretched on a blanket at its base, his head touching the cold marble and his feet upon the threshold lay the wasted form of Bartleby."

The corpse of Bartleby is not the presence of Bartleby. It is his eternal absence. In death he becomes what he has always been, a cadaver who "lives without dining," as the narrator says to the grub-man. Bartleby returns at death, in the final version of the story, to a fetal position. He is the incursion into life of that unattainable realm somewhere before birth and after death. But the word "realm" is misleading. What Bartleby brings is not a realm in the sense of place we might go. It is the otherness that all along haunts or inhabits life from the inside. This otherness can by no method, such as the long series of techniques the narrator tries, be accounted for, narrated, rationalized, or in any other way reassimilated into ordinary life, though it is a permanent part of that ordinary life. Bartleby is the alien that may neither be thrust out the door nor domesticated, brought into the family, given citizenship papers. Bartleby is the invasion of death into life, but not death as something from outside life. He is death as the other side of life or the cohabitant with life. "Death," nevertheless, is not the proper name for this ghostly companion of life, as if it were an allegorical meaning identified at last. Nor is "Death" its generic or common name. "Death" is a catachresis for what can never be named properly.

THE NARRATOR'S LAST METHOD of attempting to deal with Bartleby is his narration, going all the way from "I am a rather elderly man" to "Ah Bartleby! Ah humanity!" This narration is explicitly said to be written down and addressed to a "reader." It repeats for a more indeterminate reader, that is, for whoever happens to read it, the quasi-legal deposition he has made before the proper officer of "the Tombs, or to speak more properly, the Halls of Justice" (668). If the narrator can encompass Bartleby with words, if he can do justice to him, he may simultaneously have accounted for him, naturalized him after all, and freed himself from his unfulfilled obligation. He will have made an adequate response to the demand Bartleby has made on him. The narrator, that is, may have justified himself while doing justice to Bartleby.

This is impossible because Bartleby cannot be identified. His story cannot be told. But the reader at the end knows better just why this is so, since we have watched the narrator try one by one a whole series of strategies for accounting for someone and has seen them one by one fail. This failure leaves Bartleby still imperturbably bringing everything to to a halt or indefinitely postponing everything with his "I would prefer not to." The narrator's account is not so much an account as an apology for his failure to give an adequate account.

The narrator's writing is also an attempt at a reading, a failed attempt to read Bartleby. In this sense it is the first in a long line of attempts to read Bartleby the scrivener, though the narrator's successors do this by trying to read the text written by Melville, "Bartleby the Scrivener." Just as Bartleby by his immovable presence in the narrator's office has demanded to be read and accounted for by him, so Melville's strange story demands to be read and accounted for. Nor have readers failed to respond to the demand. A large secondary literature has grown up around "Bartleby," remarkable for its multiplicity and diversity. All claim in one way or another to have identified Bartleby and to have accounted for him, to have done him justice. They tend to exemplify that function of policing or putting things in their place which is entrusted by our society to literary studies as one realm among many of the academic forms of accounting or accounting for. In the case of the essays on "Bartleby" this accounting often takes one or the other of two main forms, as Warminski has observed. These forms could be put under the aegis of the two-pronged last paragraph of the story—

"Ah Bartleby! Ah humanity!"—or they might be said to fly in the face either of Bartleby's "But I am not particular" or of the manifest failure of the narrator's attempt to draw close to Bartleby by way of "the bond of a common humanity." Many of the essays try to explain Bartleby either by making him an example of some universal type, for example "existential man," or by finding some particular original or explanatory context for him, for example one of Melville's acquaintances who worked in a law office, or some aspect of nineteenth-century capitalism in America.[6] But Bartleby is neither general nor particular: he is neutral. As such, he disables reading by any of these strategies, any attempt to put "Bartleby the Scrivener" in its place by answering the question, "In mercy's name, who is he?"

No doubt my own reading also claims to have identified Bartleby, in this case by defining him as the neutral in-between that haunts all thinking and living by dialectical opposition. All readings of the story, including my own, are more ways to call in the police. They are ways of trying to put Bartleby in his place, to convey him where we want to put him, to make sense of him, even if it is an accounting that defines him as the nonsense that inhabits all sense-making. All readings attempt in one way or another to fulfill what the narrator has tried and failed to do: to tell Bartleby's story in a way that will allow us to assimilate him and the story into the vast archives of rationalization that make up the secondary literature of our profession. We are institutionalized to do that work of policing for our society. None of these techniques of assimilation works any better than any of the narrator's methods, and we remain haunted by Bartleby, but haunted also by "Bartleby the Scrivener: A Story of Wall-Street." I claim, however, that my accounting succeeds where the others fail by showing (though that is not quite the right word) why it is that "accounting for" in any of its usual senses cannot work, either for the story or for the character the story poses.

WHAT DOES ALL THIS have to do with Pygmalion, with prosopopoeia, and with the ethics of reading? It is easy to see the answer for the ethics of reading. We cannot identify our ethical responsibility to a person we cannot identify, whose story we cannot tell.

None of this is possible with Bartleby. On the other hand, in his ghostly way, Bartleby demands with calm authority that the narrator take responsibility for him. Where does his authority to make this demand come from? No answer is given in the text of the story, any more than an explanation is given, in the text of Hawthorne's "The Minister's Black Veil," of why Reverend Hooper dons the veil. In the case of Melville's story, the narrator's inability to fulfill his responsibility to Bartleby is analogous to our inability to read this text in the sense of providing a satisfactory interpretation based on what the text says. On the one hand the story demands to be read, with an authority like that of Bartleby himself over the narrator. Imperiously, imperatively, it says, "Read me!" On the other hand it cannot be read. It demands an impossible task, and the reader remains paralyzed by the text, called upon to act but unable to act.

Is this not a strange permutation of the story of Pygmalion and Galatea? Here the reader, like the narrator in the story, is put in the position of Galatea. Rather than being the story of the bringing to life of a statue and of a man who falls in love with the statue he has made, "Bartleby" tells about the turning of a living man into a statue. In a double reversal of the Pygmalion story, it is told by the statue, and it is a story of the petrifaction of the living.

This unsettling reversal of a model story has at least one other example in Melville's writings. The odd and powerful prefatory sketch in *The Piazza Tales,* where "Bartleby the Scrivener" first appeared in book form, is an apparently autobiographical account of how Melville had a porch built on his house in western Massachusetts. He had it built, strangely enough, on the north side of the house, where he could get a view of Mt. Greylock, standing amid smaller mountains like Charlemagne surrounded by his peers. The story he tells is of an excursion to walk to a certain house in the mountains with a window he had often seen magically catching the light. There he meets "a lonely girl, sewing at a lonely window. A pale-cheeked girl, and fly-specked window, with wasps about the mended upper panes" (629). The teller of this tale, presumably Melville himself, is not shown as consciously aware of the anterior story he is repeating, any more than the narrator of "Bartleby the Scrivener" is aware he is playing the role of Galatea.

Yet no careful reader can doubt that Melville the author as opposed to Melville the narrator of the sketch means the anecdote to be a reversed version of the story of Shakespeare's "Marianna at the moated grange" in *Measure for Measure,* and of Tennyson's new version of that, "Marianna." Melville's sketch has many echoes of Tennyson's poem, for example the detail of the flies and wasps in the window where Marianna sits sewing. What is moving about Melville's version is that it is told from the point of view of the object of this New England Marianna's perpetually unsatisfied longing. The girl he meets in the isolated farmhouse tells the narrator that she looks in longing at a distant house, the narrator's own house with its piazza facing north: "Oh, if I could but once get to yonder house, and but look upon whoever the happy being is that lives there! A foolish thought: why do I think it? Is it that I live so lonesome, and know nothing?" (634). The strangest thing of all in this strange story is that the narrator denies he is the one she seeks. He leaves her in the perpetual dissatisfaction of an "if only," neither disillusioned nor rid of her weary desire: "I, too, know nothing; and, therefore, cannot answer; but, for your sake, Marianna, well could wish that I were that happy one of the happy house you dream you see; for then you would behold him now, and, as you say, this weariness might leave you" (634). To tell the story of Marianna from the perspective of the absent beloved is to recognize that her desire can never be assuaged. Melville is by no means the happy one in the happy house, and Marianna's weariness can never leave her. To feel oneself the mistaken object of such unfulfillable desire is to feel disembodied, made unreal by one's awareness of the impossibillity of being what the other wants.

Something of the same uncannily moving effect of the reversal of a familiar story occurs in the way "Bartleby" reverses the story of Pygmalion. It might be thought at first that Bartleby is the statue, since he is so immobile, stands motionless for long hours facing the brick wall, like one of those public performers who have trained themselves to stand frozen: "His face was leanly composed; his gray eye dimly calm. Not a wrinkle of agitation rippled him" (643). And the narrator does twice compare him to some form of stone: "I should have as soon thought of turning my pale plaster-of-paris bust of Cicero out of doors" (644); "But he answered not a word, like the last column of some ruined temple" (658). But if Bartleby is the statue and not the sculptor, his immobility has a power to immobilize the narrator, to turn him at least momentarily to stone. The narrator is rendered motionless until he can leap over the hurdle of Bartleby's "I would prefer not to" and start moving again. I have already quoted these passages but cite the last again, noting that it has an extraordinary stylistic beauty: "I was thunderstruck. For an instant I stood like the man who, pipe in mouth, was killed one cloudless afternoon long ago in Virginia, by summer lightning; at his own warm open window he was killed, and remained leaning out there upon the dreamy afternoon, till someone touched him, when he fell" (659).

Repeatedly the narrator is paralyzed by Bartleby. His motion, when it begins again, becomes more and more a wandering vagrancy, no longer the careful lawyer's directed movement toward a goal. If the narrator compares Bartleby to his pale bust of Cicero, the narrator himself is turned into that bust when he tries to get Bartleby to tell him something of his earlier life: "He did not look at me while I spoke, but kept his glance fixed upon my bust of Cicero, which, as I then sat, was directly behind me, some six inches above my head" (654). This Cicero is no golden-tongued orator, master of efficacious language, under whose aegis the narrator plies his trade of conveyancing. This Cicero is forever mute.

Bartleby, moreover, has a power of petrifaction and ruination not just over the narrator but over all of Wall Street. Wall Street on Sunday, when only Bartleby is there, is as deserted as the ruined city of Petra (651). Bartleby making his home there is "sole spectator of a solitude which he has seen all populous—a sort of innocent and transformed Marius brooding among the ruins of Carthage" (651). If Bartleby is statuelike, he has power to turn those around him into statues and, in the narrator's figures, to turn Wall Street into a ruined city.

The final petrifaction performed by this strange Pygmalion in reverse is of the reader, of you and me. Although "Bartleby the Scrivener" has an inexhaustible power to generate commentary, none of it seems to get quite to the point, as if it too were fugitive and vagrant, or as if it were speech to a mute bust of Cicero. This is a Cicero whose silence reduces the one who addresses it to silence too. In the end, and in fact all along the way, the reader, no matter how voluble, is turned to stone. The reader is made like a speechless bust of Cicero, or struck by lightning like the man from Virginia, or turned into a pillar of salt like Lot's wife, as punishment for transgressing the prohibition against looking back and trying to read.

CHAPTER 5

Death Mask:
Blanchot's *L'arrêt de mort*

An important passage in George Eliot's *Daniel Deronda* (1876) speaks of the susceptibility of the heroine, Gwendolen Harleth, to sudden inexplicable fits of terror or "spiritual dread." She has these fits when faced with open spaces: "Solitude in any wide scene impressed her with an undefined feeling of immeasurable existence aloof from her, in the midst of which she was helplessly incapable of asserting herself."[1]

A strange paragraph by Maurice Blanchot entitled "Une scène primitive" (A Primitive Scene) published a century later, in 1976, describes a similar experience. The spiritual dread is ascribed this time to a child of seven or eight standing at the window and looking at a wintry scene outside:

> Ce qu'il voit, le jardin, les arbres d'hiver, le mur d'une maison; tandis qu'il voit, sans doute à la manière d'un enfant, son espace de jeu, il se lasse et lentement regarde en haut vers le ciel ordinaire, avec les nuages, la lumière grise, le jour terne et sans lointain. Ce qui se passe ensuite: le ciel, le *même* ciel, soudain ouvert, noir absolument et vide absolument, révélant (comme par la vitre brisée) une telle absence que tout 'sy est depuis toujours et à jamais perdu, au point que s'y affirme et s'y dissipe le savior vertigineux que rien est ce qu'il y a, et d'abord rien au delà.

> What he sees, the garden, the winter trees, the wall of a house; while he looks, no doubt in the way a child does, on his play area, he gets bored and slowly looks higher toward the ordinary sky, with the clouds, the gray light, the day flat and without distance. What happens then: the sky, the *same* sky, suddenly opens, black absolutely,

revealing (as if the window had broken) such an absence that everything is since forever and for forever lost, to the point at which there
is affirmed and dispersed there the vertiginous knowledge that nothing is what there is there, and primarily nothing beyond.[2]

"Rien est ce qu'il y a, et d'abord rien au delà": nothing is what
there is, and primarily nothing beyond.[3] As in the case of Wallace
Stevens' "The Snow Man," where the listener and watcher in the
snow, nothing himself, beholds "Nothing that is not there and the
nothing that is,"[4] the devastating experience of a transfiguration
that leaves the scene still exactly the same, the *same* sky, is the confrontation of a nothing that somehow is, has being, and absorbs
into itself any beyond or transcendence. In this primitive scene,
original and originating, for Blanchot's child, or possibly even for
Blanchot as a child, the sky definitely does not open to reveal heav-
enly light or choirs of angels. If the effect on Gwendolen Harleth
in Eliot's novel of confronting open space in solitude is hysterical
outbursts, the effect on Blanchot's child of an opening of a sky that
does not open is seemingly endless tears of a "joie ravageante"
(ravaging joy).

I take these details from *Daniel Deronda* and from Blanchot's "A
Primitive Scene" quite arbitrarily as parables for the dread some
readers may experience when they confront a text that seems irre-
ducibly strange, inexplicable, perhaps even mad, for example
Blanchot's *L'arrêt de mort*. As long as we have not identified the law
by which a text can be made reasonable, explicable, it is as if we
had come face to face with an immeasurable existence aloof from
us, perhaps malign, perhaps benign, in any case something we have
not yet mastered and assimilated into what we already know. It is
as if the sky had opened, while still remaining the same sky, for are
not those words on the page familiar and ordinary words, words
in our own language or mother tongue, words whose meaning we
know? And yet they have suddenly opened and become terrifying.
On the one hand, our task as readers is to transfer to reading Henry
James's injunction to the observer of life, the novice writer: "Try
to be one of the people on whom nothing is lost!"[5] A good reader,
that is to say, especially notices oddnesses, gaps, anacoluthons,
non sequiturs, apparently irrelevant details—all the marks of the
inexplicable, perhaps of the mad, in a text. On the other hand, the
reader's task is to reduce the inexplicable to the explicable, to find

its reason, its law, its ground. The task of the reader, it will be seen, is not too different from the task of the psychoanalyst.

Current criticism tends to propose one or another of the following three grounds on the basis of which the anomalies of narrative may be made lawful: (1) society, or the more or less hidden social and ideological pressures that impose themselves on storytelling and reveal themselves in oddness; (2) individual psychology, or the more or less hidden psychic pressures that impose themselves on storytelling and make it unaccountable; (3) language, or the more or less hidden rhetorical pressures, pressures from some torsion within language itself, that impose themselves on the storyteller and make it impossible for the story to maintain itself as a lucid and reasonable account.

The stories or "récits" of Maurice Blanchot, as well as his criticism, propose a fourth possibility. It is exceedingly difficult to name in so many words, though the whole task of the reader of Blanchot could be defined as an attempt to make this definition clear. This fourth possibility for the disturber of narrative sanity and coherence is a disruptive energy, but it is not society or individual psychology or language. This energy might be called religious, metaphysical, or ontological, but these words cannot be used here in a conventional way. To borrow a mode of locution familiar to readers of Blanchot, the disruptive energy is an "ontology without ontology." Nor is it to be defined as a species of negative theology.

Blanchot gives to this "something" that enters into the words, or between the words, the names of "il" (it); "la chose" (the thing); "mourir" (dying); "le neutre" (the neutral); "le retour éternel" (the eternal return); "écrire" (writing); "la pensée" (the thought); "la vérité" (the truth); "l'autre de l'autre" (the other of the other), meaning by the latter something encountered in our relations to other people, especially love, betrayal, and that ultimate betrayal, the death of the other. To list these words cannot convey much, except possibly, in their multiplicity and incoherence, a glimpse of the inadequacy of any one of them and of the way all of them must be figurative rather than literal, though figurative in a way that transcends the normal distinction between figurative and literal.

Blanchot's terms, moreover, play back and forth between the necessity of prosopopoeia and the impossibility of using prosopo-

poeia as an adequate figurative means of access to the impersonal
neutral, the other beyond the other person. This chapter will focus
on this necessity and impossibility. What sort of "thing" is it that
cannot be pinned down and labeled with a single name, so that all
names for it are improper, whether proper or generic? All Blanchot's writing is a patient, continuous attempt to answer this question, the question posed by the experience recorded in "Une scène
primitive." Only a fulfillment of the task of reading Blanchot's
L'arrêt de mort or perhaps his work as a whole will give the reader a
chance to answer this question, or at least to understand the question better. We must confront the fact that for Blanchot in his récits, as for the other authors discussed in this book, the figure of
prosopopoeia always intervenes between the author, the narrator,
the protagonist, or the reader, on the one hand, and on the other,
the "it" or "thing." The it or thing always presents itself in the
guise of a face or a person, though this presentation is as much a
barrier as a means of direct "confrontation," to use another latent
personification. But before approaching that face-to-face encounter I must identify two further features of my four proposed modes
of rationalizing, of finding grounds for the irrational or unaccountable in any narrative account.

   The first feature seems obvious, though it is evaded often
enough to need emphasizing. This is the imperialism of any one of
the four. Each as a mode of explanation demands to exercise sovereign control over the others, to make the others find their
ground in *it*. You cannot have all four at once or even any two of
them without having already implicitly grounded all but one in the
single, regal ur-explanation. Psychological explanations tend to
see linguistic, religious, or social explanations as ultimately finding their cause in individual human psychology. Social explanations see human psychology, language, and religion as epiphe-
nomena of underlying and determining social forces, the "real"
conditions of class, production, consumption, and exchange. Linguistic explanations tend to assert that society, psychology, and
religion are "all language," that is, generated by language in the
first place and ultimately to be explained by features of language.
"Religious" explanations (I call them that for want of a better term)
see society, psychology, and language as peripheral. Each of these
modes of grounding explanation asserts that it is the true principle

of reason, the true "Satz von Grund," the others bogus, an abyss. Each asserts a jealous will to power over the others.

The second feature of these four modes of explaining oddnesses in narrative is the strong resistance generated in some of those to whom they are proposed. The resistance, for instance, to Freud's assertion of a universal sexual etiology for neurosis is notorious. In Marxist theory, say Louis Althusser's in *For Marx*, "ideology" is the name given to the imaginary structures whereby men and women resist facing the real economic and social conditions of their existence. There is a tremendous resistance to totalizing explanations that say, or seem to say, "it's all language," the resistance encountered, for example, by structuralism, semiotics, and so-called deconstruction. Many people, finally, seem able to live on from day to day and from year to year, even as readers of literature, without seeing religious or metaphysical questions as having any sort of force. It appears not to be true that man is universally a religious animal. George Eliot describes eloquently Gwendolen's resistance to two of my sovereign principles of grounding. Blindness to religious questions is here strikingly equated with blindness to real economic and material conditions:

> She had no permanent consciousness of other fetters, or of more spiritual restraints, having always disliked whatever was presented to her under the name of religion, in the same way that some people dislike arithmetic and accounts: it had raised no other emotion in her, no alarm, no longing; so that the question whether she believed it had not occurred to her, any more than it had occurred to her to inquire into the conditions of colonial property and banking, on which, as she had had many opportunities of knowing, the family fortune was dependent. (pp. 89–90)

Why this resistance to looking into things, including works of literature, is so strong and so universal, I shall not attempt here to explain. Perhaps it is inexplicable, perhaps a general consensus that, as Conrad's Winnie Verloc in *The Secret Agent* puts it, "life doesn't stand much looking into."[6] It might be better not to know.

I turn now to *L'arrêt de mort*, with special attention to what the reader can learn about prosopopoeia. I shall attempt to look as far into that text as I dare or as my own resistance will allow.

The beginnings and endings of the two segments of this récit, as well as the blank space between the first and the second stories, are especially important as clues for reading the stories themselves. The beginnings and endings are places where the narrator speaks of his own resistances to writing down the account we hold in our hands. In the second paragraph the narrator tells the reader he wrote it all down once before, in 1940, and then destroyed it. In the first paragraph he says that if he has written novels, "les romans sont nés au moment où les mots ont commencé de reculer devant la vérité" (the novels have come into being just as the words begin to shrink back from the truth).[7] This warns us that the real truth is not in the words on the page, but somewhere else. In the last paragraph of the first narrative, the story of the arrested death of "J.," the narrator ends by saying: "je n'ai rien raconté d'extraordinaire ne même de surprenant. L'extraordinaire commence au moment où je m'arrête. Mais je ne suis plus maître d'en parler" (I have said nothing extraordinary or even surprising. What is extraordinary begins at the moment I stop. But I am no longer able to speak of it; 60; 30). Again, what most counts in this accounting could not be tallied up in writing. The first two paragraphs of the second narrative, about "N.," after the blank space on the page between the two narratives, assures the reader that "La vérité sera dite, tout ce qui s'est passé d'important sera dit" (The truth will be told, everything of importance that happened will be told), but then goes on to say, "Mais tout ne s'est pas encore passé" (But not everything has yet happened) and to hypothesize that in any case, "Il se peut que tous ces mots soient un rideau derrière lequel ce qui s'est joué ne cessera plus de se jouer" (It may be that all these words are a curtain behind which what happened will never stop happening; 61–62; 31). The words are a veil and the story is literally a cover for a story that never seems to get told.

The last paragraph, before the coda, asks enigmatically, "Qui peut dire: ceci est arrivé, parce que les événements l'ont permis? Ceci s'est passé, parce que, à un certain moment, les faits sont devenus trompeurs et, par leur agencement étrange, ont autorisé la vérité à s'emparer d'eux?" (Who can say: This happened, because certain events allowed it to happen? This occurred because, at a certain moment, the facts became misleading and because their strange juxtaposition entitled the truth to take possession of

them?" 146; 80). An odd proposition! Because the facts were misleading, a non sequitur or an anacoluthon, a failure in following,
the truth could take possession of them. The sentences, moreover,
are questions, not assertions. Well, who *can* say that? Can it be said
or not? The honest reader would like to know.

The narrator of *L'arrête de mort,* it can definitely be said, is reticent, evasive, and enigmatic. He withholds any direct statement of
the "truth" of his account. He insinuates repeatedly that the truth
is to be found not in the words but between them or outside them,
perphaps outside the borders of the récit altogether. As a preliminary attempt to explain this exasperating situation, I turn to the
last paragraph of all.

The last sentence of *L'arrêt de mort*—or one might even say the
last sentence beyond the last sentence, since Blanchot deleted this
sentence, and the whole coda it terminates, between the 1948 edition and the second edition of 1971—that postultimate sentence is
the following: "Et plus encore, qu'il essaie d'imaginer la main qui
les écrit: s'il la voyait, peut-être lire lui deviendrait-il une tâche sér-
ieuse" (And what is more let him [the reader] try to imagine the
hand that is writing them [these pages]; if he saw it, then perhaps
reading would become a serious task for him).

Why did Blanchot delete these words? In what sense is reading a
"task," and a serious task at that? What does this have to do with
imagining the hand that is writing the words? One remembers
Keats's phrase in the last poem he wrote, about his own hand, "this
living hand, now warm and capable / Of earnest grasping,"
marked by imminent death but caught by the words in the act of
writing about "this living hand, now warm and capable." What
writing may have to do with the hand that writes is, perhaps, inscribed in those ordinary words and phrases whose inherent figure
we tend to forget: "manuscript," "handwriting," "written by
hand," "amanuensis," "maintain," "hand" in the sense of distinc-
tive handwriting. "Maintain" means to hold in one's hand, "main-
tenir," as the reader holds a book in his hands or the writer holds
the pen, and tries to maintain control of the story he is writing or
reading. "Maintenant" is the French word for "now," the present.
If Blanchot is right to say that there is no now or "maintenant" in
the act of writing or reading, just as there is none in the act of

dying, the attempt to maintain control of a story one is writing or reading, to have it in hand in the present, is doomed to failure.

J., the dying woman in the first of the two stories making up *L'arrêt de mort,* has a cast made of her hands, while the second woman, N., has a cast made of her hands and her head. The latter is called "cette chose" (that thing; 144; 79). The face and the hand, each marked with lines that can be read as signs of the person's character, seem perhaps each a displacement of the other. And a curious reversal occurs here. The hand that writes and its double, the face, are in their replicas both survivors of and survived by the text that the living hand has written. One normally thinks that the once warm and living hand dies, decays, and vanishes into the earth, to be survived by the pages it has written. In *L'arrêt de mort* the cast of the hands, the cast of the head, will survive the deaths of the two women. As opposed to the death mask of Keats, the casts, moreover, are made on living hands and face, "opération étrange quand elle est faite sur des vivants, parfois dangereuse, sur-prenenante, opération qui . . ." (a process which is strange when it is carried out on living people, sometimes dangerous, surprising, a process which . . .)—the narrator stops and puts three points of ellipses in the text (138; 75). A process which . . . what? These casts are powerful symbols in the text for the text itself, the words on the page we are reading as survivors of the narrator, the two women, and the events in the story.

The figure of the casts suggests that the text itself is a prosopo-poeia, the giving of a face to the absent, the inanimate, the dead. The text survives as the cast or simulacrum of the events it records, life mask become death mask, just as the casts survived the two women. Anyone who reads the text of *L'arrêt de mort* becomes an-other survivor. Perhaps it might even be said that we fit the mask to our own faces, the cast to our own hands, shape our hands and faces to their shape. We maintain the story's pattern in an extended life, an arrested death, by holding it in our hands. Reading too is a kind of writing or rewriting that is an act of prosopopoeia, like Pygmalion giving life to the statue. This chain of transference goes from the events to the cast of them in the words, to the revivifying of that cast in the act of reading. But that revivifying is at the same time death-giving, or it is a way for the reader to participate in an

endless chain that maintains the perpetual act of dying, a postponement of death in an "arrêt de mort." When the narrator remains
with J. in her hospital room after the scene in which he has called
her back from the dead by uttering her first name, at one moment
she points her finger at him and says to the nurse: "voyez donc la
mort" (take a good look at death; 55; 28). Narration, like reading,
it seems, may be as much death–dealing as life–giving. It is in this
sense that reading is a serious task and that imagining the hand that
writes the words becomes a serious task. This is the task of partic-
ipating in the endless process of dying that is Blanchot's version of
the Pygmalion story.

A passage in *Le pas au-delà* affirms in another way this connection of death, writing, the hand that writes, prosopopoeia, and the
reader who brings back to life what has been written: "Mourir,
comme la main qui à peu de distance du papier se tiendrait immobile sans rien écrire ou même irait de l'avant sans rien tracer (peut-
être parce que ce qu'elle écrit ne se révélera que plus tard selon les
procédés grossiers de l'encre sympathetique)" (Dying, like the
hand which at a slight distance from the page holds itself immobile
without writing anything or even moves forward without tracing
anything [perhaps because what it writes will not reveal itself until
later on according to the crude operations of sympathetic ink]).[8]
Writing, like dying, is invisible in itself or produces only "nothing." Writing is the phantasmal movement forward over the page
by the hand that holds the pen. Reading is a serious task because it
"develops" the writing, the dying, after the fact. It makes them
visible and maintains them in visibility. Reading is the heat or the
chemical that makes the sympathetic ink visible. *Death Sentence,*
the book one holds in one's hands, in any copy or translation, is
"l'arrêt de mort" in the sense of an arrest, reprieve, or suspension
of death. The book is deferral of death in an interminable process
of dying. This arresting of death, the transformation of death into
dying, is passed on to the reader as the task of keeping that writing
hand alive by the act of reading the words on the page, being
haunted by them. Reading is a serious task in that the reader becomes, however unwillingly, the agent of the arrest of death.

This is so unpleasant a role that one would do almost anything
to avoid being caught in it, this passing on of a sentence of death,

endlessly affirmed, endlessly delayed in its execution. One might refrain, for example, from reading at all, or one might try to destroy all or part of the book, put an end to it, put it to death. But, as Blanchot says in the first sentences of the canceled coda, if you try to cancel the text as death mask, you become only more caught up in the perpetuation of this endless process of dying. You become the victim of the narrator, not the end but the beginning of his story. Far from being able to end the story, you become the agent of its continuation.

Blanchot's words about this are slightly enigmatic, as is so often the case with him. They do not say perspicuously what the reader who has undertaken the serious task of reading them may at first think they ought to say, if he assumes they will be logical. Something ("the truth"?) twists the words or enters into the spaces between the words and makes them say something else:

> Ces pages peuvent ici trouver leur terme, et ce que je viens d'écrire, nulle suite ne m'y fera rien ajouter ni rien ôter. Cela demeure, cela demeurera jusqu'au bout. Qui voudrait l'effacer de moi-même, en échange de cette fin que je cherche vainement, deviendrait à son tour le début de ma propre histoire, et il serait ma proie. Dans l'obscurité, il me verrait; ma parole serait son silence, et il croirait régner sur le monde, mais cette souveraineté serait encore la mienne, son néant le mien et lui aussi saurait qu'il n'y a pas de fin à partir d'un homme qui veut finir seul. (148)

> These pages can end here, and nothing that follows what I have just written will make me add anything to it or take anything from it. This remains, this will remain until the very end. Whoever would obliterate it from me, in exchange for that end which I am searching for in vain, would himself become the beginning of my own story, and would become my victim. In darkness, he would see me: my word would be his silence, and he would think he was holding sway over the world, but that sovereignty would still be mine, his nothingness mine, and he too would know that there is no end for a man who wants to end alone. (81)

The careful reader will note that the narrator adds something in the act of saying that nothing will make him add anything. This is a classic linguistic double bind, like a slip of paper on which is written the words, "Burn this without reading it." In order to find out the law you are forbidden to transgress, you must already have transgressed that law. In *L'arrêt de mort* the writer cannot write the words saying the text is finished without, in that enunciation of his resolve, breaking the resolve. Unless of course when he says "These pages can end here" he means to include the last page he is in the act of writing, that is, the letters he has just formed saying "These words can end here." In the latter case he would be caught in another infinite regress generated by the odd act of writing about the act of writing the words the pen is forming about the act of writing. The writer would be obliged to go on adding more and more last pages in an ever-renewed, ever-unsuccessful attempt to write after the end about the end of the writing and so put an end to the writing.

Moreover, if the last page is included in the text of which he says, "These pages can end here and nothing that follows what I have just written will make me add anything to it or take anything away from it," then when for the second edition of 1971 Blanchot deletes the last page, he is breaking the second half of his self-imposed prohibition. He is taking something away from what he said nothing would make him truncate. Either way he himself becomes subject to the curse he then invokes on the reader.

But what does Blanchot mean by "nulle suite" (nothing that follows)? He appears to mean no further events in his life, no more experiences with other women. On the other hand, he could mean nothing that follows in the sense of "no further written words," such as the words he is in the act of writing.

The curse put in the text by the writer on those who, after his death or even before it, falsify that text in any way—by alteration, erasure, or addition—has a long history. This is analogous to the tradition of the malediction on the tombstone: "Cursed be he who moves these bones." (Who, it might be asked, utters this curse? The dead man? His surviving friends and relatives? Some religious authority who speaks for God? The tombstone itself?) The analogy between the two curses is a crucial aspect of the general analogy between the act of writing and the act of dying that all Blanchot's work explores. In *Le pas au-delà* he affirms, while at the same time saying the affirmation is fallacious, that "le vivre est à l'écriture ce que serait la mort au mouvement de mourir . . . écrire, mourir sont ce qu'il y a de plus discret, toujours cependant ébruités par le Dernier Acte public, la grande pierre tombale du Livre, la souveraine publication de la présence absente" (the book is to writing what death would be to the movement of dying . . . writing, dying are what is most discrete, always nevertheless bruited about by the publicity of the Last Act, the great tomblike stone of the Book, the sovereign publication of the absent presence; 143). The published book we hold in our hands is the surviving tombstone of the living act of writing. The tombstone-book is at the same time in a strange analogical resonance with the act of dying. To add to the book or to take away from it is therefore like that extreme act of desecration, vandalizing a tomb or disturbing a buried corpse.

I have said that the tradition of the curse on whoever tampers with a book is a long one. In a drafted preface to the *Confessions,* Rousseau says:

> Qui que vous soyez que ma destinée ou ma confiance ont fait l'arbitre du sort de ce cahier, je vous conjure par mes malheurs, par vous entrailles, et au noms de toute l'espéce humaine de ne pas anéantir un ouvrage unique et utile, lequel peut servir de prémiére piéce de comparaison pour l'étude des hommes, qui certainement est encore à commencer, et de ne pas oter à l'honneur de ma mémoire le seul monument sûr de mon caractére qui n'ait pas été défiguré par mes ennemis.

> Whoever you are that my destiny or my confidence has made the arbiter of the fate of this notebook, I conjure you by my sufferings, by your entrails, and in the name of the entire human species not to destroy a unique and useful work that can serve as the primary standard for the study of men, which is certainly yet to begin, and not to take away from the honor of my memory the sole sure monument of my character that has not been disfigured by my enemies.[9]

Curses on you if you destroy this manuscript, says Rousseau, since it is the only accurate cast of my face and hands, the only sure monument of my character. All the other portraits, casts, or representations have been disfigured by my enemies, as vandals disfigure a statue. "Figure" in French, it will be remembered, means "face" as well as "form" and "figure of speech." As for Blanchot, so for Rousseau, the book is a life mask that becomes a death mask,

a funeral monument. The book arrests death in a species of prosopopoeia. To destroy it would be like defacing a tomb.

The most important allusion in Blanchot's warning against adding or taking away from his book is to the last verses of Revelation.
This book ends the New Testament in the Christian Bible. These
verses, with their terrifying curses on anyone who tampers with
the text, are also almost certainly the "source" of Blanchot's use,
at two crucial places in *L'arrêt de mort,* of the performative or vocative "Come." "Come" is vocative if it is addressed to a person,
performative if it is addressed to a "thought" that is "performed"
into existence. The words call into being a thought that does not
preexist the words "Come" and the rest. But, it could be argued,
there is a performative aspect to all vocatives, as well as a vocative
aspect to all performatives.

Three such moments punctuate *L'arrêt de mort*, though in the
first case the first name of J. is used instead of "Come." That ap-
pellation is never given in the text, as if it were a power that must
be withheld from the reader. In the most extraordinary episode of
the novel, the name is employed as a magic command to call J.
back from the dead, as Orpheus called Eurydice from the arms of
Dis or as Pygmalion brought Galatea alive by caressing the cold
marble. The passage turns on those motifs of the cast, effigy, and
hands and face so important throughout *L'arrêt de mort*:

> Elle n'était déjà plus qu'une statue, elle absolument vivante. C'est
> alors que je regardai ses mains. . . . je fus, en un instant, submergé
> par la tristesse. Je me penchai sur elle, je l'appelai à haute voix, d'une
> voix forte, par son prénom; et aussitôt—je puis le dire, il n'y eut pas
> une seconde d'intervalle—une sorte de souffle sortit de sa bouche
> encore serrée, un soupir qui peu à peu devint un léger, un faible cri;
> presque en même temps—de cela aussi je suis sûr—ses bras boug-
> èrent, essayèrent de se lever. A ce moment, les paupières étaient en-
> core tout à fait closes. Mais, une seconde après, peut-être deux, bru-
> squement elles s'ouvrirent, et elles s'ouvrirent sur quelque chose de
> terrible dont je ne parlerai pas, sur le regard le plus terrible qu'un
> être vivant puisse recevoir . . . (40–41)

She who had been absolutely alive was already no more than a
statue. It was then that I looked at her hands . . . for an instant I was
overwhelmed by sadness. I leaned over her, I called to her by her

first name; and immediately—I can say there wasn't a second's interval—a sort of breath came out of her compressed mouth, a sigh
which little by little became a light, weak cry; almost at the same
time—I'm sure of this—her arms moved, tried to rise. At that moment, her eyelids were still completely shut. But a second after-
ward, perhaps two, they opened abruptly and they opened to reveal
something terrible which I will not talk about, the most terrible
look which a human being can receive . . . (20)

In the second episode, Blanchot's narrator speaks to N., in what
is surely one of the least erotic bedroom scenes in all literature. The
relation between the narrator and N. begins with a disembodied
caress of one hand by another: "de main plus patiente, il n'y en eut
jamais, ni de plus calme, ni de plus amicale; c'est pourquoi elle ne
frémit pas quand lentement une autre main, froide, se forma
auprès d'elle, et cette main, la plus immobile et la plus froide, la
laissa reposer sur elle sans frémir" (there had never been a more
patient hand, nor one more calm, nor more friendly; that is why it
did not tremble when another hand, a cold hand, slowly formed
beside it, and that hand, so still and so cold, allowed mine to rest
on it without trembling; (127; 69). After a long time of this, the
narrator says, "un moment arriva où, la voyant toujours mortelle-
ment froid, je m'approchai encore et je lui dis: 'Viens'" (a moment
came when I saw that she was still mortally cold, and I drew closer
and said to her: "Come"; 128; 69).

In the third episode Blanchot's narrator speaks, in the last sentence before the deleted postscript, not of the woman, Nathalie,
but of the thought that the events of the récit have brought into
proximity to the narrator. This proximity is like an erotic embrace
that is also a deadly struggle: "je l'ai aimé et je n'ai aimeée qu'elle
. . . je lui ai donné toute ma force et elle m'a donné toute la sienne,
de sorte que cette force trop grande, incapable d'être ruinée par
rien, nous voue peut-étre à un malheur sans mesure, mais, si cela
est, ce malheur je le prends sur moi et je m'en réjouis sans mesure
et, à elle, je dis éternellement: 'Viens,' et éternellement, elle est là"
(I have loved it and I have loved only it . . . I gave it all my strength
and it gave me all its strength, so that this strength is too great, it
is incapable of being ruined by anything, and condemns us, perhaps, to immeasurable unhappiness, but if that is so, I take this

unhappiness on myself and I am immeasurably glad of it and to that thought I say eternally, "Come," and eternally it is there; 146–147; 80). The French word for "thought" is feminine and therefore is spoken of as "elle," she. This means that there is an implicit identification of N. or J. and "that thought." The invocation of J. and N., the calling to them by saying "Come" or a proper name, ultimately reveals itself to be a narrative prosopopoeia for the performative invocation of a strange "thought" that is the hidden theme of the récit, as it is the theme of all Blanchot's work.

Here are the last five verses of the book of Revelation:

17 And the Spirit and the bride say, Come. And let him that heareth say, Come. And let him that is athirst come. And whosoever will, let him take the water of life freely.
18 For I testify unto every man that heareth the words of the prophecy and of this book. If any man shall add unto these things, God shall add unto him the plagues that are written in this book:
19 And if any man shall take away from the words of the book of this prophecy, God shall take away his part out of the book of life, and out of the holy city, and from the things which are written in this book.
20 He which testifieth these things saith, *Surely I come quickly.* Amen. Even so, come, Lord Jesus.
21 The grace of our Lord Jesus Christ be with you all. Amen. (King James Version)

After having said that the human spirit as the bride of Christ says "Come," John, the author of Revelation, says "Come," in answer to Christ's promise to come: "Surely I come quickly." John performs in the text the "Come" rather than merely citing it or mentioning it. His figure of the human soul as the bride of Christ means that the erotic sense of "Come," employed of course by Blanchot, is also present in Revelation. Between the "Come" as citation and the "Come" as performative comes the terrifying interdict against changing the text. It is as if the efficacy of "Come" as an invocation of the second coming, the last unveiling of the apocalypse, were dependent on just this collection of words in just this order, no more, no less. If you add to them, the plagues written in the book will be added to you. If you take any words away, all the promises written in the book will be taken away from you.

If you tamper with the book, the book itself will become a malediction, not an invocation.

Something of the same sort happens in that canceled ending of *L'arrêt de mort*. The narrator says that what he has written will remain until the very end ("jusqu'au bout"). End of what? End of his life? End of the world? In any case, the end of the end, the end beyond the end, "le pas au-delà." The narrator's end is deferred by the activity of reading that might try to assist the narrator in reaching the end: "Whoever would obliterate it [the récit] from me, in exchange for that end which I am searching for in vain, would himself become the beginning of my own story."

Blanchot here adds a new twist, a notion of interminability, the endless deferment of the end, to Christ's promise in Revelation to come quickly. In Blanchot's case, the curse of the reader who would arrest *L'arrêt de mort* by ending it, obliterating the text, is to become condemned to repeat the text. The reader will become haunted or possessed by the text so that he or she will be the beginning once more, all over again, of the story told by the text. This is another double bind. If you try to obliterate the text, so that it does not have to be read, you are condemned to begin it again. If you do read it, you are condemned to begin it again. You will become the next in an endless chain of repetitions, haunted by the story. Either way you have had it, and you have had it in the very act whereby you read the words that tell you you have had it.

Author, reader, and, finally, critic, all three in a chain, are condemned to transgress the interdict in the act of understanding it. As soon as the critic comments on the text, she is adding to it more words, words that are not already there, as I am now caught in the act of doing. On the other hand, she commits also the sin of taking away, since she does not, except in a few exceptional cases such as Roland Barthes's *S/Z*, cite all of the text to which she is adding her commentary. And what of translation, for example the translation of *L'arrêt de mort* into *Death Sentence*? Does it not also both add and take away, desecrate the text by adding all those new words in a foreign language while at the same time obliterating, defacing, the original? The text of *L'arrêt de mort*, like the text of the Bible, both demands commentary and at the same time forbids it as a dangerous desecration.

The wish to write "I write my death"[10] as a meaningful sentence is impossible to fulfill. If one does not die alone or finish alone, one does not die in company either. Dying in company is instead an interminable process of dying, passed on from story to story, from author to narrator to reader to critic to translator, ad infinitem, each doomed to incarnate a new form of Blanchot's version of Pygmalion.

WHAT IS THE relation of translation to prosopopeia? Walter Benjamin in a famous essay speaks of "the task of the translator," "Die Aufgabe des Übersetzers." The word "Aufgabe" in Benjamin's title means task, debt, obligation, or burden. The word implies that the effort of carrying over the meaning of a work from its original language to a second language is a tremendous responsibility. In fact, translation may be an impossible task, though that does not keep works from getting translated. But the shoulders of the translator always bend and break under the burden, the "Aufgabe." This, according to Benjamin, is because the "original" is not original. It is already a wandering of language in perpetual exile from a lost original language. The result is that both the original and the translation are recognizable "wie Scherben als Bruchstück eines Gefässes, als Bruchstück einer grösseren Sprache" (as fragments of a greater language, just as fragments are part of a vessel").[11]

No gluing together of fragments will put the Humpty Dumpty of that lost "greater language" together again. As Benjamin says: "In dieser reinen Sprache, die nichts mehr meint und nichts mehr ausdrückt, sondern als ausdrucksloses und schöpferisches Wort das in allen Sprachen Gemeinte ist, trifft endlich alle Mitteilung, aller Sinn und alle Intention auf eine Schicht, in der sie zu erlöschen bestimmt sind" (In this pure language—which no longer means or expresses anything but is, as expressionless and creative Word, that which is meant in all languages—all information, all sense, and all intention finally encounter a stratum in which they are destined to be extinguished; 67; 80).

The paradox is that the most original and expressive language, that which all languages, *L'arrêt de mort* in French and *Death Sentence* in English, mean is at the same time expressionless, "ausdruckslos," the place where meaning or information, all that a

critic can discuss, is destined to be extinguished. The locus of truth
is incompatible with the articulation of truth.

Something of the same sort is said by Blanchot himself in an
essay from *Amitié*, "Traduir." The essay is a review of Maurice
Gandillac's translation of Benjamin's *Illuminationen*:

> on suppose que chaque langage aurait un seul et même mode de
> visée, et toujours de même signification, et que tous ces modes de
> visée pourraient devenir complémentaires. Mais Benjamin suggère
> autre chose: tout traducteur vit de la différence des langues, toute
> traduction est fondée sur cette différence, tout en poursuivant, ap-
> paremment, le dessein pervers de la supprimer. (L'oeuvre bien tra-
> duite est louée de deux façons opposées: on ne la croirait pas tra-
> duite, dit-on; ou encore, c'est vraiment la même oeuvre, on la retrouve
> merveilleusement identique; mais, dans le premier cas, on efface, au
> bénéfice de la nouvelle langue, l'origine de l'oeuvre; dans le second
> cas, au bénéfice de l'oeuvre, l'originalité des deux langues; dans tous
> les cas, quelque chose d'essentiel est perdu.) A la vérité, la traduc-
> tion n'est nullement destinée à faire disparaître la différence dont elle
> est au contraire le jeu: constamment elle y fait allusion, elle la dissi-
> mule, mais parfois en la révélant et souvent en l'accentuant, elle est
> la vie même de cette différence, elle y trouve son devoir auguste, sa
> fascination aussi, quand elle en vient à rapprocher orgueilleusement
> les deux langues par une puissance d'unifcation qui lui est propre et
> semblable à celle d'Hercule resserant les deux rives de la mer.

One supposes that each language would have a single and self-same
kind of perspective, always with the same meaning, and that all the
kinds of perspective could become complementary. But Benjamin
suggests something else: each translator lives off the difference
among languages, even while pursuing, apparently, the perverse design of suppressing it. (The well-translated work is praised in two
opposed ways: one would not believe it to be translated, people say;
or again, it is truly the same work, one rediscovers it again marvel-
ously the same; but, in the first case, one effaces, for the sake of the
new language, the origin of the work; in the second case, for the
sake of the work, the originality of the two languages; in both cases,
something essential is lost.) In truth, translation is in no way destined to efface the difference of which it is on the contrary the play:
constantly it alludes to it, it dissimulates it, but sometimes in revealing it and often in accentuating it, it is the very life of this difference,
finds there its august duty, its fascination also, when it happens

proudly to bring close to one another the two languages by a power
of unification that is proper to it and that is like that of Hercules
bringing together the two shores of the sea.[12]

In a later text, *Le pas au-delà,* Blanchot writes of the strange relation of writing and speaking according to a metaphor of original
text and translation. Writing both creates and cuts the inextricable
knot of speaking and writing, at once binding them together and
distinguishing them: "comme un livre ouvert, avec sur une page
un texte dit de traduction et sur l'autre page le même texte dit original, sans qu'on puisse jamais décider de quel côté l'un de quel côté
l'autre, ni même qu'il s'agit d'un texte en deux versions, tant iden-
tité et différence se recouvrent" (like an open book, with on one
page a text said to be a translation and on the other page the same
text said to be original, without it being possible ever to decide on
which side is the one, on which side the other, nor even if it is a
question of a single text in two versions, so completely do identity
and difference overlap; 128).

But there are surely other versions of this situation of a translation that is "free" not because it falsifies the so-called original text,
but because both "original" and "translation" are freely wandering
transpositions, metaphors, or transferences of an original that can
never be given as such? "Free" in these cases has the not altogether
happy meaning of unauthorized, unsponsored, ungrounded.
Translation, metaphor, transference—all have the same etymological meaning of carrying over, a lateral movement from here to
there, as implied by the German words for translation, "Überset-
zung" and "Übertragung." Translation is a physical action of pick-
ing a meaning up here and putting it down again over there.

Is not the influence of one writer on another—Homer on Virgil;
Virgil on Dante; all three on Milton; Shelley on Thomas Hardy;
Benjamin or Heidegger on Blanchot—another example of translation? Does not the anxiety of influence stem from the fear that
the translation may be secondary, without force? But "Übertragung" is also of course a key word in psychoanalysis. A passage in
Freud's *Dora* defines "Übertragungen," transferences, as either
"Neudrucke" (new impressions) or "Neubearbeitungen" (revised
editions) of an old text. But the first edition was already secondary

to an original, a primal trauma or fixation that can never be recovered as such, only given in translated form.[13] The question about the efficacy of psychoanalysis, the "talking cure," is this: can the transferred or translated version of the original trauma, the new edition as Freud calls it, gain purchase on the buried trauma, cure it by reenacting it in different form? This is another way of asking whether a translation can have performative efficacy.

Two more important examples must be mentioned of this strange relation of translation to a so-called original whose originality is put in question by the act of translation. Are these examples to be defined as translations or as new editions of one another? The first example is the relation of criticism to text. The critic attempts to translate the original into other terms, into one or another of the languages of criticism, while at the same time remaining faithful to the text, repeating its truth in another tongue. The fulfillment of this task is a transposition, translation, or "allegory" of the serious task of reading that Blanchot, at the end of *L'arrêt de mort,* defines in terms of thinking of the hand engaged in writing the words the reader is reading. I shall return later to the question of the relation of criticism to "literature proper."

The second example will return the reader to the text of *L'arrêt de mort,* in either language. Is not the second story, the story of N., a translation of the same narrative materials as are found in the story of J.? Both stories narrate an erotic relation that is in one way or another, literally in the first story and figuratively in the second, a calling back of the loved woman from the dead, as Orpheus spoke his "Come" to Eurydice or Jesus his "Lazarus, come forth." One function of prosopopoeia is its use as a fictive raising of the dead. But if the second story is the double of the first, could the reader not just as well call the first the translation of the second? No clear indication, except that of the sequence in which the two stories are told, is given of any relation between them. It is as if the narrator were a different person in each case. The reader is drawn once more to ask which is the original, which the translation. Both stories are, finally, translations of and translated by the act whereby what Blanchot calls "cette pensée" is called into existence by the right words. By way of the ambiguity of *elle,* the final sentence of the second récit identifies "that thought" and "N." Both respond to the "Come": "à elle, je dis éternellement: 'Viens,' et éternellement, elle est là." Does the translation not falsify this by choosing a referent for *elle* and saying: "to that thought I say eternally, 'Come,' and eternally it is there"?

If you think I have added something here, stretched my evidence, you need only turn to the page where the narrator has missed a meeting with N. and sees her with a young man he does not know:

> Au théâtre, à l'entr'acte, accompagnée d'un garçon inconnu, elle était là. Elle me parut extrêmement belle. Je la voyais passer devant moi, aller et venir dans un lieu tout proche et infiniment séparé et comme derrière une vitre. Je fus frappé d'une idée folle. J'aurais sans doute pu lui parler, mais je ne le désirais pas et peut-être, en effet, ne le pouvais-je pas. Elle se tenait en ma présence avec la liberté d'une pensée; elle était dans ce monde, mais dans ce monde je ne la recontrais encore que parce qu'elle était ma pensée; et quelle connivence s'établissait donc entre elles, quelle complicité pleine d'horreur. (112)

> At the theater, during the intermission, I saw her with a young man I did not know. [The translation misses the premonitory echo of the ending in "elle était là."] She seemed very beautiful to me. I saw her passing in front of me, walking back and forth in a place that was very near and infinitely separated from me, as if it were behind a window. I was struck by an insane idea. No doubt I could have talked to her, but I did not want to and maybe I actually was not able to. She remained in my presence with the freedom of a thought; she was in this world, but I was encountering her again in this world only because she was my thought; and what tacit understanding was therefore being established between her and my thought, what terrifying complicity. (60)

The way the invocation in words of a thought, or perhaps its performative creation, may be thought of as analogous to storytelling, leads to a final question. What is the relation, for Blanchot, of storytelling to philosophy, criticism, or literary theory? He is of course a distinguished writer in both modes. Are Blanchot's *récits* no more than translations of his ideas in his philosophical criticism? Is *L'arrêt de mort* no more than a transposition of Blanchot's thoughts about death, writing, literature, the eternal return, and so on, to the conventional modern narrative categories of loving, making love, mortal illnesses, death and dying, adultery, betrayal, interpersonal relations generally, incompetent doctors, bureaucratic jobs, letters, telegrams, phone calls, business cards, door keys, wallets, hotel rooms, apartments, halls, stairways, streets, episodes in modern history like the Munich crisis, the beginning of World War II, the bombing of Paris—in short, all the decor or paraphernalia of realistic fiction with an urban setting? Such things seem to have little in themselves to do with abstract thought or philosophical criticism. Does that narrativization add nothing to Blanchot's thought, or at worst sugar-coat it for those who prefer novels to essays on philosophy, literature to the criticism of literature? One hopes that the récits say something more or different, since if this is not the case, then the conscientious reader would hardly bother with Blanchot's frivolous récits. It would be better to spend one's time reading Blanchot's serious writing.

One might say, plausibly enough, that the récits persuade the serious reader that Blanchot's abstract themes are not just words or ideas, off somewhere among those names that will never hurt you. Blanchot is concerned with matters of life and death, things that are rooted in history and that might intervene in the most everyday occurrences, for example when you get to know someone who lives in your apartment building. Living, or rather dying, is the same thing as writing or reading. The récits might be taken as proving on the reader's pulses both forms of this analogy. Living/dying is like reading; reading is like dying or like being called from the dead.

This abstract analogy is not what is most serious here, since it depends on what the récits say or represent rather than on what they do. Is it not that, as Blanchot says, the récits on the one hand and the criticism on the other each provide unique collocations of words that function as the calling forth, by a different "Come," of a unique truth that enters between the words or beyond the words or form which the words shrink: "à elle [cette pensée], je dis éternellement: 'Viens,' et éternellement, elle est là" (to it [that thought] I say eternally, "Come," and eternally it is there).

If, as Blanchot says, something happened "because, at a certain moment, the facts became misleading and because of their strange juxtaposition entitled the truth to take possession of them" (80), does not that taking possession both occur and get betrayed at the moment the "facts" are turned into either narration or criticism? A moment before the passage just quoted, the narrator says N., in telling her story of having a cast made of her face and hands, "ait obéi à un commandement mystérieux, et qui était le mien, et qui est en moi la voix à jamais renaissante, voix jalouse elle aussi, d'un sentiment incapable de disparaître" (was obeying a mysterious command, which came from me, and which is the voice that is always being reborn in me, and it is vigilant too, the voice of a feeling that cannot disappear; 146; 79–80). That voice is the neuter voice behind the personal voice, the "it" behind any "he" or "she." It is a neuter that can only be reached or glimpsed through the operations of what in Blanchot's case might be called a self-canceling prosopopoeia—or, as he might put it, a prosopopoeia without prosopopoeia. I mean that, in the case of the récits, the shadowy personality of the narrator and the invocation of the personalities of the female protagonists, N. and J., are the indispensable means of reaching beyond personification to the voice that is not so much impersonal as neuter, "ne-uter," neither the one nor the other.

Just before the passage about the "mysterious command," the narrator asserts that "the truth is not contained in these facts. I can imagine suppressing these particular ones. But if they did not happen, others happen in their place, and answering the summons of the all powerful affirmation which is united with me, they take on the same meaning and the story is the same" (79). Though the facts must be turned into answers to an all-powerful summons, that is, turned into language, once this happens, the meaning of all stories, for example of the two récits in *Death Sentence*, is the same. Any one could be substituted for any other and release or repel the same truth, though only just these words in just this sequence, neither more nor less, on pain of malediction, will work as an extended form of saying "Come." Only just these words will work as an effective death sentence, arrest of death, but the words may be either narrative or criticism. The relation between Blanchot's criticism and his récits, then, is like the relation between the first story

and the second in *L'arrêt de mort*. They are forms of "le même," but
of a same that at the same time is capable of taking infinitely different forms.

THE WORDS OF each narrative are different, unique, but each is an
answer to the same summons and has the same meaning. How can
this be? As an attempt to formulate an answer to this question and
as the last step in my trajectory, trying to fulfill the serious task of
reading Blanchot, I turn to a single strange episode in the second
story of *L'arrêt de mort*. This is the episode in which the narrator
proposes marriage to N. in her own mother tongue. The latter is a
language almost wholly unknown to the narrator. It is never given
by name to the reader or exemplified by one single word in that
language in the text of Blanchot's story. This alien language is forever irrecoverable, as much so as the song the sirens sang to Ulys-
ses. The episode comes just after the moment when the narrator
sees N. as the embodiment of his "thought," very near and yet
infinitely distant as if she were behind a window (112; 60), just as
the child in "Une scène primitive" sees that scene through a window that seems suddenly to shatter. The proposal in N.'s mother
tongue comes right before the climactic episode of the second récit, the narrator's discovery of N. in his room and his iteration of
the apocalyptic "Come." I cite, or perhaps I should say "recite,"
what I declare to be the essential sentences, committing of course
once more the crime of both taking away by not quoting all and of
adding by citing again, and by citing in translation as well as in the
original. The ellipsis dots are the silent signs of my sins of omis-
sion; the indentation of a quoted block, the silent signs of my sins
of commission. I have added to the text by recitation, with the
accent on either the third or first syllable, saying it out loud or
citing it once more: reci*ta*tion or *re*citation, in French and in
English.

> Depuis quelque temps, je lui parlais dans sa langue maternelle, que
> que je trouvais d'autant plus émouvante que j'en connaissais moins
> les mots. Pour elle, elle ne la parlait pour ainsi dire jamais, du moins
> avec moi, et cependant, si je commençais à ânnoner, à lier ensemble
> des termes maladroits, à former des locutions impossibles, elle les
> écoutait avec une sorte de gaîté, de jeunesse, et à son tour elle me

répondait en français, mais un français différent du sien, plus enfan-
tin et plus bavard, comme si sa parole fût denenue irresponsable, à
la suite de la mienne, employant une langue inconnue . . . (114)

For quite some time I had been talking to her in her mother tongue,
which I found all the more moving since I knew few words of it. As
for her, she never actually spoke it, at least not with me, and yet if I
began to falter, to string together awkward expressions, to form impossible idioms, she would listen to them with a kind of gaiety, and
youth, and in turn would answer me in French, but in a different
French from her own, more childish and talkative, as though her
speech had become irresponsible, like mine, using an unknown language . . . (61)

Passage of an admirable power to provoke or to invoke thought!
Ordinarily one opposes speech to silence, or perhaps that which
may be spoken to the unspeakable, what is beyond the limits of
speech or writing, though perhaps only a "pas au delà," one step
beyond. Speech-act theorists distinguish, on the other hand, between genuine speech acts, those performed in just the proper circumstances or as texts with the right contexts, from etiolated,
nonserious, or inefficacious speech acts, for example those in
poems, in novels, in weddings performed on the stage, in practice
masses (what are called "White Masses" performed by accolite
priests), or perhaps in translations into a foreign tongue of a sacred
text. Could the same thing be said of reading *L'arrêt de mort* in
translation rather than in the original? Can reading in translation
ever be a serious task, or is it perhaps always irresponsible?

The distinction between valid speech and etiolated, "whitened,"
speech seems clear. But what of promises, contracts, bets, excuses,
or any other kind of performative speech act, exchanged between
two persons who have different mother tongues? Such an exchange would be a strange dialogue in which one or the other, or
both, will be speaking frivolously, fictively. Can I or she be expected to be held to vows one of us must utter in an unknown
language or at any rate in a language that has not flowed from the
mother to the tongue of the speaker, has not been taken in with
mother's milk?[14]

Just such a dialogue takes place between the narrator and N. The
narrator speaks N.'s language, which he knows only imperfectly,

and N. answers him not in that language, which she knows, but in French, which is an alien language to her. The result is a strange irresponsibility or gaiety. Each partner in the dialogue says things he or she would not otherwise have said or could only say in "an unknown language." Each speaker more or less invents either language on the spot, stammering, creating impossible or ridiculous idioms, speaking like a child who is learning to talk.

What is strangest, most serious, about this frivolous nonserious speech is that it does cross limits and is efficacious. It is an act of transgression that makes something happen:

> Et il est vrai que, moi aussi, je me sentais irresponsable dans cet autre langage, si ignoré de moi; et ce que je n'aurais jamais dit, ni pensé, ni même tu à partir de mots véritables, ce balbutiement, ir-réel, d'expressions à peu près inventées, et dont le sens se jouait à mille lieues de ma tête, me l'extorquait, m'invitait à le faire en-tendre, me donnait, à l'exprimer, une petite ivresse qui n'avait plus conscience de ses limites et allait hardiment au delà de ce qu'il fallait. (114–115)

> And it is true that I too felt irresponsible in this other language, so unfamiliar to me; and this unreal stammering of expressions that were more or less invented, and whose meaning flitted past, far away from my mind, drew from me things I never would have said, or thought, or even left unsaid in real words: it tempted me to let them be heard, and imparted to me, as I expressed them, a slight drunkenness which was no longer aware of its limits and boldly went further than it should have. (61–62)

Though the words each speaks are not real words, if one means by "mots véritables" words that are emitted with full intention by a self in command of its thought and in command of the process whereby thought is transformed into words spoken in the mother tongue, still these words have an active power. Rather than being the expression of thought, they create thoughts and feelings. These words in a strange language create thoughts and feelings in the narrator, drive him to speak them out and to let them be heard by N. These words create a new intimacy between them, ulti-mately bringing N. to the narrator's room and to his bed.

That the words exchanged in two languages are truly performative is indicated in the next sentences in Blanchot's story. But they are odd performatives. They are not fictitious because they really make something happen, but they differ from "normal" performatives in not being used intentionally by the "I" who speaks them as the instruments of effective action in the world. These words act autonomously, on their own. They make something happen that is not intended by the speaker. He is speaking frivolously, irresponsibly. A marriage, with all its attendant language— proposal, promise to marry, performance of the marriage—is a classic example of performative as opposed to constative language. A marriage is a way of doing things with words. Yet the narrator marries N. not in French but in her language:

> Je lui faisais donc dans ce langage les plus aimables déclarations, habitude qui m'est bien étrangère. Je lui offris au moins deux fois de l'épouser, ce qui prouve le caractère fictifs de mes propos, étant donné mon éloignement pour cet état (et mon peu d'estime), mais je l'épousais dans sa langue, et cette langue, non seulement je l'employais à la légère, mais surtout, l'inventant plus ou moins, j'exprimais par elle, avec l'ingénuité et la vérité d'une demi-conscience, des sentiments inconnus qui surgissaient effrontément sous cette forme et me trompaient moi-même, comme ils auraient pu la tromper. (115)

> So I made the most friendly declarations to her in this language, which was a habit quite alien to me. I offered to marry her at least twice, which proved how fictitious my words were, since I had an aversion to marriage (and little respect for it), but in her language I married her, and I not only used that language lightly but, more or less inventing it, and with the ingenuity and the truth of half-awareness, I expressed in it unknown feelings which shamelessly welled up in the form of that language and fooled even me, as they could have fooled her. (62)

"Je l'épousais dans sa langue"—is this a real marriage or a fictitious marriage? Blanchot's point is that it is neither quite the one nor the other. It is "neuter" in the etymological sense of "ne-uter," neither/nor. This marriage is performed with fictitious words, but the words have creative power. They call, "Come," and the strange thought and feelings they invoke are eternally there. Blanchot's

implicit contribution to the theory of speech acts is a demonstration of the existence of this third possiblilty, neither the red language of contracts, promises, excuses, christenings, and marry-
ings in the "real" world, nor the white language of frivolous or
"poetic" performatives that make nothing happen. These speech
acts are expressed in the neuter of a fictitious language that nevertheless is productive. Such performatives are detached, like a translation or like a formula I utter in an foreign tongue, from all the
subjective, intentional, and social contexts that tie the Austinian
performative to the presupposition of a speaking and intending
"I." Still they function to call forth something—it, the thing, the
thought, the truth, a truth beyond any "I" or any social context.
All narrative, for Blanchot, is the translation of ordinary language
into a foreign tongue, the language of the neuter, even if the words
remain those of the familiar speech of the reader. Only when they
are translated in this way can they be efficacious as performative
invocations.

The relation to translation of this strange mode of speech act, in
which the language functions automatically as an invocation, is indicated in the passage following the ones I have just cited from
L'arrêt de mort:

> Elle s'était mariée une fois, mais cette histoire ne lui avait laissé que
> le souvenir des ennuis du divorce. Le mariage, pour elle non plus,
> n'était donc très important. Et cependant, pourquoi, lui ayant pro-
> posé ce mariage, la seule fois, ou l'une des seules fois que je reçus
> d'elle une résponse dans sa langue, ce fut à cet instant: un mot
> ètrange, de moi parfaitement inconnu, qu'elle ne voulut jamais me
> traduire, et quand je lui dis: "Bien, moi je vais le traduire," elle fut
> prise d'une véritable panique à la pensée que je pourrais tomber
> juste, de sorte que je dus garder pour moi seul et ma traduction et
> mon pressentiment. (116)

> She had once been married, but that business had left her only the
> memory of the unpleasant details of the divorce. So that marriage
> was not very important to her either. And yet why was it that the
> only time, or one of the only times, she answered me in her own
> language, was after I had proposed marriage to her: the word was a
> strange one, completely unknown to me, which she never wanted
> to translate for me, and when I said to her: "All right, then I'm going
> to translate it," she was seized by real panic at the thought that I

might hit on it exactly, so that I had to keep both my translation and my presentiment to myself. (62–63)

Here for once the dialogue between the narrator and N. takes place in a single language, but the narrator has no comprehension of the other half of the dialogue, though he makes a guess at the meaning of the word N. speaks. That word is a response to his proposal of marriage. It might or might not seal the contract that would transform them from free to bound or "engaged." Such a speech act takes two utterances, the proposal—"Marry me!" [15]—and an affirmative response to the proposal: "I will." In this case the proposal is etiolated, fictional. It is spoken in a language in which the speaker cannot be other than frivolous, and Nathalie's answer is never translated, neither for the narrator nor for the reader. There is no way to tell whether the answer is yes or no. Still the exchange, in the same language on both sides of the dialogue, has efficacy. It initiates the series of events that brings N. to the narrator's room and allows him (and the reader) once more to invoke the thought that is "eternally there," just behind the surface of all words and all events, or between their interstices, and at the same time at an infinite distance.

The dialogue in two languages in this episode recalls Benjamin's paradigm of the original and its translation, both of which are extinguished as intention, information, and meaning in a stratum that is nevertheless what is meant by all language: an expressionless and creative Word. Although each word, expression, episode, narrative, or *récit* in any language has its unique performative power, all, in relation to that expressionless Word, mean the same thing, namely "il" or "elle," "it." But all are at the same time at an infinite distance from "it," like the narrator's lovemaking with N. N. tells the narrator she wants to meet him "Nulle part" (Nowhere). In the hotel room his cold caress of her hand takes place "infiniment loin" (at an infinite distance), as if it were behind unbreakable glass. In the same way, each of the two narratives in *L'arrêt de mort* is unique and calls forth its own commentary. Each is at the same time, in relation to that thing to which both call "Come," the translation or double of the other. Each is an example of translation as forgetting and obliteration of the so-called original, as each story covers over the other and makes the reader forget it. In the same way, the translation of *L'arrêt de mort* into *Death Sentence* covers over the French "original" with an English substitute, though neither is original or proper in relation to the "it."

In both cases, however, the "it" is called forth by the personifications making the story possible and, at the same time, is kept at a distance by the incompatability between the "it" and any person. "La chose," "la mort," "la pensée," even "le neutre," are personified as "elle," but this prosopopoeia does not constitute a mastery over death or over the thing. It initiates instead an interminable series of repetitions that arrests death, holds it off. The personification inveigles protagonist, narrator, author, and reader not into death but into a perpetual process of dying. This indefinite postponement of death is named in one of the meanings of the title phrase, "l'arrêt de mort." If for Dylan Thomas "death is all metaphors,"[16] for Blanchot all prosopopoeias are allegories of death.

THIS BRINGS US full circle, in conclusion, to the questions posed earlier about the relation between Blanchot's philosophical criticism, his *récits*, and any reading of Blanchot or commentary on his work. Each is initiatory, the bringer of unique thoughts, but each is also no more than secondary, a translation of the others. All are translations in relation to the original Word that can never be given. Reading, like translation, like criticism, like writing, is the endless and perhaps impossible task, "Aufgabe," of invoking that Word.

The end point, for now, of this trajectory through one small region of Blanchot's writings is a juxtaposition of those two fundamental motifs in his work, the impossibility of dying and the eternal return. The latter is formulated in a series of not quite congruent fragments, each a "translation" of the last, in an early section of *Le pas au-delà*. Blanchot's version of the difficult thought of the eternal return rejects the traditional logocentric idea of a time oriented to the presence of the present, so that the past is what once was present and the future a present to be. Blanchot substitutes the notion of a present moment that is never present, for example as the phenomenal making manifest of the "it," the thing behind the screen. Blanchot's present is rather the interruption without interruption of a past that never was present but that has already repeated the future. The future, on the other side of the nonpresent screen or gulf of the present, will repeat the past in the eternal return of a "same" that is always different, since it is governed by no available original Word on the basis of which the sameness of the eternal return can be measured. To one of Blanchot's formulations of this I give the last word, or rather I give the last word to my "translation" of one of Blanchot's "translations" of that thought, one of his ways of saying "Come" to the thought of the eternal return:

> L'exigence du retour serait donc l'exigence d'un temps sans présent, temps qui serait aussi celui de l'écriture, temps futur, temps passé, que la radicale disjonction (en l'absence de tout présent) de l'un et de l'autre, fussait-ils les mêmes, empêche d'identifier autrement que comme la différence que porte la répétition.
>
> Entre passé, futur, la plus grande différence est donnée en ceci que l'un répéterait l'autre sans la commune mesure d'un présent: comme si entre passé et futur régnait l'absence de présent sous la forme simplifiée de l'oubli.
>
> Qu'est-ce qui reviendra? Tout, *sauf* le présent, la possibilité d'une présence. (27)

> The exigence of the return would be therefore the exigence of a time without present, a time which would be also that of writing, future time, past time, that the radical disjunction (in the absence of any present) of the one and the other even if they were the same, forbids identifying other than as the difference which carries repetition.
>
> Between past, future, the greatest difference is given in this that the one repeats the other without the common measure of the present: as if between past and future reigned the absence of the present under the simplified form of forgetting.
>
> What is it that will return? Everything, *except* the present, the possibility of presence.

What does Blanchot's thought of the eternal return have to do with prosopopoeia in his work? What returns, in *L'arrêt de mort* and in Blanchot's work as a whole, even in the criticism, is a situation of close proximity and immense distance involving two persons, a man (the protagonist-narrator) and another, the other in the récits usually a woman ("elle," "la pensée"). These personages approach one another with a movement that is infinitely slow and yet has infinite force. The force makes an ultimate demand on the one who receives it, a new form of ethical, legal, political, and social responsibility. What returns, then, for Blanchot, is prosopopoeia. All his work might be defined as a prolonged meditation about prosopopoeia and a mobilization of its resources, in patient repetition. Prosopopoeia is the essential means, but also the essential obstacle, to thinking of death, the thing, all those "pensées sans pensées" that Blanchot must think, in response to an irresistible "Come." His work calls on the reader to think those thoughts again.

CHAPTER 6

Facing It:
James's "The Last of the Valerii"

Can a work of art, something belonging to the category of the aesthetic, serve as the bridge between epistemology and ethics, as Kant said it must—if there is to be any way to get from the one to the other? Can a fictive narrative showing someone choosing in terms of the moral imperative give readers of the fiction access to that law for their own ethical choices? The reading of *What Maisie Knew* culminated in a recognition that for James ethical choice is made in response to "something still deeper than a moral sense," something other than the economic round of taking and giving that governs Maisie's elders. This something appears to be unique for each person, and it makes ethical decision solitary and inaugural. It is solitary because it cannot give a legible law to anyone else's action. It is inaugural in the sense that though it is without discernible antecedents, and cannot be formulated as a rational law, nevertheless it proposes a universal standard valid for all men and women at all times. We should all act like Maisie. We should all renounce. The difficulty, perhaps the impossibility, is to know in a given case what that would mean. At a certain moment, when she becomes an independent moral agent, Maisie becomes unknowable for the other characters, for the narrator, unknowable even for James and for the reader. She is wholly other and she is a mediator of the wholly other.

This means that at the farthest reaches of the attempt to understand *What Maisie Knew* the reader encounters the question of prosopopoeia. Though the law as such is not a person, it appears to be accessible only through the mediation of a figurative person, for example those fictive persons who are the necessary presupposition of any novel or short story. There is no storytelling without prosopopoeia, just as there is no access to the moral law without the intervention of some human figure. The problem of anthropomorphism has emerged as a fundamental part of thinking about the relation of ethics to narrative.

Though all James's fiction depends on the initiating act of prosopopoeia that creates the protagonists of each story or novel, personification is a special issue in one set of his works. These form a double group: on the one hand the ghost stories, on the other the stories about portraits or statues. I propose to read here one of the latter.

"The Last of the Valerii" (1874) belongs to the group of stories by James about art and, within that, to the subgroup in which works of sculpture or painting figure prominently: "The Beldonald Holbein," "The Aspern Papers," "The Real Thing," "Covering End," *Roderick Hudson,* and many others. "The Last of the Valerii" also belongs to the group of ghost stories, stories of the uncanny and quasi-supernatural. "The Jolly Corner" and "The Turn of the Screw" are the best known of these. Many of both sets have something fabulous or sensational about them. One can imagine the stories they recount being reported in some tabloid: "Scholar Tries to Extort Papers of Dead Poet from Poet's Aged Mistress"; "Expatriate Meets Ghost of Self in Greenwich Village Mansion"; "Governess Bewitches Her Two Young Charges." In the case of "The Last of the Valerii" the headline would run: "Italian Hubby Betrays American Heiress in Love Affair with Statue."

What can be said about this improbable story? It was, by the way, excluded from the New York Edition. Is "The Last of the Valerii" at all serious, or is it a mere light-hearted jeu d'esprit? Like most of James's over one hundred short stories, even the many not in the New York Edition, "The Last of the Valerii" is a subtle text. Recognition of its complexity has emerged, for me, only through prolonged interrogation of details, on the assumption that everything counts. An example is the fact that the narrator is an American and also the heroine's godfather, whereas her real father is never mentioned. It is as if the latter had never existed. Martha has a mother, but for father she appears to have only the "unscrupulous old *genre* painter"[1] who tells the story and who stands in loco parentis to Martha, confessing that he "took a godfatherly interest in what it had not always seemed to me crabbed and pedantic to talk of as her moral development" (96).

If it is true that all texts are allegories of the way their own clarity about tropes cannot be read,[2] something strange happens when the trope in question is a prosopopoeia. James's "The Last of the Valerii" is exemplary of this strangeness and of the way it involves what, for want of a better word, may be called materiality. The strangeness results from the fact that the generative trope is not just this or that fallacious tropological substitution, but the founding trope (though it is not a trope in the ordinary sense of the word) that makes storytelling possible in the first place. An allegory may be about anything under the sun, but in order to have allegory at all there must be posited the possibility of talking about anything under the sun in terms of imaginary people. In this story the personages are the American heiress Martha, her Italian husband, Count Camillo Valerio, and the other characters, including the narrator, an unsuccessful American painter of picturesque subjects, with a "passion for bedaubing old panels with ineffective portraiture of mouldy statues against screens of box" (96). A story about prosopopoeia takes as its subject the conditions of its possibility of being. This might be a dangerous operation, since a story may end up by demonstrating its own impossibility and so dissolve before the reader's eyes. That this might not be entirely bad must, for the moment, remain an open possibility.

That "The Last of the Valerii" is also about personification there can be no doubt. The historical context for the story (if "context" is the right word) is not only actual transatlantic marriages in the late nineteenth century between rich American girls and impecunious Italian peers, for example the marriage of Margaret Fuller to the Count d'Orsini. The context also includes the splendid array of nineteenth-century work on comparative religion and mythology that culminated in Frazer's *The Golden Bough*.

Victorian study of myth is, among other things, a demonstration of personification's power that includes a critique of that trope, sometimes under the name of "primitive animism," sometimes under the Ruskinian name of "pathetic fallacy." James almost

certainly knew some of the works in this tradition. "The Last of
the Valerii" might almost seem a proleptic narrative meditation on
one of the most splendid of such works, Walter Pater's "The Myth
of Demeter and Persephone." The latter was originally published
in two parts in the *Fortnightly Review,* in January and February 1876
(two years after the publication of "The Last of the Valerii"), and
then in the book *Greek Studies* in 1895. There is no time here to
recapitulate the intricate theoretical and historical argumentation
of Pater's essay. It joins Ruskin's "Of the Pathetic Fallacy" as one of
the great reflections on prosopopoeia. The crucial pages, however,
after arguing for a combination of literalism and figuration in the
allegorical temper, culminate in a claim that the personification of
nature had by no means disappeared:

> But there are traces of the old temper in the man of to-day also; and
> through these we can understand that earlier time—a very poetical
> time, with the more highly gifted peoples—in which every impres-
> sion men received of the action of powers without or within them
> suggested to them the presence of a soul or will, like their own—a
> person, with a living spirit, and sense, and hands, and feet; which,
> when it talked of the return of Kore to Demeter, or the marriage of
> Zeus and Here, was not using rhetorical language, but yielding to a
> real illusion; to which the voice of man "was really a stream, beauty
> an effluence, death a mist."[3]

A full reading of what Pater has to say about prosopopoeia would
not be simple, especially if works other than "Demeter and Persephone" were included in the account, the essays on Greek sculpture in *Greek Studies,* for example, or the two extraordinary stories
dramatizing what Heine called "the gods in exile": "Apollo in Pi-
cardy," and "Denys l'Auxerrois." In the passage I have just quoted,
however, Pater stresses global wholeness, the integrating powers
of prosopopoeia, as well as the power of this trope to unify man
and nature, subject and object, in an enclosed economy of tropological exchange. The old Greeks projected a single god or goddess as bringing together within a person and within the name of
that person a complex of fluctuating impressions of nature. According to Pater, "that older unmechanical, spiritual, or Platonic,
philosophy envisages nature rather as the unity of a living spirit or
person, revealing itself in various degrees to the kindred spirit of

the observer, than as a system of mechanical forces" (96). The myth of Demeter is an example of this: "And a large part of [early Greek] experience—all, that is, that related to the earth in its changes, the growth and decay of all things born of it—was covered by the story of Demeter, the myth of the earth as a mother . . . thus naming together in her all their fluctuating thoughts, impressions, suspicions, of the earth and its appearances, their whole complex divination of a mysterious life, a perpetual working, a continuous act of conception there" (97). Pater emphasizes the priority of the phenomenal and experiential over the linguistic in this transaction. Nature is first seen or felt to be a person and then named as such. But if man's kinship to nature is affirmed by the giving of a face and a story to what is in fact inanimate, in what Pater calls "not using rhetorical language, but yielding to a real illusion," the reciprocal of this, in the balanced substitution of inner for outer, outer for inner, is the literalization of natural metaphors for human bodily realities. Men or women get depersonified as inanimate objects are personified. To men and women in that "very poetical time," the voice of man was really a stream, beauty was a physical effluence, and death was literally a mist darkening consciousness. The tropological operation that is overtly excluded is nevertheless implicitly revealed in Pater's description of a reciprocal interchange, though he is right to see personification as a transformation that has always already occurred and is therefore presupposed to have occurred at the level of substance, not as a superficial matter of the transposition of names.

What happens when James borrows this tropological system from the same tradition of mythological speculation to which Pater's essay belongs? There is one reference in "The Last of the Valerii" to Demeter and Persephone—of that more later. James's story seems to fit perfectly both the paradigm established in Pater's essay and a paradigmatic definition of a text as the allegory of the unreadability of a system of tropes affirmed and then deconstructed. Martha, the pretty blond American heiress of James's story, marries the handsome but poor Count Camillo Valerio. "Martha": the name is sturdily New Testament and Protestant, though it does not seem to fit in this case except ironically. Martha in Luke's Gospel is the woman who does the housework while her sister Mary

sits at Jesus' feet and listens to the word. Martha is rebuked by
Jesus when she complains and asks Jesus to get Mary to help her
with the serving: "Martha, Martha, thou art careful and troubled
about many things: But one thing is needful; and Mary hath chosen that good part, which shall not be taken away from her" (Luke
10:41–42). It is not recorded how Jesus proposed to get the housework done if both Mary and Martha sat at his feet and listened. In
any case the biblical Martha hardly seems a prototype of James's
Martha, who is too rich to need to do any housework, though she
does have "plans of study, of charity, of worthily playing her part
as a Contessa Valerio" (96) and is shown at the end occupying herself with embroidery, drawing "her silken stitches like an image of
wifely contentment" (121).

Although one of Martha's half-joking projects for Camillo is to
convert him from Catholicism to her own American Protestantism (or be converted herself to his ancestral faith), the fact is that
the Count is "a poor Catholic." In him lurk remnants of the ancient Roman faith in the old gods who dwelt "in caves and woods
and streams, in earth and air and water" (111). "Yes, by Bacchus,"
says the Count to the narrator, "I am superstitious! . . . There have
been things seen and done here which leave strange influences behind! They don't touch you, doubtless, who come of another race.
But they touch me, often, in the whisper of the leaves and the odor
of the mouldy soil and the blank eyes of the old statues. I can't bear
to look the statues in the face. I seem to see other strange eyes in
the empty sockets, and I hardly know what they say to me. I call
the poor old statues ghosts. In conscience, we've enough on the
place already, lurking and peering in every shady nook" (98–99).
In spite of her husband's warning—"Let them lie, the poor disin-
herited gods . . . and don't break their rest"—Martha makes the
mistake of hiring a crew of excavators and an archaeologist, "an
ugly little dwarfish man who seemed altogether a subterranean ge-
nius, an earthy gnome of the underworld" (99), to dig on the
Count's estate. They find a splendid antique statue of Juno. The
Count falls in love with it, executing complicated obeisances to the
statue by moonlight, including blood sacrifice, and ceasing to care
at all for his new wife. "His Juno's the reality," Martha cries; "I'm
the fiction!" (117). Camillo's infatuation is cured and his alienated

affections are returned to his wife only when she has the Juno buried again in the dark earth, the "mouldy soil" that has been so often mentioned in the story as the place of burial and death. As the narrator says, "After the fable, the moral!" (117). The moral of the story, the ethical command the reader seems to receive from it, is apparently clear enough: Be faithful to your lawful wedded wife, and do not go whoring after strange gods or committing that version of the error of prosopopoeia that leads to the personifying of stones in an act in which worship cannot be distinguished from illicit sexual desire.

But things, as is usual with James, are not quite so simple as they seem. It is easy to see how the story can be read as the narrative presentation of a trope along with its deconstruction followed by the reassertion of the first error, to make a third narrative superimposed on the first two. I say "along with" since the three narratives are superimposed and simultaneous, interwoven throughout the text.

The fundamental presupposition generating this story is the use of a first-person narrator who is intelligent, perceptive, and ironic but who nevertheless cannot be counted on to draw out the full implications of what he says. Nor is it certain that he is even aware of these implications. James flatters his readers by this narrative procedure. We feel we are pretty smart if we can second-guess not the ordinary "unreliable narrator" but even a narrator so intelligent as this one.

One form of such second guessing is the way the narrator, without explicitly calling attention to what he is doing, sets up the transformation of statues into people and of people into statues. On the one hand he speaks of Camillo as like a statue: "Strong the Conte Valerio certainly was; he had a head and throat like some of the busts in the Vatican. To my eye, which has looked at things now so long with the painter's purpose, it was a real perplexity to see such a throat rising out of the white cravat of the period. It sustained a head as massively round as that of the familiar bust of the Emperor Caracalla, and covered with the same dense sculptural crop of curls . . . his large, lucid eyes seemed to stare at you like a pair of polished agates" (90). Later the narrator says of Martha: "I more than once smiled at her archaeological zeal, and declared that I believed she had married the Count because he was like a statue of the Decadence" (93). Yet the narrator also speaks of statues as if they were alive, thereby commiting in his own narration the error that in the case of Camillo has such disastrous results. Of the "disinterred fragments of sculpture,—nameless statues and noseless heads and rough-hewn sarcophagi" that stand in the ilex walk on the Count's estate even before Martha begins digging for more buried treasures, the narrator says: "The statues used to stand there in the perpetual twilight like conscious things, brooding on their gathered memories. I used to linger about them, half expecting they would speak and tell me their stony secrets,—whisper heavily the whereabouts of their mouldering fellows, still unrecovered from the soil" (94). And of his first sight of the newly dug-up Juno, the narrator says, in an unashamed Pygmalion-like yielding to the temptation of anthropomorphism: "My pulses began to throb, for I felt she was something great, and that it was great to be among the first to know her. Her marvellous beauty gave her an almost human look, and her absent eyes seemed to wonder back at us" (100–101).

The story of the Count's unfortunate infatuation with the disinterred Juno seems to function as a deconstruction of the system of tropes that is affirmed by the narrator in the process of telling the story, apparently without awareness that he is doing so. The trope of prosopopoeia, in this case giving a face, a body, and a name to an inanimate chunk of stone, and its reverse, the depersonification of the living by seeing them as statues, is posited by the narrator always with some degree of reserve or ironic undercutting, as a matter of "like," "as," "almost," or "seem." Count Camillo is "like" a statue of the Decadence, the statues are "like" conscious things, the narrator only "half" expects them to speak, and the great Juno has an "almost" human look.

Camillo makes the disastrous mistake of taking this figure of speech literally. He makes the error that Ovid dramatized in the story of Pygmalion. Camillo abandons his wife for love of the statue, though as the earthy archaeologist, "the little expert in disinterment," cynically observes: "He keeps her under lock and key, and pays her solitary visits. What does he do, after all? When a beautiful woman is in stone, all he can do is to look at her" (105).

If the statue of Juno comes alive for Camillo, though remaining tantalizingly unembraceable, his wife becomes more and more like a statue. As in James's *The Sacred Fount,* if vitality flows into one place or person it has to be subtracted from another place. "Her [the Juno's] beauty be blasted!" says the narrator to the little archaeologist. "Can you tell me what has become of the Contessa's? To rival the Juno, she's turning to marble herself" (116).

The happy ending of the story is obtained by a reversal of this reversal. Martha takes it upon herself to rebury the Juno. She makes it once more a piece of marble covered with earth, a stone in the soil: "The ropes were adjusted and the Juno was slowly lowered into her earthy bed. The Countess took a handful of earth and dropped it solemnly on her breast. 'May it lie lightly, but forever!' she said" (121). The Juno becomes again a piece of hard matter, an "it," like those stones against which the picks of the excavators ring when they are digging to find her: "He [Camillo] sniffed delightedly the odor of the humid earth, and stood watching the workmen, as they struck constantly deeper, with a kindling wonder in his eyes. Whenever a pick-axe rang against a stone he would utter a sharp cry, and be deterred from jumping into the trench only by the little explorer's assurance that it was a false alarm" (99). By the reciprocal balancing that tells us we are dealing here with a closed economic system of figures, the Count is immediately cured of his infatuation when the statue is buried. He straightway returns all his affection to his wife in a long look into her eyes and in an act of obeisance that repeats his earlier gestures of bowing before the statue: "At last she raised her eyes and sustained the gaze in which all his returning faith seem concentrated. He hesitated a moment, as if her very forgiveness kept the gulf open between them, and then he strode forward, fell on his knees and buried his head in her lap. I departed as the Count had come in, on tiptoe" (121–122).

What seems an unequivocally happy ending is, however, shadowed. It is shadowed, for one thing, by the somewhat disquieting way that the long gaze of the Count and Countess into one another's eyes anticipates the terrifying ending of *The Golden Bowl,* written three decades later. There Prince Amerigo, utterly defeated by Maggie's forgiveness, looks into her eyes and says, "I see only

you." The unequivocal happy ending is also shadowed by the way
the Count's return of affection for his wife is described not as a
shift back to wholesome feeling, but as a shift from one illusion to
another. The Juno is initially described as "a majestic marble image" (100), and the Count is described as "staring at the image"
(101). Just before the Juno is reburied, the little archaeologist is
described as "privately scanning the recumbent image with an eye
which seemed to foresee a malicious glee in standing on a certain
unmarked spot on the turf and grinning till people stared" (120).
When the Count tiptoes in to his wife after that image has been
reconsigned to the earth, he sees Martha, according to the language of the narrator, not as a person but as another image. The
word is insisted on: "The Countess kept her eyes fixed on her
work, and drew her silken stitches like an image of wifely contentment. The image seemed to fascinate him: he came in slowly, almost on tiptoe, walked to the chimney-piece, and stood there in a
sort of rapt contemplation" (121).

Far from righting the balance in a closed-circuit economy of tropological substitution, leaving reality and fiction restored to their
right places, the last scene leaves the reader with one trope left
over, with an excess of illusion over reality. The Count's love for a
real person is modeled on the fictional personification of a piece of
marble, not the other way around. To put this in terms of the paradigmatic definition of narrative with which I began, the deconstruction of the system of tropes centering on prosopopoeia and
generating the story does not prevent the repetition of the error
that the deconstruction had identified. It seems as if neither the
characters, the narrator, nor the author have any power to prevent
the recurrence of the aberration whose disastrous consequences
have been so clearly demonstrated and made available as knowledge by the story itself. It is as if the characters, the narrator, and
the author cannot read the evidence before their eyes. In this way
"The Last of the Valerii" fulfills de Man's claim that in each narration the deconstruction of the generating trope coexists with what
he calls an allegory of the unreadability not of the trope but of the
deconstruction of the trope.

I BEGAN BY asserting that the trope of prosopopoeia is not just any
trope having the potential to generate a narrative. Personification

is the inaugural trope of narration, and without it there is no story-telling. This means that the deconstruction of this particular trope pulls the rug, so to speak, out from under the whole enterprise of narration. Although the reaffirmation of this trope in the allegory of unreadability may make the characters, the narrator, the author, and the reader guilty of what is shown to be a potentially disastrous aberrancy, still it restores the possibility of storytelling. Or the reaffirmation tells the reader that the foundation of storytelling is in fact invulnerable to deconstruction. This might be said to be a lucky thing for storytelling and even for social and domestic life generally. What would happen to marriage if all wives learned that their affection for their husbands is submission to a false trope? What would happen to storytelling if we readers or listeners did not yield to the "real illusion" that the story is of real people, with thoughts and feelings like our own?

The basic presupposition of this book has been that we should take seriously the claim that the reading of stories has a positive ethical function. It is hard to see how this function could be fulfilled if prosopopoeia were disabled or undermined, unless the one thing needful is to learn to distrust this trope. Insofar as narratives cannot carry out their good work unless their readers yield to the "real illusions" generated by anthropomorphisms, we may rejoice that this learning is not likely to take place, however often insight into this dangerous fallacy is iterated in novels and stories. On the other hand, works like "The Last of the Valerii" and the other narratives read in this book show that yielding to the power of this figure is by no means wholly innocent or an entirely constructive social act. The moral of our story at this point would seem to hover between the contradictory assertions that "the truth will make you free," that is, it is better to know the full truth about the way prosopopoeia works, and, on the other hand, that there may be some truths that it is better not to know.

But I have so far not accounted for an important feature of the positing of prosopopoeia. The text of "The Last of the Valerii" gives to the careful reader, if not to the narrator, to the characters, or perhaps even to the author (who knows, in this case, about James himself?), two further forms of knowledge of the way prosopopoeia works. It may be that this knowledge will protect the reader from the dangerous folly to which the story shows the characters succumbing. One of these comes by way of the persistent motif of fragmentation or mutilation that runs all through the story, culminating in an odd coda to the ostensible happy ending.

Many examples of fragmentation, disfigurement, or disarticulation punctuate the story. Far from being a trope that confers wholeness, as Pater affirms, whatever may be its putative origin in a global sense that nature is alive with an animation like that of man, the actual articulation of prosopopoeia in language always dismembers. It names bits and pieces of the human body here and there throughout the world. Dismemberment is already there in the technical definition of prosopopeia. It does not, according to that definition, confer a soul, an anima, on the absent, the inanimate, or dead. It ascribes, through language, a face or a mask, a voice, and a name to representatives of one or another of those three classes. Prosopopoeia projects not the wholeness of a self, body and soul together, but fragments that stand for the whole, as the face stands for the person who presents that face to the world. Each prosopopoeia therefore contains in itself the traces of its inaugural violence and artifice.

Mutilation is present in one way or another in all the versions of the Pygmalion story in this book, in "Der Findling," *L'arrêt de mort,* and "Bartleby the Scrivener." In "The Last of the Valerii" it appears most significantly in the narrator's insistence on the way the antique statues standing on the grounds of the estate are all disfigured. He says that he became familiar with "every moss-coated vase and mouldy sarcophagus and sad, disfeatured bust of those grim old Romans who could so ill afford to become more meagre-visaged." He tells the reader that the ilex walk "was filled with disinterred fragments of sculpture,—nameless statues and noseless heads and rough-hewn sarcophagi" (94). As these passages indicate, the motif of disfeatured statues is consistently associated with burial in the damp earth. An ilex walk is often found in cemetaries, the ilex and yew traditionally being associated with death. Sarcophagi are several times mentioned in the story. Roman portrait busts were tomb sculptures, placed over the moldering bodies of those grim Romans to show what they looked like when they were alive and thereby to perpetuate their memory. A Roman portrait sculpture for a tomb is a species of materially substantiated prosopopoeia. Such a bust gives a marble face and a name carved in stone to the absent and inanimate as these occur in a specific form: a dead body.

Just as any naming substitutes for the immediate presence of what is named and presupposes some form of unavailability, so personification kills just when it ascribes life. It presupposes the absence, inanimation, or death of what it resurrects. The theme of death and resurrection as the performative scene of prosopopoeia is the paradoxical drama of "The Last of the Valerii." The Juno, who was never more than a chunk of carved marble, is dug up, then treated as though she were a real person by Camillo, the narrator, and Martha. The statue is ultimately buried again in a ritual ceremony that is a parody of the burial of a dead body. She is "slowly lowered into her earthy bed" and the Countess solemnly drops a handful of earth with a prayer, just as one does with a casket containing a real body before it is covered up with earth.

A more pervasive and perhaps less easily noticed form of this "disfeaturing" recurs in the narrator's discourse. This is the way he describes real people in terms of pieces of their anatomy. The Count is described as like a bust in the Vatican rising, grotesquely, from nineteenth-century clothes and, says the narrator, "his large, lucid eyes seemed to stare at you like a pair of polished agates" (90). To speak, in descriptive passages in a narrative, of a person's "eyes" or "hands" or "cheek" or "brow" without mentioning the rest of the body is of course a linguistic necessity of such descriptions, but once the reader has been sensitized to the way this dismembers the characters, and once the reader begins to notice the frequency of such locutions in "The Last of the Valerii," the story seems to be peopled not by whole persons but by fragments of bodies no more whole and perhaps no more alive (as indeed they are not, since they exist only as black marks on paper) than those disinterred fragments of sculpture that stand in the perpetual twilight of Camillo's ilex walk.

The initial description of Camillo mentions not only those agate eyes but the fact that "neither his nose nor his mouth was delicate," but "powerful, shapely, and manly." The reader is told that Martha "most prized" his "slow-coming, slow-going smile" (91) as if it were a detachable element floating in the air, like the smile of the

Cheshire cat. The reader's attention is called to the fact that Martha had "a rosy glow in her cheeks" (92) and later to the moment when, "taking the young girl's hand, he was about to raise it affectionately to his lips" (93), as if it too were a separate entity. During the happy early days of their marriage, the reader is told how it delighted her to "feel her husband's arm about her waist and his shoulder against her cheek," or how she "would place her finger on her lips" to warn the narrator not to waken him when he "lay picturesquely snoozing," and of the way he used to spend his time "strolling about looking at his fingernails" (95). Camillo, in one of those commonplace locutions that use a part of the body figuratively to name a psychological or subjective trait, is said to have had an excellent "eye" for comparing the narrator's landscapes to their originals. As Martha waits for the Count's return after she has reburied the statue, she sits embroidering with "her eyes fixed on her work." Such images become bizarre if for some reason we are beguiled into taking them literally, as my daughter once did as a small child when she pressed her face against her mother's knee and said, "I've got my eye on you!" The emphasis on detached body parts in "The Last of the Valerii" is likely to make the reader momentarily into such a childlike literalist. One momentarily sees the oddity of the rhetorical displacements in such bits of ordinary language.

Such locutions, both the literal ones isolating a part of the body in the midst of a narrative description and the figurative ones that are clichés, are no doubt a necessary part of any narration. How could one do otherwise in any storytelling that is at all circumstantial, just as in the real world we interpret our fellows by focusing on the gestures and expressions of one or another part of their bodies. But in "The Last of the Valerii" attention is called to this procedure. It is foregrounded, as might be said, by its iteration next to all the attention to fragmented statues. The reader comes to see a disquieting similarity between the way we read other people through individual body parts and the way a "senseless pagan block," as the narrator calls another statue on the Count's estate, can be made to seem alive if it is carved in the likeness of the human body. Both procedures depend on prosopopoeia, which always involves linguistic procedures of fragmentation and grotesque mutilation in the very act of ascribing the wholeness of a personality to a lump of marble or a lump of flesh. The trope always bears, out in the open, where any reading eye can see them, the traces of the linguistic artifice projecting a whole out of detached parts.

The implication of the disturbing reciprocity between statue-making and person-making comes to the surface especially in two passages in "The Last of the Valerii." In one James explicitly juxtaposes Martha's hands and the Juno's hands: "She laid her two rosy, ungloved hands upon the stony fingers of the goddess, and remained for some moments pressing them in her warm grasp, and fixing her living eyes upon the inexpressive brow" (102). Martha is alive and the Juno is mere marble, but Martha is about to be abandoned for this lump of stone. A little later the reader is told of a statue on the estate that Camillo especially admires: "The Hermes, for a wonder, had kept his nose; and when I reflected that my dear Countess was being neglected for this senseless pagan block, I secretly promised myself to come the next day with a hammer and deal him such a lusty blow as would make him too ridiculous for a sentimental tête-à-tête" (108–109). Here again a statue is associated with mutilation.

This occurs most disturbingly in the scene when the narrator and Martha discover that the Count has set up a makeshift altar before the Juno, "composed of a nameless fragment of antique marble, engraved with an illegible Greek inscription," and has performed a blood sacrifice. "A curious glitter on the face of the low altar" is a trickle of blood, and though it is no doubt, as the narrator assures Martha, "very innocent," the blood merely of "a lamb, a kid, or a sucking calf!" (118), Martha, the narrator, and perhaps even the reader are "agitated": "A swarm of hideous conjectures pressed into my mind, and for a moment I was sickened." That crimson trickle reveals the association of taking literally a prosopopoeia with a mutilation in which real blood flows, animal blood as a substitute for human blood. At the same time that a personification confers life and wholeness, it takes them away. The altar is a "nameless fragment of antique marble," and its Greek inscription is "illegible." Prosopopoeia seems always liable at any moment to shatter into fragments that are a revelation not of a ubiquitous spiritual life but of the senseless, shapeless, and illegible matter of which both statues and human bodies are made.

The most grotesque emphasis in the story on this dark side of prosopopoeia is the elaborated detail about the Juno's hand. The left hand of the statue has been broken off and is dug up first. The rest of the statue is the synecdochic completion of the detached part first encountered by the diggers in that damp earth. The hand then mysteriously disappears, after the rest of the Juno, minus the hand, is set up for Camillo to love and worship. The archaeologist tells the narrator that the Count has stolen it and is keeping it in a secret shrine: "And what does he do with that precious hand? He keeps it in a silver box; he has made a relic of it!" (105). The text of the story ends not with the Count's long gaze of returning affection for his wife but, after that, with a coda set off from what precedes it by an extra space. Here the narrator tells the reader an anecdote to show that Camillo "never became a thoroughly modern man." The Count, years after the main events, shows a visitor, in his cabinet of antiquities, "a marble hand, suspended in one of its inner recesses." When the visitor becomes "inquisitive":

> he looked grave and turned the lock on it. "It is the hand of a beautiful creature," he said, "whom I once greatly admired."
> "Ah,—a Roman?" said the gentleman, with a smirk.
> "A Greek," said the Count, with a frown. (122)

The Count, it seems, is not wholly cured of his primitive infatuation. This final image contains in itself both a reassertion of the irresistible power of prosopopoeia and also, once more and for the last time, indicates the way that trope always involves the projection of wholeness from a base of mutilation. The narrator's phrase, "a marble hand," is straightforwardly literal and referential. It names a hand made of marble. It is an example of the necessary referential moment in even the most elaborately overdetermined play of figurative language. On the other hand, the phrase is of course not really a literal expression. It is a kind of obscure catachresis. To say "marble hand" is like saying "table leg." It is a hand and not a hand, just as a table leg is a leg and not a leg. The Count's response to the visitor's question is also, on one level, perfectly literal. It returns to the literalism that has characterized him from the beginning. He does not say "the hand of a beautiful woman" but "the hand of a beautiful creature." "Creature" is an appropriate word for a piece of marble that has been shaped by a sculptor, created. On the other hand, the expression is also a perfectly ordinary one for a beautiful woman: "It is the hand of a beautiful creature."

Camillo is still a fetishist and an idolator, though he is now able to hide that fetishism in an elaborate irony. But for Camillo, the marble hand is a relic, an actual hand. Though a fetish may be a way of living out, as Freud says, the threat of the absence/presence of the maternal phallus, a threat much at work in Camillo's relation to the Juno, the basis of this living out is a real object, the "material base" of all the superstructure of tropological meaning. That marble hand still gives Camillo illusory access to the whole woman, or rather to Juno minus her left hand and her wand of power. Or at least it gives him access to his memory of the episode of his infatuation with her: "It is the hand of a beautiful creature . . . whom I once admired."

The inquisitive visitor apparently understands the hand to be part of a sculptural representation of a woman the Count once loved: "'Ah,—a Roman?' said the gentleman, with a smirk." The Count's answer, "A Greek," functions on three levels at once. It is meant to mislead the visitor into thinking the hand is part of a statue of a Greek woman he once admired. It accurately names the Juno as a Greek statue. And it reaffirms that the Count still yields to the fallacy of prosopopoeia. Part of him still sees the marble woman as a real Greek goddess, the hand as a part of her that still gives him access to the broken whole.

The set of different ways in which the marble hand may be taken, and is taken throughout the story, is still present in the phrasing of the coda. Perceptive readers will of course at this point reflect that we have been engaged in a similar alternation among various ways of personifying a set of material signs, the words on the page that give us access to the characters and their story. The law of personification is that for a sharp reader it uncovers as it covers over. Prosopopoeia effaces, defaces, and disfigures even as it confers, ascribes, or prescribes a face and a figure. That defacing reveals the linguistic artifice by which the trope operates, projecting a wholeness extrapolated from parts, pieces, and fragments— a face, not a whole body; perhaps a face without a nose; a voice that is imagined to speak certain words; a proper name that is both

idiosyncratic and at the same time the ascription of putative wholeness; an inscription that may become illegible, mere marks on
stone.

The uncovering is also apparently of the materiality veiled by
linguistic device. The damp earth shows through the fissures
where the statue is broken, a nose or a hand missing, or through
breaks in the text, for example that blank space between the happy
ending and the coda that contradicts it. These textual details function, if I may be allowed a neologism, as paraprosopopoeias, lay-
ing bare and canceling the power of the figure. They show the
mechanism whereby it projects a wholeness by naming a part.
They lead readers to think they have a glimpse, through the cracks
or at the edges of the broken statues, of a shapeless materiality that
lies behind this conferring of organic wholeness and form. Such
materiality is present at the semantic level in all the emphasis
throughout the story on the earth of the Count's estate and especially on its smell, "the odor of the mouldy soil," "the odor of the
humid earth" within which the Juno and who knows what other
antique sculptures are buried.

So far I have been talking primarily about the motif of fragmentation by way of details of language that express the theme semantically, as in the description of statues without noses or hands.
Mutilation appears in "The Last of the Valerii" in more disquieting, even if less ostentatious, ways. These ways are disquieting because they occur not at the semantic level but at the level of what
might be called the materiality of the letter, those letters on the
page the reader is reading. A fragmentation at this level, insofar as
it is present and has power, renders powerless even the unequivocal
semantic affirmation of the theme of fragmentation. A mutilated
text cannot even speak clearly and forcefully about mutilation.
How does this more radical unmanning take place?

It confronts the reader where the pervasive irony of the narration leads toward a suspension of clear, identifiable meaning. That
the narrator of "The Last of the Valerii" speaks ironically no adept
reader can doubt. This text, like all James's first-person narratives,
exemplifies three major features of irony.

The first is the notorious fact that irony is not signaled by any
identifiable linguistic features, as other tropes are. A simile is indi-

cated by the presence of "like" or "as." The same kind of proof by citation can be made for metaphor, metonymy, prosopopoeia, catachresis, and most other figures of speech. But it is impossible to cite a passage from an ironical text and say, "See, that is ironic," as acrimonious disagreements about ironic texts make evident. Nothing is more annoying than to find that you have been fooled into taking "straight" a statement meant to be ironic. The reaction of government officials when they discovered that Defoe's "The Shortest Way with the Dissenters" was ironic is one example. A sensitivity to irony, it can even be said, distinguishes the sheep from the goats among readers. It is the one thing needful if you want to be a good reader, though it may be the one thing most difficult to learn or teach.

The second feature of irony is that it is by no means necessarily a local trope, present in this sentence or that of an otherwise un-ironic text. A literary work often is ironic through and through, from the first word to the end. "The Last of the Valerii" is an example of that.

The third feature of irony is that, even when it can be generally agreed that a text is pervaded by irony, this is only the beginning of the problem of reading it. The questions then become, "Ironic in what way? Just how does the irony function to qualify or even to suspend meaning in this particular text?"

In the case of James's first-person stories, the "reading" of irony depends on adjudicating the difficult question of how much the narrator knows of the implications of what he says. An ironic narrator is a special case of the so-called unreliable narrator. James's characteristic first-person narrator is intelligent, perceptive. He is clearly ironic, and in the special sense of implying more than he is willing to say outright. Nevertheless, the reader is still apparently intended to understand the story better than the narrator does. Or at any rate the reader is able to do that, whether James intended it or not. The text is therefore permeated by a double form of irony. First there is the irony apparently intended by the narrator, as when he says that Martha would have been willing for Camillo's sake "to say her prayers to the sacred Bambino at Epiphany" or when he speaks of his own "passion for bedaubing old panels with ineffective portraiture of mouldy statues against screens of box."

But beyond that conscious irony are the ironies apparently not intended by the narrator. It is tempting to think of the latter as the use, through a strange kind of ventriloquism, by James himself as author, of a fictional first-person narrator to convey meanings that are not said directly. But we do not have direct access to James's conscious intentions, not even, in this case, in the form of notes, commentary, or prefatory analysis before or after the writing of the story. We are left pretty much on our own, a precarious place to be when it comes to reading an ironic text.

Although every aspect of the narration is permeated by irony's power to suspend ascertainable meaning, the most important effect of the ironic tension between what the narrator says and what is said by a kind of ghostly "undertext" is the putting in question of the happy ending. Camillo is cured of his horrid regression to paganism and becomes the last of the Valerii, the first of the almost but not quite thoroughly modern Valerios. He is brought back into the everyday world of the late nineteenth century by the patience and love of his American wife, "in her blond prettiness, so tender, so appealing, so bewitching." The narrator assists Martha in performing this feat. To him the Count in his unfortunate infatuation with the Juno "for the most part . . . seemed to me simply an unhappy young man, with an unwholesome mental twist which should be smoothed away as speedily as possible" (113).

A clue to a quite different undertext of possible meaning, playing ironically against the manifest meaning, is given by the odd episode of the German scholar who comes to the Count's door, after word of the Juno gets around. This personage tells Camillo that "your new Juno . . . is, in my opinion, much more likely to be a certain Proserpine" (103). The Count turns the German rudely away, but the reader is left wondering, "Why drag Proserpine in at this point? For that matter, why did James choose to have the statue a Juno rather than, say, an Aphrodite or a Minerva, both also mentioned in the text?"

The answer to the second question is somewhat easier to give. The Juno is described as "an embodiment of celestial supremacy and repose. Her beautiful head, bound with a single band, could have bent only to give the nod of command; her eyes looked straight before her; her mouth was implacably grave; one hand, outstretched, appeared to have held a kind of imperial wand, the arm from which the other had been broken hung at her side with the most classical majesty" (101). The Juno is a mother figure of the sort that demands of her male children the ultimate sacrifice of their masculinity. This sacrifice is mimed in the blood sacrifice Camillo performs. Like Dante Gabriel Rossetti's painting of the majestic and implacable Mnemosyne, James's Juno is endowed with a ghostly phallic imperial wand, now gone but once held in her outstretched right arm, while her left hand is broken off, in another discrete emblem of the castration she represents and will impose on those men who worship her. The Juno both has and has not the phallus, in the no-win situation Freud analyzed in his discussion of the moment that the male child discovers his mother lacks a penis. If the Juno has it, Camillo does not. If she does not have it, Camillo does not or may not. In order to grow up both historically and psychologically, Camillo must free himself from his atavistic bewitchment by this mother figure that implacably unmans all her male children. He must turn to the opposing bewitchment of the blond, American, Protestant Martha. Martha comes from his own generation and from outside Camillo's national and racial family. He must replace Juno with Martha, just as all men must turn from their mothers to women outside the family in order to grow to adulthood.

All that seems clear enough, but why then does James bring in Proserpine? The answer is given in a long speech the narrator makes to Martha when they are planning together how to cure the Count. The narrator is responding to Martha's lament for "the gulf of silence and indifference" that has opened between her and her husband. As she says, "His Juno's the reality; I'm the fiction!" the narrator replies:

> I've lately become reconciled to this gulf of silence, and to your fading for a while into a fiction. After the fable, the moral! The poor fellow has but half succumbed: the other half protests. The modern man is shut out in the darkness with his incomparable wife. How can he have failed to feel—vaguely and grossly if it must have been, but in every throb of his heart—that you are a more perfect experiment of nature, a riper fruit of time, than those primitive persons for whom Juno was a terror and Venus an example? He pays you the

compliment of believing you an inconvertible modern. He has
crossed the Acheron, but he has left you behind, as a pledge to the
present. We'll bring him back to redeem it. The old ancestral ghosts
ought to be propitiated when a pretty creature like you has sacrificed
the fragrance of her life. He has proved himself one of the Valerii;
we shall see to it that he is the last, and yet that his decease shall leave
the Conte Camillo in excellent health. (117)

The right reading of "The Last of the Valerii" depends on the right
reading of this passage. But it is by no means easy to read. The
gnomic and traditional formula, "After the fable, the moral,"
comes at an exceedingly odd place. Normally it would come at the
end of the recounting of an exemplary story, just before the drawing of ethical conclusions. Here the reader expects something like:
"The moral of the story is: 'Don't believe in personifications.'" But
in this case the formula is inserted in the middle of the story and is
followed not by a moral, but by an analysis of the situation that is
made the basis of a plan to save Martha's marriage. Moreover, the
word "fable," coming so soon after the word "fiction," seems to
echo that word and to suggest a strange reading for the formula.
Camillo's reversal of reality and fiction, turning Martha into a
statue and taking the Juno as a real person, is fabulous. It is the
fable. The moral to come after is not the drawing of general ethical
conclusions, but the reversal of the reversal that puts fiction and
reality back in their right places and returns the Count to a real
world in which moral evaluations and obligations are in their right
places, that is, in the places "modern" American Protestantism
would put them.

But just what place would that be? The Count is a double man,
half modern and half pagan. His doubleness has been given an odd
definition. Handsome as he is, Camillo is "perhaps a little stupid.
"He had a sort of sunken depth of expression, and a grave, slow
smile, suggesting no great quickness of wit, but an unimpassioned
intensity of feeling which promised well for Martha's happiness"
(89). He has a tendency to go to sleep when Martha reads the
newspapers to him. He has no understanding of the spiritual com-
plexities of Catholicism. He has an exceedingly sharp eye for the
photographic accuracy of the narrator's paintings, but apparently
no other appreciation of them. He is able to amuse himself indefi-

nitely playing a childish game: "he carried in his pocket a collection of precious fragments of antique pavement,—bits of porphyry and malachite and lapis and basalt,—disinterred on his own soil and brilliantly polished by use. With these you might see him occupied by the half-hour, playing the simple game of catch-and-toss, ranging them in a circle, tossing them in rotation, and catching them on the back of his hand. His skill was remarkable" (96). Camillo is, in short, "the natural man" (95). With his "slow-coming, slow-going smile" he is all body, a body perhaps without a soul, splendid no doubt in the physical sense as a lover for Martha but good for little else. "He had no beliefs nor hopes nor fears,—nothing but senses, appetites, and serenely luxurious tastes . . . He had moods in which his consciousness seemed so remote and his mind so irresponsive and dumb, that nothing but a powerful caress or a sudden violence was likely to arouse him" (95, 96). The modern Camillo is an absolute literalist, with no gift for understanding the exchanges, transfers, and substitutions of figurative language. His mode of transposition is to substitute one stone for another in the game of pitch and toss.

The digging up of the Juno changes all that. The one part of his mind that is not "irresponsive and dumb" is his superstitious responsiveness to the statues on his estate. The discovery of the Juno leads him to take literally the materially embodied prosopopoeia of such a statue. That in turn transforms him into someone with enough spirit to make ironic jokes, as when he tells the learned German visitor that he is "sorry you should have the trouble of carrying your little note-book so far." As the narrator ironically observed of Camillo's irony, "The Count had suddenly become witty!" (104) Camillo's new wittiness, like wit in general, involves a skill in handling figurative exchanges and in using that most difficult of tropes, irony.

Paradoxically, in order to attain enough consciousness and "soul" to be a fit husband for Martha, Camillo has to revert to a paganism that leads him to abandon her. This paganism is a strange transposition of Camillo's modern literalism. This now takes the form of an ancient taking literally of anthropomorphism, just as Pater says the ancient Greeks did. "There *is* a woman in the case," says the narrator to Martha. "Your enemy is the Juno. The

Count—how shall I say it?—the Count takes her *au sérieux*" (116).
In order to rescue the marriage, Martha and her godfather must
cure the Count of the only sort of wittiness he seems capable of.
They must return him to the condition of a man whose mind is
"irresponsive and dumb" or at any rate responsive only to Martha,
as Prince Amerigo sees only Maggie or as Drowne, in Hawthorne's "Drowne's Wooden Image," returns to his talentless carving of figureheads after his brief infatuation with a beautiful
woman inspires him to fashion a splendid statue of her. The story
defines the return of Camillo's affection to Martha as a displacement of his idolatry of the statue. He substitutes one image for
another and remains in the dangerous condition of a man who
takes tropes literally.

The countertexture of ironic meaning in the description of the
treatment of Camillo by Martha and the narrator goes against the
grain of the manifest meaning. This is made clear to the reader if
we attempt to follow out the implications of the narrator's figure
of Camillo as a man who has crossed the Acheron—an allusion
that refers us obliquely back to that seemingly trivial reference to
Proserpine. The two passages together define Camillo's relation to
his wife as an odd version of the myth of Demeter and Persephone
or of the myth of Orpheus and Eurydice. In this version the sexes
and the location of underworld and overworld are reversed.

The relation of Martha to Camillo has been from the beginning
defined in terms of the transgressive crossing of borders—the border between American and European, between unmarried and
married, between Protestant and Catholic, between Catholic and
pagan, between male and female. In the first sentence of the story,
the narrator tells the reader, "I had had occasion to declare more
than once that if my god-daughter married a foreigner I should
refuse to give her away." To "give her away" is to send her across
the frontier between virgin and married. "The Last of the Valerii"
is an early version of that theme of disastrous transatlantic court-
ships, adulterous couplings, or marriages so fundamental in
James's work. The moral of all might be: "Don't marry a foreigner." Martha is not unaware of what is transgressive in her romantic love for Camillo. "I want," she says, "to do something
more for him than girls commonly do for their lovers,—to take

some step, to run some risk, to break some law, even! I'm willing to change my religion, if he bids me." To which Camillo responds that he is "a poor Catholic," that his confessor long ago told him that he "was a good boy but a *pagan*!" (93).

Taking risks, breaking laws, and stepping across boundaries seem to be performed more by Camillo than by Martha. Demeter lost Persephone to the underworld, as Orpheus lost Eurydice. Both were able to get the lost woman back by a descent into the underworld or, in the case of Demeter, by the delegated descent of Zeus to negotiate with Dis the partial release of Persephone for part of each year. Camillo, on the other hand, has himself descended into the underworld of pagan belief, leaving his wife behind as a pledge to modernity. "He has crossed the Acheron, but he has left you behind, as a pledge to the present. We'll bring him back to redeem it" (117). This reversal of the elements of the myth relocates them, in a way that brings into the open the ironic ambiguity of what Martha does to her husband, what Maggie, in *The Golden Bowl,* does to the Prince in taking him off to American City. Martha has expressed herself as willing first to be converted to Catholicism and then to become a pagan herself in order to keep him: "he's welcome to any faith, if he will only share it with me. I'll believe in Jupiter, if he'll bid me!" Rather than redeeming his wife in the sense of bringing her across the threshold from death to life as Orpheus tries to do with Eurydice and as Demeter succeeds in getting done with Persephone, Camillo comes back himself to a realm of modern daylight that has been surreptitiously defined as the place of his death. It is as if Orpheus had gone to stay in the underworld with his lost wife or as if Demeter had descended permanently into the underworld to live with her daughter, leaving perpetual winter behind on the surface.

The transformation of the pagan Camillo, last of the Valerii, into an almost modern man, the Count Valerio, is explicitly defined as his death, or at least as the death of the pagan half of him: "He has proved himself one of the Valerii; we shall see to it that he is the last, and yet that his decease shall leave the Conte Camillo in excellent health." Camillo as the last of the Valerii has to be buried too, like the Juno, in order to make possible the resurrection of the modern Camillo.

This is a chilling implication of the last example before the coda of the naming of a part of the body rather than the whole body. The Count's reconciliation with his wife is described in straight-forward, even banal, language, the imagery of nineteenth-century popular magazine fiction or of sentimental genre painting: "he strode forward, fell on his two knees and buried his head in her lap." That is what a husband does who has betrayed his wife and has been forgiven by her. But the expression is not entirely straightforward, in fact not unlike "I've got my eye on you." As long as the phrase is taken as a cliché, there is no problem with it. But if the reader happens to take it literally, as we have been encouraged to do by those other features of the text I have discussed, it becomes ominous and violent, another image of fragmentation and mutilation. Just as Martha has reburied the Juno, so in her triumph over Camillo she has not so much buried him as led him to bury a piece of himself, his own head grotesquely detached from his body. This is that handsome head with its splendid curls already described as separated from the rest of him, perched incongruously above "the white cravat of the period" and "as massively round as that of the familiar bust of the Emperor Caracalla." The Count buries his own head as if it were a marble bust. He buries it, moreover, in his wife's lap. This image of birth in reverse or of a sexual act suggests that he has transferred to his wife his submission to Juno as majestic and emasculating mother, just as the falling on his knees echoes his prayerful submission by moonlight to the statue.

The following out of this ironic undertext leaves the reader face to face with a story that has two incompatible meanings, both of which may be supported by an elaborate integument of textual references. In one reading, Martha and the narrator cure Camillo of a dangerous mistake in the reading of signs, the pathological error of taking a statue for a real person. A healthy and happy marriage is thereby saved. Who can argue that this is not a good thing? In the other reading, Martha and the narrator "see to it" that this handsome pagan Italian is made prisoner of their own values, in an unscrupulous violence of expropriation and spiritual coercion that mimes the political and commercial imperialism of the United States over Europe. The only good European is a dead European. Martha and the narrator see to it that Camillo the pagan dies for good, that he becomes the survivor of his own death, the last of the Valerii. Who can argue that this is not a way the story can be read, and that treating another person like this is not an exceedingly bad thing to do? The attempt to read the irony of "The Last of the Valerii" leads the reader in the end to the experience of a radical suspension of unequivocal meaning. The text becomes unreadable, dead words on the page, provocative hints at meaning that cannot be satisfactorily put together in a totalizing act of comprehension. The text may be read this way or it may be read that way, but the text itself justifies the reader neither in choosing between the two nor in reconciling them in some dialectical synthesis.

This materialization of letters on a page drains them of identifiable unified meaning in an experience that matches the theme of fragmentation and mutilation. This exists in another form in the iteration of certain key words in incompatible contexts. The word "image" is used both for the statue and for Martha. In one case the word defines a fiction, the cunningly carved marble as a representation of the goddess. In the other case the word describes the warm reality of Martha, as an "image of wifely contentment." To this image Camillo must return if he is to be saved from his horrid pagan ways. If the word "image" applies properly in one context, it cannot, so it would seem, be used properly in the other context. Such simultaneous usage and counterusage drains such words of clear semantic meaning. It leaves the reader face to face with the word as such, the marks on the page or the sound of the word uttered, another form of materiality.

The text in these ways—in the theme of fragmentation, in the pervasive irony suspending unified sense, and in the materializing of words through their contradictory use—may give the reader liberating knowledge of the way prosopopoeia is imposed on a senseless materiality. It appears to give a glimpse, through the cracks, of the inaugural creative posing that has already happened, the imposition of an initiating catachrestic prosopopoeia, the hiding of an aboriginal ignorance. But to say "catachrestic prosopopoeia" is to proffer an odd sort of oxymoron. It shows the difficulty of finding appropriate terminology for a linguistic moment that could never be confronted face to face. Although the region of catachresis and the region of prosopopoeia overlap, they by no means coincide. Only the "first" prosopopoeia, it may be, was a catachresis and only some, but not all, catachreses are prosopopoeias.

A prosopopoeia in ordinary language normally substitutes for available, nonpersonifying, literal language and is oriented toward the past. A prosopopoeia is usually at least implicitly an apostrophe, an invocation, an attempt to bring back something that was presumably once present but no longer is present. A prosopopoeia ascribes a face, a voice, or a name to the absent, the inanimate, or the dead by addressing them as if they were persons who could answer back: "Ye knew him well, ye cliffs and islands of Winander." A catachresis, on the other hand, is normally oriented toward the present. It supplements or covers for a lack of literal language to name some segment of the present phenomenal world by bringing over a word from some other realm.

That the realm from which the terms are borrowed is so often a part of the body has profound significance. It indicates the human propensity to personify the surrounding world, to spread the human body everywhere around in ways that are neither figurative nor unfigurative. The ways are figurative because these entities are not really bodies or body parts, but unfigurative because the catachreses do not substitute for literal words that are part of normal language: face of a mountain, leg of a table, headland, eye of a storm. Those are "proper" unfigurative locutions. They may not be cured by a return to some nonpersonifying literal language, since the terms are themselves the literal, proper ones. But at the same time they are improper, since a mountain has no face, a table no leg, a storm no eye. The first prosopopoeia is the one that can never be reached by a backward movement of memory or of rational analysis, since it has already occurred in order to create language, time, and consciousness. This first prosopopoeia is the wholly unavailable converging point where catachresis and prosopopoeia cannot be distinguished and from which they diverge and go their own ways.

THIS UNAVAILABLE CONVERGING point is also the birthplace (to use another prosopopoeia) of ethical obligation, as I have attempted to argue throughout. To say that the point of origin is "unavailable" for a face-to-face confrontation by no means, and in no degree, takes away from its ethical obligation, the "I must" that is the ethical moment in the reading of narrative.

This unavailability does, however, place obstacles in the way of a rational comprehension of ethical obligation, as Kant long ago formulated in the last paragraph of *Grundlegung zur Metaphysik der Sitten* (Foundations of the Metaphysics of Morals), though my concentration on the linguistic and rhetorical dimension of ethics, the ethics of narrative, would give Kant's words a different sense and require a change in his formulation. Kant wrote: "Und so begreifen wir zwar nicht die praktische unbedingte Notwendigkeit des moralischen Imperativs, wir begreifen aber doch seine *Unbegreiflichkeit*" (And so we do not indeed comprehend the practical unconditional necessity of the moral imperative; yet we do comprehend its *incomprehensibility*).[4] I should say rather that we do not even comprehend its incomprehensibility, if one means by that a rational or phenomenal confrontation. That incomprehension, however, in no way lessens the practical unconditional necessity of the ethical obligation we incur when we read a narrative. We do not comprehend because neither that inaugural figure-nonfigure nor its material base was ever present as such to consciousness as something to be comprehended. The first prosopopoeia preceded consciousness and time. It generates them. Both "precedes" and "generates" are used figuratively here. They are words borrowed from a traditional paradigm of linear and causal time to name by figurative displacement an occurrence that is neither causal nor linear. Any words for it are already within the field that presupposes it. There is, for example, a latent personification in "generates." The word presupposes the situation to be explained, namely the situation in which such prosopopoeias are ineffaceable parts of ordinary language.

Of the first prosopopoeia it can be said, "Let's face it; you cannot face it." Since the first prosopopoeia was never a present event for consciousness, it cannot later be recalled either in the sense of being remembered, recollected, gathered together again as a present phenomenal object, or in the sense of being canceled, revoked, abjured, abdicated, disowned, abnegated, renounced, as for example Prometheus, in Shelley's play, attempts to "recall" his curse of Jupiter. The question at the heart of the ethics of narrative is the question of how we can be held responsible for something we cannot remember, recall in either sense, either call back in memory and so master or rescind in the sense that a defective car is recalled.

The first prosopopoeia is not available as knowledge. The apparent knowledge of it forgets it by regularizing it as "theory," say as the theory of prosopopoeia, of fragmentation as paraprosopopoeia, and of the material base. These theoretical concepts forget as they remember. They cover over in the act of apparently exposing. The initial prosopopoeia was sui generis, unique, incompatible with ordinary language, and any naming falsifies it. As Wittgenstein says at the end of the *Tractatus logico-philosophicus,* in a notorious formulation: "Wovon man nicht sprechen kann, darüber muss man schweigen" (Whereof one cannot speak one should or must remain silent).[5] The "muss" names both a necessity and an obligation. The attempt to reach back to that inaugural moment of positional language and name it is a defiance of this prohibition. The initial prosopopoeia has always already happened, and there is no way to recall it, or to name it, since all our names belong to what is derived from it, including all the names of the material base presumed to underlie the first prosopopoeia and to be covered over by it. The allegory of this failure of knowledge in "The Last of the Valerii" is the way theoretical knowledge of the dangerous mechanism of prosopopoeia, given by the story, does not prevent the reader from forgetting this insight, from having already forgotten it, necessarily, in order to read the story.

How does this happen? By the time the reader comes to understand that the trope of prosopopoeia is a linguistic error possibly leading to social and domestic disaster, it is too late. The reader has thought of the narrator, Martha, Camillo, and the rest as if they were real people. We project names, faces, voices into those inanimate black marks on the page. Nor do we cease at the end of the story to go on thinking of those characters as if they were real people. The reading of stories depends on taking prosopopoeias literally (in however subtle and sophisticated a suspension of disbelief) and is impossible without it. We repeat the mistake in an act of reading that is not so much constative as performative. The reader posits the existence of the characters, repeating in that act the act of the author in writing. The reader must take responsibility for the ethical, political, and aesthetic results of that performative act. The formulation of a moral for the fable is not the place to locate the ethics of reading narrative. The ethical act in question here is rather personifying the inanimate. This act must occur as a presupposition whatever the overt ethical themes of the story may be.

The reading of "The Last of the Valerii" is a performative speech act. It brings the black marks on the page alive and so repeats the act of Camillo before the reader learns what that act was. It does so, moreover, by necessity if the reader is to find out what that act entails. It is not that we learn ethics from reading stories, but that reading "The Last of the Valerii" is itself a paradigmatic ethical act. It posits the law, "Thou shalt not make unto thee any graven image" (said by Kant to be the most sublime expression in the Bible). At the same moment it breaks that law and must take responsibility for the lawbreaking.

This taking of responsibility might be phrased as a positive answer to a variant of Stanley Cavell's question—not "Must we mean what we say?" but "Must we do what we read?" The first law of reading is that we must do what we read. One remembers the old adage, present in Chaucer: "to make a virtue of necessity." All virtue, including the virtue that comes of reading, is of necessity. What happens when we read happens. It happens, however, by a strange nonnecessary linguistic necessity, a "necessity without necessity," as Blanchot might say. By this I mean that such necessity is not incompatible with the most strenuous freedom, though at the same time the necessity in question is more imperative in the obligation it sets up than the most irresistible material cause. Here is a case (however it may be with performatives in general) where the efficacy of a performative does not depend on the intention or knowledge of the one who performs it.

Reading opens the field for ethics, politics, aesthetics, and epistemology, but only as arenas of action that follow this inaugural doing. We must not only do what we read. We must also take responsibility thereafter for the doing of our reading, even though we did not intend to do it. This categorical imperative is an obligation to a law that did not predate the initial event of positing by reading, though it seems to have been there eternally once we become aware of it. The law was brought into existence, for us at least, in that act of positing by reading. The violence of this positing finds its figure, in "The Last of the Valerii," in the power of the long-dead ancient sculptor to chisel marble into the shape of a human body, itself the figure of an imperial and commanding goddess. All narratives, it may be, are in one way or another stories of this shaping.

The reader of "The Last of the Valerii" is like the recipient of a message on a scrap of paper: "Burn this without reading it." "The Last of the Valerii" exposes for its readers the linguistic mechanism whereby prosopopoeia occurs. It shows the disasters that can follow from taking the figure literally. But this exposing happens too late to prevent the recurrence of the prosopopoeia in the reading and the resulting incurring of responsibility for what we have done and for what that doing does. This, I conclude, is the ethics of narrative.

The understanding of this form of ethical obligation, paradigmatic for ethical obligation in general, may finally explain why renunciation, for James, is the highest virtue, and why it is so problematic. For him, only if we can undo what we have already done can we fulfill an obligation that we must incur if we are to learn what our ethical obligation is. So we must renounce. But "The Last of the Valerii," like James's more celebrated later works, indicates the way renunciation is an act of power that repeats in another form the act from which it would refrain. Renunciation would withdraw by a new speech act annulling the first. Like Isabel, Maisie, Strether, Milly, or Maggie, Martha exerts a great power over the one who has wronged her. Her power over him is her "forgiveness," her renunciation of her right to avenge the wrong. Camillo, the reader is told, "hesitated a moment, as if her very forgiveness kept the gulf open between them, and then he strode forward, fell on his two knees and buried his head in her lap."

The original act, to which we can give the general name of prosopopoeia, Pygmalion's creative act, can be recalled in the sense of remembered, neither by an inner, phenomenal recollection nor by a rational procedure of retracing a chain of signs, in some detective procedure like that of Sherlock Holmes or Sigmund Freud. But neither can the prosopopoeia be recalled in the sense of being revoked or renounced. Or this can only occur in a performative speech act that undoes the done in a new act of enunciation, annunciation, or just "-nunciation." This "-nunciation," as the "re" or "ab" or "a" in these double antithetical words indicates, can cross out an earlier speech act only by a positing that repeats the first performative in a new form and incurs a new round of obligation in its turn. The series forms an endless sequence in which the renunciation can never quite catch up with the obligation.[6] But the first positing was already as secondary as any of its later repetitions or re-enunciations.

This perpetual belatedness is present in one way or another in all the stories discussed in this book. It finds its emblem in the way Pygmalion fashioned Galatea, a new painted lady, in compensation for all the fallen and painted ladies who haunted his imagination, so repeating what was done in the act that would make up for it. But these acts, like those performed in the stories read here and like writing, reading, and teaching them, are also oriented toward the future. They are affirmative, productive, inaugural. They enter the cultural and historical world to change it and keep it going forward. Each of my texts not only tells how that happens but, as a work of importance in our culture, is an example of it. We appropriate these stories for our own performative uses. Each also helps us to understand what is at stake in such appropriations, for example Kleist's demonstration of the political efficacy of thoughts improvised while speaking or the analyses by Melville and Blanchot of attempts through narration to account for another person.

Notes

Proem

1. P. Ovidius Naso, *Metamorphoseon Libri XV*, ed. Hugo Magnus (New York: Arno Press, 1979, reprint of the 1914 edition published by Weidmann, Berlin), 10.228, 232–234. For the English translation I have used *Metamorphoses*, trans. Mary M. Innes (Harmondsworth: Penguin Books, 1955), p. 231. Further citations from the *Metamorphoses* are given in text, first by book and line numbers from the Latin, followed by page numbers from the English.

2. See Paul de Man, "Anthropomorphism and Trope in the Lyric," *The Rhetoric of Romanticism* (New York: Columbia University Press, 1984), p. 241.

1. The Ethics of Narration

1. Henry James, *The Golden Bowl*, vol. 23, Charles Scribner's New York Edition of 1909 (reprint New York: Augustus M. Kelley, 1971), p. xxiv. Further citations from James's novels and tales are from this edition, unless otherwise noted.

2. Ibid., p. xxiv.

3. Anthony Trollope, *He Knew He Was Right* (New York: Dover Publications, 1983), 1.104.

4. James, 11.354.

5. Franz Kafka, *The Trial*, trans. Willa and Edwin Muir (Harmondsworth: Penguin Books, 1953), p. 7.

6. Paul de Man, foreword to Carol Jacobs, *The Dissimulating Harmony* (Baltimore: Johns Hopkins University Press, 1978), p. xi.

7. Sylviane Agacinski, *Aparté: Conceptions and Deaths of Søren Kierkegaard*, trans. Kevin Newmark (Tallahassee: Florida State University Press, 1988), p. 3.

2. Reading, Knowing, Doing

1. See J. A. Ward, *The Search for Form: Studies in the Structure of James's Fiction* (Chapel Hill: University of North Carolina Press, 1967); Walter Isle, *Experiments*

in Form: Henry James's Novels, 1896–1901 (Cambridge: Harvard University Press, 1968); Juliet Mitchell, "*What Maisie Knew:* Portrait of the Artist as a Young Girl," *The Air of Reality: New Essays on Henry James,* ed. John Goode (London: Methuen, 1972), pp. 168–189; Merla Wolk, "Narration and Nurture in *What Maisie Knew,*" *Henry James Review,* 4.3 (1983), 165–206; Dennis Foster, "Maisie Supposed to Know: Amo(u)ral Analysis," *Henry James Review,* 5.3 (1984), 207–216; Carren Kaston, *Imagination and Desire in the Novels of Henry James* (New Brunswick: Rutgers University Press, 1984); Donna Przybylowicz, *Desire and Repression: The Dialectic of Self and Other in the Late Works of Henry James* (University: University of Alabama Press, 1986); Sharon Cameron, *Thinking in Henry James* (Chicago: University of Chicago Press, 1989). I am also indebted to brilliant unpublished work on *What Maisie Knew* by Julie Rivkin (in a book forthcoming from Stanford University Press); Deborah Esch; and Shiela Teahan.

2. In *Thinking in Henry James.*

3. James, *The Ambassadors,* 22.326.

4. James, *What Maisie Knew,* 11.viii.

5. David Oberhelman has kindly prepared for me the following summary of changes in divorce laws in England from 1700 to the present:

"Divorce continued to be obtainable by an Act of Parliament through the 1700s, although the ecclesiastical courts still in principle controlled all divorce proceedings. The number of applications rose steadily, however, up to the end of the century, forcing the Lords to restructure the procedure for making a petition. Lord Chancellor Loughborough authored a set of resolutions which imposed harsh restrictions on husbands seeking divorce: they had to secure a decree of divorce *a mensa et thoro* from the ecclesiastical courts and an award of damages against their wives' seducers in the secular courts, in addition to meeting certain elegibility requirements, before they could approach the House of Lords. The effect of these resolutions was that aggrieved husbands alone could petition, and the limitations made divorce an even more costly and difficult procedure.

"In 1850 a Royal Commission headed by Lord Campbell was created to suggest changes in the structure of divorce laws. The Campbell Report's conclusions led to the passage of the Matrimonial Causes Act of 1857, the most important piece of divorce legislation in the nineteenth century. The Act removed divorce from the jurisdiction of the ecclesiastical courts, placing it entirely with 'the court for Divorce and Matrimonial Causes,' and did away with the requisite Act of Parliament to finalize divorce proceedings. The Act made divorce accessible to middle-class petitioners who previously could not afford it. Yet the substance of the old divorce laws was essentially transferred into the new ones: the old decree of divorce *a mensa et thoro* was renamed a decree of judicial separation, and the husband still had the advantage in the proceedings (the husband could file for divorce based on his wife's adultery alone; the wife had to bring charges of adultery aggravated by incest, cruelty, desertion, etc.).

"The legislation led to a larger number of petitions, but the remedies were still limited to the monied sections of the British populace. Dissatisfaction with the new law, especially with its harsh treatment of wives, grew in the next century.

The 1909 Gorell Report was the first to recommend that 'the law should be amended so as to place the two sexes on an equal footing as regards the grounds on which divorce may be obtained.' Further legislation passed in 1923, 1937, and 1946 followed that advice and led to the current structure of British divorce laws."

6. See Lawrence Stone, *The Family, Sex and Marriage in England, 1500–1800* (New York: Harper and Row, 1977). I am also indebted to an admirable unpublished paper presented at Irvine on Defoe's *Roxana* by David Oberhelman, " 'I would be a *Man-Woman*': *Roxana* and Ideological Representations of the Female Subject."

7. Henry James, *Complete Notebooks*, ed. Leon Edel and Lyall H. Powers (New York: Oxford University Press, 1987), p. 146, henceforth abbreviated N in text.

8. James, *The Awkward Age*, 9.v.

9. James, *Roderick Hudson*, 1.vii.

10. "Embedded" is Stephen Greenblatt's word (or figure). See his *Renaissance Self-Fashioning: From More to Shakespeare* (Chicago: University of Chicago Press, 1980), p. 5.

11. But the matter is of course note quite so simple in Plato. For a discussion of virtue, see my "Face to Face: Plato's *Protagoras* as a Model for Collective Research in the Humanities," *The States of "Theory": History, Art, and Critical Discourse*, ed. David Carroll (New York: Columbia University Press, 1989).

12. This phrase modifies Charles du Bos's splendid definition of the power that Robert Browning wields in his dramatic monologues, the power of *l'introspection d'autrui*, the introspection of others (*Etudes anglaises*, 7 [1954], 1964). The product of Browning's imaginative power of introspection, however, is a first-person present tense, miming of the speech of another. In James's case, as is the case of narration generally in novels not told in the first person by a character, the product of imaginary introspection of another speaks of that other in the third person, mingles two languages inextricably in indirect discourse (that of the introspecting person and that of the person introspected), and is in the past tense. It is the retrospective introspection of another. It should be remembered, by the way, that strictly speaking a "third-person narration" is as much in the first person as any autobiographical novel. The anonymous "omniscient" narrator of *Middlemarch* is as much an "I" as Marlow in *Lord Jim*.

13 For an authoritative essay on this topic, see Michal Peled Ginsburg, "Free Indirect Discourse: A Reconsideration," *Language and Style*, 15 (1982), 133–149.

14. See Jean-Jacques Rousseau, *Pygmalion*, in *Oeuvres complètes*, ed. Bernard Gagnebin and Marcel Raymond, vol. 1 (Paris: Gallimard, 1961), pp. 1224–31. For a discussion of this text, see Paul de Man, "Self (*Pygmalion*)," *Allegories of Reading* (New Haven: Yale University Press, 1979), pp. 160–187.

15. The sex of the reader might make a difference, but this would be hard to define, since it is subject to so many social and personal variables.

16. There would be much to say about "Oh!" in James. "Oh!" is an exclamation on the border between word and inarticulate cry. "Oh!" in one sense means nothing: it has no semantic content. On the other hand, it serves an indispensable

function: it may be a means of expressing or at any rate indicating the inexpressible, the "unspeakable." This inexpressible that nevertheless gets expressed by the "Oh!" may be what in another person is truly "other," or it may be something "other" than any person, for example the absolute otherness of death. *The Wings of the Dove* is so punctuated by crucial confrontations pivoting on "Oh!" that it might almost be said that learning to read this novel means learning to read "Oh!" The reader's attention is called early in the novel to "Oh!" in a passage where Densher admires Lord Mark's superior command of its use, in this case to respond to Kate's introduction of Densher to him: "'Oh!' said the other party while Densher said nothing—occupied as he mainly was on the spot with weighing the sound in question. He recognised it in a moment as less imponderable than it might have appeared, as having indeed positive claims. It wasn't, that is, he knew, the 'Oh!' of the idiot, however great the superficial resemblance: it was that of the clever, the accomplished man; it was the very specialty of the speaker, and a great deal of expensive training and experience had gone to producing it. Densher felt somehow that, as a thing of value accidentally picked up, it would retain an interest of curiosity" (*The Wings of the Dove*, 20.57). On the next page: "'Oh!' said Lord Mark again—and again it was just as good. That [the 'Oh!'] was for Densher, the latter could see, or think he saw" (58). If Densher begins as a good reader of the "Oh!"s of another, the novel ends, after many intermediate "Oh!"s, with a passage demonstrating that Densher too has learned its uses. In response to Kate's assertion that she will give up Milly Theale's money and marry him if he gives his word of honor that he's not in love with Milly's memory, Densher says only: "Oh—her memory!" (405). This one "Oh—" means they will never be again as they were and separates them forever. Sir Claude's "Oh!" in *What Maisie Knew* anticipates Densher's. It lets Maisie know she has lost everything.

17. Published in pamphlet form as "Is There an Ethics of Reading?" (Tokyo: English Literary Society of Japan, 1986), 25 pp., reprinted in *Reading Narrative: Form, Ethics, Ideology*, ed. James Phelan (Columbus: Ohio State University Press, 1989), pp. 79–101.

18. The phrase "vicious circle" reappears, used in somewhat the same way, in a crucial scene in *The Golden Bowl*, the scene of Fanny Assingham's midnight colloquy with her husband at the end of the first book. As is often the case with James, for example in the relation between *Roderick Hudson* and *The Ambassadors*, the later novel is a transformational rewriting and reinterpretation of the earlier one. Maggie, says Mrs. Assingham, "has done the most" to bring things among the four principal protagonists to their present pass: "Well, she did it originally—she *began* the vicious circle. For that—though you make round eyes at my associating her with 'vice'—is simply what it has been. It's their mutual consideration, all round, that has made it the bottomless gulf; and they're really so embroiled but because, in their way, they've been so improbably *good*." She goes on, in a new variation on the economic imagery for moral relations so important in *Maisie*, to define Maggie's part in the vicious circle as a constant impossible attempt to "make up" first to her father and then to the Prince for having taken

attention away from either one of them in order to fulfill her obligation to the other. "Before she knew it at any rate," says Mrs. Assingham, "her little scruples and her little lucidities, which were really so divinely blind—her feverish little sense of justice, as I say—had brought the two others [Charlotte and the Prince] together as her grossest misconduct couldn't have done" (23.394, 396). Maggie's goodness, like Maisie's, proliferates vice in these around her; it also makes bad worse.

19. See Neil Hertz, "Dora's Secrets, Freud's Techniques," *Diacritics*, 13 (Spring 1983), 65–76. "*What Maisie Knew*, James seems to be claiming," says Hertz, "could not have been written if he hadn't had access to what Maisie in fact knew" (p. 67). Hertz's fine essay has been reprinted in his *The End of the Line* (New York: Columbia University Press, 1985).

20. For a discussion of the principle of reason, see Martin Heidegger, *Der Satz vom Grund* (Pfullingen: Günther Neske, 1957). See also Jacques Derrida, "The Principle of Reason: The University in the Eyes of Its Pupils," trans. Catherine Porter and Edward P. Morris, *Diacritics*, 13 (Fall 1983), 3–20.

21. Maurice Blanchot, "La voix narrative (le 'il,' le neutre)," *L'entretien infini* (Paris: Gallimard, 1969), pp. 556–567.

22. In the formulations in this and the previous paragraph I am indebted to questions posed by Jeffrey Belnap and Linette Davis. My remarks about the depersonalizing of the narrator were instigated by a question from Laura Zakarin. These questions and comments came out of a seminar I gave at Irvine.

23. See "Re-Reading Re-Vision: James and Benjamin," the last chapter of my *The Ethics of Reading*, pp. 101–127.

24. "The invention of the other" is Jacques Derrida's phrase. See "Psyché: L'invention de l'autre," *Psyché: Inventions de l'autre* (Paris: Galilée, 1987), pp. 11–61.

3. Just Reading

1. Heinrich von Kleist, *Sämtliche Werke und Briefe*, vol. 2 (Munich: Carl Hanser Verlag, 1961), pp. 319–324; translated in Philip B. Miller, *An Abyss Deep Enough: Letters of Heinrich von Kleist, with a Selection of Essays and Anecdotes* (New York: E. P. Dutton, 1982), pp. 218–222. Further page references to these volumes are given in text, German edition first and then the English.

2. See Paul de Man, *The Resistance to Theory* (Minneapolis: University of Minnesota Press, 1986), pp. 3–20.

3. Jacques Derrida, "The Conflict of Faculties: A *Mochlos*," trans. Cynthia Chase, Jonathan Culler, and Irving Wohlfarth, forthcoming in a book from Columbia University Press, edited by Michael Riffaterre. For the French original see Derrida, "Mochlos, ou le conflit des facultés," *Philosophie*, 2 (1981), 4.

4. Johann Wolfgang Goethe, *Die Wahlverwandtschaften* (Munich: Deutscher Taschenbuch, 1963), p. 34.

5. Johann Wolfgang von Goethe, *Elective Affinities* (New York: Frederick Ungar, 1962), p. 38.

6. Sigmund Freud, *Jokes and Their Relation to the Unconscious,* trans. James Strachey, *Standard Edition of the Complete Psychological Works of Sigmund Freud* (London: Hogarth Press and the Institute of Psycho-Analysis, 1953–1974), 6.115.

7. Paul de Man, *The Rhetoric of Romanticism* (New York: Columbia University Press, 1984), p. 122.

8. See Immanuel Kant, *Grundlegung zur Metaphysik der Sitten, Werkausgabe,* ed. Wilhelm Weischedel, vol. 7 (Frankfurt am Main: Suhrkamp, 1982), p. 102: "Und so begreifen wir zwar nicht die praktische unbedingte Notwendigkeit des moralischen Imperativs, wir begreifen aber doch seine *Unbegreiflichkeit,* welches alles ist, was billigermassen von einer Philosophie, die bis zur Grenze der menschlichen Vernunft in Prinzipien strebt, gefodert werden kann." English translation: Kant, *Foundations of the Metaphysics of Morals,* trans. Lewis White Beck (Philadelphia: Bobbs-Merrill Educational Publishing, 1969), p. 94: "And so we do not indeed comprehend the practical unconditional necessity of the moral imperative; yet we do comprehend its incomprehensibility, which is all that can be fairly demanded of a philosophy which in its principles strives to reach the limit of human reason."

9. Here is Kleist's formulation of this in the letter to Wilhelmine: "*Bildung* schien mir das einzige Ziel, das des Bestrebens, *Wahrheit* der einzige Reichtum, der des Besitzes würdig ist" (*Education* seemed to me the only goal worth the striving, and *Truth* the only wealth worth the having; 633; 95).

10. See Friedrich Nietzsche, *Untimely Meditations,* trans. R. J. Hollingdale (Cambridge: Cambridge University Press, 1983), p. 140; in German: Nietzsche, *Werke in Drei Bänden,* ed. Karl Schlechta, vol. 1 (Munich: Carl Hanser, 1966), pp. 302–302: "it seems to me, indeed, that Kant has had a living and life-transforming influence on only a very few men. One can read everywhere, I know, that since this quiet scholar produced his work a revolution has taken place in every domain of the spirit; but I cannot believe it. For I cannot see it in those men who would themselves have to be revolutionized before a revolution could take place in any whole domain whatever. If Kant ever should begin to exercise any wide influence we shall be aware of it in the form of a gnawing and disintegrating scepticism and relativism [eines zernagenden und zerbröckelnden Skeptizismus und Relativismus]; and only in the most active and noble spirits who have never been able to exist in a state of doubt would there appear instead that undermining and despair of all truth [jene Erschütterung und Verzweiflung an aller Wahrheit] such as Heinrich von Kleist for example experienced as the effect of the Kantian philosophy."

11. See Jacques Derrida, "Déclarations d'indépendence," *Otobiographies* (Paris: Galilée, 1984), pp. 13–32.

12. This recalls the story of André Gide's jealousy when he learned that his friend Paul Valéry discussed his latest ideas every morning with someone he met on the streetcar traveling to work. The unknown interlocutor turned out to be an intellectually undistinguished Parisian, who played for Valéry the role of Molière's housemaid.

13. See Paul de Man's brief comment on Kleist's "On the Gradual Fabrication" at the end of his essay on "On the Puppet Theater." The sentence is an example

of what it talks about, since it turns on the "accidental" fact that the German syllable "fall" has been, within the German language, combined with a series of different prefixes to produce a cluster of words that do not form a logical system, though to use any one of the words is to invoke the possibility of the others as a shadowy background: "As we know from another narrative text of Kleist [his footnote here refers to "On the Gradual Fabrication"], the memorable tropes that have the most success ('Beifall') occur as mere random improvisation ('Einfall') at the moment when the author has completely relinquished any control over his meaning and has relapsed ('Zurückfall') into the extreme formalization, the mechanical predictability of grammatical declensions ('Fälle')." "Aesthetic Formalization in Kleist," *The Rhetoric of Romanticism* (New York: Columbia University Press, 1984), p. 290. De Man's insight into the power of language conceived of as the random or arbitrary filling out of preexisting grammatical or syntactical patterns is expressed repeatedly in his later work, but the most rigorous working out of the implications of this insight is made in the final pages of his reading of Shelley's "The Triumph of Life" in "Shelley Disfigured," *The Rhetoric of Romanticism,* esp. pp. 111–123.

14. Translation of the French: "As for the shepherd . . . one might say . . . he well deserves to suffer . . . being one of those people . . . who builds himself a chimerical empire over the animals."

15. The example is Tom Keenan's. For a superb discussion of the most notorious dash (Gedankenstrich) in Kleist's work, see Deborah Esch, "Toward a Midwifery of Thought: Reading Kleist's 'Die Marquise von O . . . ,'" *Textual Analysis: Some Readers Reading,* ed. Mary Ann Caws (New York: Modern Language Association, 1986), pp. 144–155. I am grateful for observations about Kleist's "On the Gradual Fabrication" made by Keenan and Werner Hamacher.

16. A Kleistian bottle was the German name for a Leyden jar, which an ancestor of Heinrich von Kleist had independently invented in 1745.

17. Cited by Martin Greenberg in the Introduction to Heinrich von Kleist, *The Marquise of O and Other Stories,* trans. Martin Greenberg (New York: Ungar, 1973), p. 33.

18. Heinrich von Kleist, *Plays,* ed. Walter Hinderer, The German Library, vol. 25 (New York: Continuum, 1982), p. 114.

19. For a brilliant discussion of the latter, as well as of "Improbable Veracities" and "The Foundling," see Carol Jacobs, "The Style of Kleist," *Diacritics,* 9 (Winter 1979), 47–61.

20. See Matthew 11:33: "For I am come to set a man at variance against his father, and the daughter against her mother, and the daughter in law against her mother in law."

21. See Philippe Lacoue-Labarthe, *La Fiction du politique: Heidegger, l'art et la politique* (Paris: Christian Bourgois, 1987), esp. the section entitled "Mimétologie," pp. 114–133.

22. Paul de Man, *Allegories of Reading* (New Haven: Yale University Press, 1979), p. 245. De Man is speaking of Kleist's plays, but the observation applies just as well to the stories.

23. Andrzej Warminski, "A Question of an Other Order: Deflections of the Straight Man," *Diacritics*, 9 (Winter 1979), 70–78.

24. Immanuel Kant, *Critique of Pure Reason*, trans. Norman Kemp Smith (New York: St Martin's Press, 1965), p. 233; *Kritik der reinen Vernunft, I, Werkausgabe*, ed. Wilhelm Weischedel, vol. 3 (Frankfurt am Main: Suhrkamp, 1976), p. 231. For an authoritative discussion of Kant's theory of causality, see Gerd Buchdahl, "The Kantian 'Dynamic of Reason,' with Special Reference to the Place of Causality in Kant's System," *Kant Studies Today*, ed. Lewis White Beck (La Salle, Ill.: Open Court, 1969), pp. 341–374.

25. Warminski, "A Question of an Other Order," p. 75.

26. Ibid., pp. 71ff.

27. This passage is cited and discussed by Jacques Derrida in *D'un ton apocalyptique adopté naguère en philosophie* (Paris: Galilée, 1983), pp. 53–57, trans. John P. Leavey, Jr., "Of an Apocalyptic Tone Recently Adopted in Philosophy," *Oxford Literary Review*, 6.2 (1984), 18–20. For the original German see Kant, "Von einem neuerdings erhobenen vornehmen Ton in der Philosophie" (1796), *Werke*, ed. Ernst Cassirer, vol. 6 (Berlin, 1923), pp. 494–495. I have borrowed some sentences in my discussion here from my "Prosopopoeia in Hardy and Stevens," *Alternative Hardy*, ed. Lance St. John Butler (London: Macmillan, 1989), pp. 110–127.

28. For a brilliant essay on another region of Kant's thought in which personification appears as a way of thinking about what cannot be known directly, see Cathy Caruth, "The Force of Example: Kant's Symbols," *Yale French Studies*, 74 (1988), 17–37.

29. See my analysis of this in "Reading Telling: Kant," *The Ethics of Reading* (New York: Columbia University Press, 1987), pp. 13–39.

4. Who Is He?

1. Herman Melville, "Bartleby, The Scrivener," *Pierre; Israel Potter; The Pizza Tales; The Confidence Man; Uncollected Prose; Billy Budd, Sailor* (New York: Library of America, 1984), pp. 663–664. Page numbers in text refer to this edition. I have followed convention in dropping the comma from the title, but the comma signals the gap between Bartleby as name and as social function.

2. I owe this detail, as well as some other features of my reading, to an unpublished lecture on "Bartleby" by Andrzej Warminski.

3. See Brook Thomas, "The Legal Fictions of Herman Melville and Lemuel Shaw," *Critical Inquiry*, 11 (September 1984), 24–51, and "'Bartleby, the Scrivener,' Fellow Servants and Free Agents on Wall Street," *Cross-Examinations of Law and Literature: Cooper, Hawthorne, Stowe, and Melville* (Cambridge: Cambridge University Press, 1987), pp. 164–182.

4. I have discussed this story in an essay published in part in "Literature and History: The Example of Hawthorne's 'The Minister's Black Veil,'" *Bulletin of the American Academy of Arts and Sciences*, 41 (February 1988), 15–31. The full study is scheduled for publication in 1990 by Blackwell as *Hawthorne and History*.

5. Maurice Blanchot, in a remarkable paragraph on "Bartleby" (*L'ecriture du désastre* [Paris: Gallimard, 1980], pp. 33–34), stresses this passivity or "patience" and its effective force in opening "à la défaillance, à la perte d'être, à la pensée" (to exhaustion or default, to the loss of being, to thought): "'Je ne le ferai pas,' aurait encore signifié une détermination énergique, appelant une contradiction énergique. '*Je préférerais ne pas . . .*' appartient à l'infini de la patience, ne laissant pas de prise à l'intervention dialectique: nous somme tombés hors de l'être, dans le champ du dehors où, immobiles, marchant d'un pas égal et lent, vont et viennent les hommes détruits" ("I shall not do it" would still have signified an energetic determination, calling for an energetic contradiction. "*I would prefer not to . . .*" belongs to the infinity of patience, not leaving any purchase for dialectical intervention: we have fallen outside being, in the region of the outside where, immobile, walking with a slow and even pace, go and come the destroyed men).

6. The essays by no means fall neatly into the two categories I have defined as typical strategies of "accounting." Nor do the ones that invoke history agree on just which historical facts ought to be adduced or, more importantly, on just how these contextual facts account for the text. Their diversity is striking, as is the energy with which they respond to the story's urgent demand for an explanation. About forty articles exist, going from Leo Marx, "Melville and the Parable of the Walls," *Sewanee Review*, 41 (Autumn 1953), 602–627, to recent essays like John Carlos Rowe, "Ecliptic Voyaging: Orbits of the Sign in Melville's 'Bartleby the Scrivener,'" *Through the Custom-House: Nineteenth-Century American Fiction and Modern Theory* (Baltimore: Johns Hopkins University Press, 1982), pp. 111–138; Michael Paul Rogin, *Subversive Genealogy: The Politics and Art of Herman Melville* (New York: Alfred A. Knopf, 1983), pp. 192–201; Michael Clark, "Witches and Wall Street: Possession Is Nine-Tenths of the Law," *Texas Studies in Language and Literature*, 25.1 (1983), 55–76; Ann Smock, "Quiet," *Qui parle*, 2 (Fall 1988), 68–100.

5. Death Mask

1. George Eliot, *Daniel Deronda*, in *Works*, vol. 1, Cabinet Edition (Edinburgh and London: William Blackwood and Sons, n.d.), chap. 6, p. 90.

2. First published in *Première livraison* (1976), my trans. The same text reappears but with a question mark after the title—"une scène primitive?"—and a paragraph break after "sans lointain," in *L'écriture du désastre* (Paris: Gallimard, 1980), p. 117. See also Blanchot's remarkable commentaries on this text later on in *L'écriture du désastre*, pp. 176–179; 191–196. For a translation see *The Writing of the Disaster*, trans. Ann Smock (Lincoln: University of Nebraska Press, 1986).

3. See Blanchot's commentary on this, given within quotation marks, as if it were cited from some other writer: "'—Mais "l'au-delà," arrêté par la décision de ce mot évidé "rien" qui n'est lui-même rien, est au contraire appelé dans la scène, dès que le mouvement d'ouverture, dès que la révélation, ainsi que la tension du rien, de l'être et de l'il y a interviennent et provoquent l'ébranlement interminable. —Je le concède: "rien est ce qu'il y a" interdit de se laisser dire en tranquille

et simple négation (comme si à sa place l'éternel traducteur écrivait: "Il n'y a rien.").—Nulle négation, mais des termes pesants, stances juxtaposées (sans voisinage), suffisance fermée (hors signification), chacun immobile et muet, et ainsi usurpant leur rapport en phrase dont nous serions bien embarrassés de désigner ce qui voudrait s'y dire. —Embarras est peu: passe par cette phrase ce qu'elle ne peut contenir qu'en éclatant. —Pour ma part, j'entends l'irrévocable de l'*il y a* que être et rien, houle vaine, déployant, reployant, traçant, effaçant, roulent selon le rythme de l'anonyme bruissement'" ("But 'the beyond,' brought to a stop by the decision of this emptied out word, 'nothing,' that is in itself nothing, is on the contrary called on the scene, as soon as the movement of opening, as soon as the revelation, along with the tension of nothing, of being, and of the 'there is,' intervene and provoke the interminable shaking. —I concede it: 'Nothing is what there is there' cannot be said in tranquil and simple negation (as if in its place the eternal translator wrote: 'There is nothing there'). —No negation, but weighty terms, standing juxtaposed (without closeness), firm sufficiency (beyond meaning), each one immobile and mute, and thereby usurping their relation within the sentence, of which we would be very hard put to say what is meant to be said by it. —'Hard put' is hardly adequate: that sentence is traversed by what it cannot contain without breaking into pieces. —For my part, I hear the irrevocable of the 'there is' that being and nothing, vain swell, spreading out, building up again, tracing, effacing, roll according to the rhythm of the anonymous rustling of the wind"). *L'écriture du désastre,* p. 178, my trans.

4. Wallace Stevens, *Collected Poems* (New York: Alfred A. Knopf, 1954), p. 10.

5. Henry James, "The Art of Fiction," *Literary Criticism: Essays on Literature; American Writers; English Writers* (New York: Library of America, 1984), p. 53.

6. Joseph Conrad, *The Secret Agent* (Garden City: Doubleday, Page, 1925), p. xiii.

7. Maurice Blanchot, *L'arrêt de mort* (Paris: Gallimard, 1948), p. 7; Maurice Blanchot, *Death Sentence,* trans. Lydia Davis (Barrytown, New York: Station Hill Press, 1978), p. 1. Page numbers in text are first to the French and then to the English.

8. Maurice Blanchot, *Le pas au-delà* (Paris: Gallimard, 1973), p. 136, my trans. The infinitive "mourir," in Blanchot's usage, means an interminable process of dying. It is opposed to "mort," the fait accompli of death. Yet another passage in Blanchot, this one in "La solitude essentielle," associates the act of writing with "l'interminable, l'incessant" and, as in the case of passages of beginning and ending I have cited from *L'arrêt de mort,* affirms that mastery begins where writing stops, begins, that is, with the nonwriting performed by "the other hand," the hand that does not write: "La maîtrise de l'écrivain n'est pas dans la main qui écrit, cette main 'malade' qui ne lâche jamais le crayon, qui ne peut le lâcher, car ce qu'elle tient, elle ne le tient pas réellement, ce qu'elle tient appartient à l'ombre, et elle-même est une ombre. Le maîtrise est toujours le fait de l'autre main, celle qui n'écrit pas, capable d'intervenir au moment où il faut, de saisir le crayon et de l'écarter. La mâîtrise consiste donc dans le pouvoir de cesser d'écrire,

d'interrompre ce qui s'écrit, en rendant ses droits et son tranchant décisif à l'instant" (The writer's mastery does not lie in the hand that writes, the "sick" hand that never lets go of the pencil, that cannot let it go because it does not really hold what it is holding; what it holds belongs to shadow, and the hand itself is a shadow. Mastery is always the achievement of the other hand, the one that does not write, the one that can intervene just when it has to, grasp the pencil and take it away. Mastery, then, consists of the power to stop writing, to interrupt what is being written, giving its rights and its exclusive cutting edge back to the instant). Maurice Blanchot, "La solitude essentielle," *L'espace littéraire* (Paris: Gallimard, 1955), pp. 15–16; "The Essential Solitude," *The Gaze of Orpheus and Other Literary Essays,* trans. Lydia Davis (Barrytown, N.Y.: Station Hill Press, 1981), pp. 67–68.

9. Jean-Jacques Rousseau, *Oeuvres complètes,* ed. Barnard Gagnebin and Marcel Raymond, vol. 1 (Paris: Gallimard, 1959), p. 3, my trans. The odd accenting of the French is Rousseau's.

10. "I write my death" is Cathy Caruth's phrase, in an unpublished lecture at Yale.

11. Walter Benjamin, *Illuminationen* (Frankfurt am Main: Suhrkamp, 1969), p. 65; Walter Benjamin, *Illuminations,* trans. Harry Zohn (New York: Schocken Books, 1969), p. 78.

12. Maurice Blanchot, "Traduire," *L'amitié* (Paris: Gallimard, 1971), pp. 70–71, my trans.

13. Sigmund Freud, "Bruchstück einer Hysterie-Analyse," *Gesammelte Werke,* vol. 5 (Frankfurt am Main: Fischer, 1942), p. 280; "Fragment of an Analysis of a Case of Hysteria," *Standard Edition of the Complete Psychological Works,* 7.116.

14. William Faulkner, or rather Henry Sutpen in Faulkner's *Absalom! Absalom!,* asks this question and gives a positive answer: "Suppose I assume an obligation to a man who cannot speak my language, the obligation stated to him in his own and I agree to it: am I any the less obligated because I did not happen to know the tongue in which he accepted me in good faith? No: the more, the more." (New York: Vintage Books, 1972, p. 118).

15. This is the phrase in Bathsheba's valentine in Hardy's *Far From the Madding Crowd.* Bathsheba's "Marry Me!" is emitted, like the narrator's proposal in *L'arrêt de mort,* frivolously, by accident, so to speak. "Marry Me!" is chosen by Bathsheba somewhat maliciously from among other conventional valentine mottoes. Still the words have a terrible performative effect on poor Farmer Boldwood, who takes them seriously.

16. Dylan Thomas, "Altarwise by owl-light," *Collected Poems* (New York: New Directions, 1953), p. 80.

6. Facing It

1. Henry James, "The Last of the Valerii," *Complete Tales,* ed. Leon Edel, vol. 3 (Philadelphia: J. B. Lippincott, 1962), p. 93.

2. See Paul de Man, "Allegory: *Julie,*" *Allegories of Reading* (New Haven: Yale

University Press, 1979), p. 205. See also my commentary on this passage in "Reading Part of a Paragraph of *Allegories of Reading*," *Reading de Man Reading*, ed. Lindsay Waters and Wlad Godzich (Minneapolis: University of Minnesota Press, 1989), pp. 155–170.

3. Walter Pater, "The Myth of Demeter and Persephone," *Greek Studies* (London: Macmillan, 1910), p. 100.

4. Immanuel Kant, *Grundlegung zur Metaphysik der Sitten, Werkausgabe,* ed Wilhelm Weischedel, vol. 7 (Frankfurt am Main: Suhrkamp, 1982), p. 102; *Foundations of the Metaphysics of Morals,* trans. Lewis White Beck (Indianapolis: Bobbs-Merrill Educational Publishing, 1969), p. 94.

5. Ludwig Wittgenstein, *Schriften* (Frankfurt am Main: Suhrkamp, 1960), p. 83.

6. The prefix in these words is the signal of their status as a peculiar form of repetition, undoing by redoing. Each names a new speech act whose purpose is to cancel an earlier speech act, just as a postage stamp, a configuration of signs that sends a letter from here to there, is "canceled" by the superimposition of another configuration of signs that is both necessary to the proper functioning of the stamp and at the same time makes it impossible to use it again on another letter. These words fall into two groups, one in "re-" and one in "ab-" or "a-." Each word desingnates a different form of the operation of canceling by repetition. Each would deserve a long analysis of its specific working in ordinary language. This would involve also an analysis of the adjacent family of words with the same root: "vocation" and "invoke" along with "revoke"; "call" along with "recall"; "sign," "design," and "ensign" along with "resign," and so on.

Here are some of the words in the series: resign, revoke, rescind, recollect, recall, recant, renege, repudiate, reflect, renounce, retake, reprise; abdicate, abjure, abnegate, abrogate, annul. Insofar as the "original" prosopopoeia or any of its innumerable repetitions was a linguistic act, the conferring of a face where there is none, the word "deface" may be added to this list. But, as I argue, the ascription of a face and the effacing or defacing of that face are simultaneous acts in any prosopopoeia.

Acknowledgments

Much of this book was drafted with the help of a Research Fellowship from the National Endowment for the Humanities. I am extremely grateful for this support. Some sentences and paragraphs in Chapters 1 and 2 have appeared in earlier forms in two versions of "Is There an Ethics of Reading?"—one presented as a lecture at the fifty-eighth general meeting of the English Literary Society of Japan and then published as a pamphlet in Tokyo in 1986 by the Society, the other published in *Reading Narrative: Form, Ethics, Ideology,* ed. James Phelan (Columbus: Ohio State University Press, 1989). Parts of the beginning of Chapter 5 appeared in an earlier version in "The Search for Grounds in Literary Study," published first in *Genre* (Spring–Summer, 1984), and then in *Rhetoric and Form: Deconstruction at Yale,* ed. Robert Con Davis and Ronald Schleifer (Norman: University of Oklahoma Press, 1985). Permission to reuse this material in revised form is gratefully acknowledged. And I thank Maud Wilcox, on the occasion of her retirement as editor-in-chief at Harvard University Press, for her help and confidence in me over many years.

Index